ROBERT BURNS
AND
CULTURAL AUTHORITY

ROBERT BURNS
AND
CULTURAL AUTHORITY

Edited by

Robert Crawford

EDINBURGH UNIVERSITY PRESS

for Robert Fergusson's Alma Mater
with sly thanks

© The Contributors, 1997

Edinburgh University Press
22 George Square, Edinburgh

Typeset in Bulmer
by Pioneer Associates, Perthshire, and
printed and bound in Great Britain
at the University Press, Cambridge

A CIP record for this book is available from the
British Library

ISBN 0 7486 0740 4

CONTENTS

ACKNOWLEDGEMENTS

This book draws very substantially on the University of St Andrews / British Library Centre for the Book Robert Burns Bicentenary Lectures delivered at the University of St Andrews, at the British Library, London, at BBC Scotland, Edinburgh, and at the Church of St Andrew and St George, Edinburgh, in 1996. Without the generous sponsorship of the University of St Andrews, the University of St Andrews Scottish Studies Institute (SASSI) and the British Library Centre for the Book, the lecture series could not have been mounted. I would like to thank the Principal of the University of St Andrews as well as Mr Mike Crump and Dr Richard Price of the British Library Centre for the Book for putting their money where our mouths were. Thanks are also due to Dr Price for his deft organisation of the London lectures.

At St Andrews, Mrs Frances Mullan, Secretary of SASSI, provided invaluable support in arranging the smooth running of the lecture series; Ms Anna Mullan and Mrs Jane Sommerville of the School of English provided secretarial assistance; the University's Public Relations Officer, Mrs Lesley Lind, and the University's Alumnus Officer, Ms Heather Walker, kept us in touch with the wider world; and other colleagues at St Andrews, including Mr A. H. Ashe, Mr Giles Dove, Dr Susan Sellers and Dr C. J. M. MacLachlan, were generous with their time, talent and fellowship. Mr Andrew Nash acted as general troubleshooter, and has shot accurately at some troubled footnotes in this typescript. Mr Jeremy Thurlow, the University's Composer in Residence, enlivened the lectures with his specially composed Burns music and his St Andrews Suite. Mr Alan Jack and Mr Geoff Baskerville at BBC Radio Scotland hosted and broadcast Seamus Heaney's lecture. The Rev. Andrew McLellan and Dr Robin Hill of the Church of Scotland helped host Dr Susan Manning's lecture.

At Edinburgh University Press, Ms Jackie Jones, who commissioned this book, deserves thanks for her trust and patience; thanks are also due to Ms Alison Bowden, to the copy-editor, Mr Ivor Normand, and to the indexer Dr Campbell Purton, as well as to Ms Alison Munro and Ms Kath McLean.

Books involve more debts than can be tabulated neatly. The contributors have come up trumps, defying many logistical problems to produce their essays. As editor, I would like to thank them for their generosity; to thank the generations of Burns scholars, not least those of the later twentieth century, on whose work this book builds; and to reserve my culminating thanks for my wife, Alice, who knows about the making of books.

R. C.
St Andrews
April 1996

INTRODUCTION

Robert Crawford

Robert Burns's poetic career is a subtle, full-throated flyting with cultural authority. Burns crosses swords with Kirk, language, literati, King, government and, not least, himself. Yet, after his death in 1796 at the age of 37, the Burns who had so slyly contested cultural authority in his work was made into a posthumous patron whose name might validate a bewildering variety of projects. Clubs, ceilidhs, countries and causes, not to mention critics and writers, all boasted that directly or indirectly they bore his *imprimatur*.

This book is about Robert Burns and cultural authority – his own and other people's. It assembles a nimble, informed and occasionally disputatious team to write about the poet who did more than any other in his century to reinforce the art of verse through vernacular voice. Before Wordsworth, Byron or any other of the Romantic poets, Burns advanced the popular line in his work, learning from Robert Fergusson and others to blend demotic and high-cultural timbres in order to produce what Seamus Heaney calls an 'art speech'. Byron's slangy, informed tone owes as much to Burns as to the *salon*. Keats's 1819 'Ode to Psyche' and 'Ode on a Grecian Urn' muse on mortality and move from 'happy, happy dove' ('Psyche') to the hymning in the Grecian urn ode:

> Ah, happy, happy boughs, that cannot shed
>   Your leaves, nor ever bid the spring adieu;
> And, happy melodist, unwearièd,
>   For ever piping songs for ever new!
> More happy love, more happy, happy love!

In these lines, Keats's ear is haunted by the Burns to whose country and whose home he had made a pilgrimage the previous year and whose poetry ghosts some of Keats's greatest work. It is the Keatsian Burns who writes in 1786 in 'The Cotter's Saturday Night':

> O happy love! where love like this is found!
> O heart-felt raptures! bliss beyond compare!

Sometimes fleetingly, sometimes in a sustained way, Burns both produces and nourishes Romantic poetry. He is social, yet also sublime. Yet, like his lesser Scottish contemporary James Macpherson (who also died in 1796), Burns is an eighteenth-century writer whose output underpinned Romantic writing and has been misunderstood, not least by great nineteenth-century critics such as the Oxonian Matthew Arnold whose poetic theory recognises in Burns's work a challenge with which it is unable fully to deal. In the twentieth century, Burns's example, tones and achievement are even more acutely present, whether we consider the work of Robert Frost, Hugh MacDiarmid, Seamus Heaney and Les Murray, or that of other poets whose vernacular negotiations with cultural authority are not just comparable with, but even alert to, Burns's exemplary stance and music. The cunning, ambitious future farmer-poet Frost knew Burns's poetry from early childhood, and quoted it in correspondence with his first editor. MacDiarmid drew on Burns's example time after time, rewriting 'Tam o' Shanter' as *A Drunk Man Looks at the Thistle*, his 1926 masterpiece. If Frost's Burns is a poet of vernacular voice, MacDiarmid's is mixed daringly with the modernism of T. S. Eliot, but is no less potent for that. 'Robert Burns . . . mostly recited by men who were drunk' was part of the earliest education of the poet from a New South Wales farm whose own 'Variations on a Measure of Burns' articulates both Les Murray's fidelity to and suspicion of Burns and his cultural authority in Scots Australia.[1]

Written in Standard Habbie, later called the 'Burns stanza', Seamus Heaney's verse-letter to Sorley MacLean recalls that

> this Burns stanza was the first
> Art speech I heard. His lines conversed
> In local accents and rehearsed
> A local rhythm.[2]

From his own farming background, not in Ayrshire but across the water in Northern Ireland, Seamus Heaney has gone on to learn from, negotiate with, and include in his poetry the world of the late twentieth-century literati. Yet Heaney rightly locates in Burns not only a sense of cannily social poetry, but also a lyric depth and intensity that some readers too easily elide. Burns for Heaney is foreign as well as oddly native; but Burns's work may have this mixture of qualities even for modern Scottish readers, and that can make him all the more elusively fascinating. Certainly his poetry remains a living, formative presence in the work of contemporary Scottish poets from Douglas Dunn to Kathleen Jamie and beyond. When the late Norman MacCaig edited his 1959 volume *Honour'd Shade*, he produced an act of poetic homage, what that book's subtitle calls *An Anthology of New Scottish Poetry to mark the Bicentenary of the Birth of Robert Burns*. This present book arises from lectures which I organised at the University of St Andrews to commemorate the 1996 bicentenary of Burns's death. It presents mere prose, but its mixture of essays by writers of poetry, fiction and criticism is deliberate and attests to the continuing way in which Burns's work provides cultural nourishment. Today, too, writers may wish to claim something of Burns's cultural authority and to question, even dispute, aspects of that power.

The book begins by considering Burns and cultural authority in the area of gender. The first essay looks at how he learned from Fergusson certain tones, stances and linguistic strategies, and (just as importantly) at how Burns followed Fergusson into the homosocial, often masonic world of eighteenth-century Scottish clubland where he found his 'brothers'. Burns's brotherly activities conditioned not least the Burns clubs which developed after his death, and his attitude to women. In considering her own experience of a Burns club and examining the literary lover presented in Burns's letters, the novelist A. L. Kennedy writes with acute insight into Burns's dealings with his female correspondents. Kirsteen McCue's consideration of Burns and women lyricists examines in detail the frequently female world of song transmission which was for a long time eclipsed by the contributions of Burns. This essay sets Burns's work as song-collector fully and carefully in the world of native culture, at the same time alerting us to other, female voices which sounded alongside his own.

In drawing on the cultural authority of native tradition, Burns worked nowhere to greater effect than in the area of what Douglas Dunn follows T. S. Eliot in calling his 'metric'. Dunn's essay shows more fully and convincingly than before how Burns harnessed the energies of traditional metrical forms with *brio*, using them in turn to contest that configuration of ideological forces represented by such a figure as Hugh Blair, not to mention Holy Willie. Considering the aesthetics and politics of metre, Dunn's essay precedes Marilyn Butler's treatment of the difficult topic of Burns and Burns and politics. Attending both to Burns the internationalist, alert to the revolutions of America and France, and Burns the nationalist, attuned to the political energies of his immediate society, Marilyn Butler presents a Burns who is an inventor of modern cultural nationalism, assembling a nation through his literary art. If his politics were dangerous, and so at odds with the authorities in eighteenth-century Scottish and British culture, then Burns's religious beliefs are even more awkward terrain. Yet in considering Burns and God (two figures whom later writers sometimes conflate), Susan Manning is dealing with the ultimate cultural authority, as well as with certain problems and limitations in Burns's language. Her treatment of this topic cuts through swathes of critical verbiage to present concisely what can be said, and to acknowledge what cannot.

The essays which follow Susan Manning's deal with the posthumous reception of Burns's work by later writers and critics in America and in Britain. Burns's popularity in the United States led both to spectacular excesses and to powerful and enabling misinterpretations, crisply set forth by Carol McGuirk. On Burns's own side of the Atlantic, Wordsworth and Keats were only two of a vast legion of later writers who looked to Burns as a figure of example and warning. Not least, Nicholas Roe's essay suggests how, more and more as the nineteenth century developed, anxiety about the nature of the 'authentic' Burns was linked to concern about the uncertain status of Scotland. Andrew Nash's essay picks up on this theme, showing how later critics presented a Burns, particularly a carefully-edited Burns, poet of 'The Cotter's Saturday Night', whose cultural authority could be used to mould and validate Kailyard visions, the very visions which were so antithetical to the temperament of Hugh MacDiarmid. Alan Riach's essay makes it clear that MacDiarmid's relations with Burns were full and complex ones, and cannot be seen in terms of any simple opposition. Yet their strength testifies to Burns as an inescapable and enduring figure for the Scottish poets of later ages. One thing which Seamus Heaney's concluding consideration of Burns's 'art speech' reminds us is that it is not only for Scottish poets that Burns matters. Unless we consider Burns as a poet whose work, born out of a love of voice and a sometimes complicitous contest with cultural authority, has acquired a remarkable cultural authority of its own, we are unduly narrowing our range.

Substantial sections of this book focus on Burns's poetry itself. Yet to ignore the part played in Burns's own cultural authority by his later readers and critics (not least those in Burns clubs) would be naive. Since *A Drunk Man Looks at the Thistle*, it has become something of an orthodoxy among intellectuals to deride Burns Suppers and Burns clubs, taking their lead from MacDiarmid's dauntingly splenetic attack in that poem's early stanzas:

> No' wan in fifty kens a wurd Burns wrote
> But misapplied is a 'body's property,
> And gin there was his like alive the day
> They'd be the last a kennin' haund to gi'e –
>
> Croose London Scotties wi' their braw shirt fronts
> And a' their fancy freen's, rejoicin'
> That similah gatherings in Timbuctoo,
> Bagdad – and Hell, nae doot – are voicin'
>
> Burns' sentiments o' universal love,
> In pidgin English or in wild-fowl Scots,
> And toastin' ane wha's nocht to them but an
> Excuse for faitherin' Genius wi' *their* thochts.[3]

Yet MacDiarmid's engagement with the Burns movement was at root an attempt to reconnect that movement with modern poetry. The earliest Burns clubs, not least that in Paisley, were passionately interested not just in Burns but also in poetry. So we find the poet Robert Tannahill as one of the Paisley Burns club's founders, and if one looks at the programme of the 1859 Burns Birthday Centenary celebrations in Paisley's Exchange Rooms, one sees that the canon of writers recognised by the organisers is much wider than that which would have been recognised by the literary curricula of contemporary universities, for instance. Toasting not just Burns and Shakespeare, but also Tennyson, Tannahill, Longfellow, Moore and other English, Irish, Scottish and American poets, the gentlemen at table were alert to recent international poetic developments as well as to those of their native tradition.[4] It is just such an awareness that Burns himself had possessed and that MacDiarmid, like any sensible poet, wished to develop and preserve. So this present book is not clumsily directed against all who have toasted the immortal memory of Robert Burns on 25 January. They too are tribute to the cultural authority which Burns and his work acquired, though too often they seem to have lost their predecessors' sense of a wider literary culture and its vital interconnectedness. If only they incorporated in their ritual observances the passing-round of a hat for contemporary literature, and paused to reflect on Burns's place within the poetry of his day and our own, we might all be a little the richer, and we might move towards a spryer understanding of Robert Burns and cultural authority.

NOTES

1. For more on Burns and these poets, see my *Devolving English Literature* (Oxford: Clarendon Press, 1992) and *Identifying Poets: Self and Territory in Twentieth-Century Poetry* (Edinburgh: Edinburgh University Press, 1993).

2. Seamus Heaney, 'To Sorley MacLean', in Angus Peter Campbell (ed.), *Somhairle: Dàin is Deilbh, A Celebration on the 80th Birthday of Sorley MacLean* (Stornoway: Acair, 1991), p. 59.

3. Hugh MacDiarmid, *A Drunk Man Looks at the Thistle* (1926), ed. Kenneth Buthlay (Edinburgh: Scottish Academic Press, 1987), p. 8.

4. The programme is reproduced in Robert Brown, *Paisley Burns Clubs 1805–1893* (Paisley: Alexander Gardner, 1893), plate facing p. 192.

ROBERT FERGUSSON'S
ROBERT BURNS

Robert Crawford

We value the work of Robert Burns because it is the most alert and renovating literary channel of vernacular culture produced anywhere in the English-speaking world of the eighteenth century. More than that, Burns made better use of vernacular material than any other poet in the history of Scottish literature. The vernacular nature of much of his achievement is unsurprising if we look forwards to Wordsworth's poetry with its emphasis on using 'a selection of language really used by men' and its fidelity to rural nature; or if we look to the developing democratic consciousness with which such linguistic theories can be aligned.[1] Yet in the Scotland of Burns's day where the leading literary theorists – men like Adam Smith and Hugh Blair – were establishing in print and through academic teaching a culture which insisted on adherence to linguistic propriety according to Anglocentric norms, Burns's resolute deployment of the Scots vernacular is especially striking. This is the aspect of Burns's poetry which we most admire today. The Burns who matters most to us is Robert Fergusson's Robert Burns.

When the poet whom Burns would call his 'brother' matriculated as a student at the University of St Andrews in 1765, he signed his name on the matriculation roll simply as 'Rob Fergusson'.[2] He put no full stop after his first name, nor did he call himself 'Robertus' or 'Robert' as did his student namesakes of that year. Instead, what he did when joining an institution committed to Anglocentric standards of linguistic propriety was to matriculate in the vernacular.

That tiny, subversive gesture is typical of Fergusson, and typical of what attracted Burns to his work. The strength of Burns's attachment to Fergusson is well known. In 1787, while the Edinburgh edition of his own poems was in press, one of Burns's most significant public acts in the Scottish capital was to campaign and pay for the erection of a memorial to Fergusson. Burns took to task the Bailies of the Canongate because 'the

1

remains of Robert Ferguson [*sic*] the so justly celebrated Poet, a man whose talents for ages to come will do honor to our Caledonian name, lie in your church yard among the ignoble Dead unnoticed and unknown'.[3] Burns wrote three poems on Fergusson (more than he wrote about any other poet), and they all date from the period in early 1787 when the Edinburgh edition of his own poems was in press, so that we can with some justice relate Burns's view of Fergusson to his own position as a poet emerging in the literary Edinburgh of Hugh Blair and other arbiters of correct taste in writing.

One of these poems in particular draws on the language which had just been used of Burns in the most famous early review of his works, written by Henry Mackenzie in *The Lounger*. There, in December 1786, Mackenzie, author of Burns's favourite novel, *The Man of Feeling*, had discussed the Kilmarnock edition of Burns's *Poems* in terms of 'genius' and called its author a 'Heaven-taught ploughman'.[4] Burns opens one of his Fergusson poems by addressing the dead poet as 'Ill-fated Genius! Heaven-taught Fergusson' (*Poems and Songs*, 258), and I want to spend a little time pondering the significance of those words. If the *OED* can be trusted, Mackenzie is the first person in English to use the striking compound adjective 'Heaven-taught', but his discussion of natural literary genius is of a piece with the view of genius put forward by Blair and other eighteenth-century teachers of Rhetoric and Belles Lettres, and dates back at least to the seventeenth-century *Réflexions sur la Poétique d'Aristote* (1674) by René Rapin, who writes of a poet's 'elevation of Soul that depends not on Art nor Study, and which is purely a Gift of Heaven, and must be sustain'd by a lively Sence and Vivacity'.[5] This notion of being essentially 'Heaven-taught' clearly appealed to the widely-read and self-schooled Burns, who also used the term in two other poems of 1787 (*Poems and Songs*, 265 and 280); but in applying the term to Robert Fergusson he was doing something odd, since, unlike Burns, Fergusson, educated at Edinburgh High School, Dundee High School and the University of St Andrews, had been taught according to sophisticated curricula.

We might like to think that, in calling Fergusson 'Heaven-taught', Burns is giving a most favourable assessment to the University of St Andrews; but this would be a naive assumption. As a St Andrews student, among other things Fergusson would have had to study Rhetoric under Robert Watson, whose teaching, like that of his academic colleagues in other Scottish universities, was designed to discourage the use of Scots and Scotticisms. Shortly after Fergusson left university, Watson would be one of Dr Johnson's most admiring hosts when the great lexicographer visited St Andrews and the two men discussed English composition.[6] Fergusson's sympathies, however, lay elsewhere. He was quite a wild student. The Principal recalled that Fergusson was reprimanded for taking part in a St Andrews 'Riot' or

student brawl, and, more revealingly, that he behaved 'wantonly' during one
of the university's rituals. The details of this offence are recorded by
Fergusson's fellow student, Charles Webster:

> He was considered the best singer at the university, of consequence, he
> was oftener than he inclined, requested to officiate as clerk at morning
> and evening prayers. In order to get quit of this drudgery, he meditated
> the following scheme. It is usual, according to the Scottish mode of
> Presbyterian worship, to mention the names of persons, who are rec-
> ommended in prayer; our poet, who, as usual, was in the precenter's
> desk, rose up with great composure, and with an audible voice, as if
> reading from a paper he held in his hand, said 'Remember in prayer
> [John Adamson] a young man (who was in the hall at the very instant)
> who, from the sudden effects of inebriety, there appears but small hope
> of recovery'[7].

Unsurprisingly, this threw all the students into 'convulsive merriment' and
almost led to Fergusson's expulsion from the university. He was saved only
by the intervention of William Wilkie, poet and Professor of Mathematics,
who had become his mentor.

Such an action of taking an established ritual and subverting it, producing
a parodic or play-ritual which mocks irreverently even as it enacts a set cultural pattern, so that we're not quite sure how much is being mocked and
how much is being left in place, is typical of the eighteenth century, which
offers us the Popean mock-heroic produced by the very poet who translated
Homer. In Scottish poetry, this ambiguous territory, a debatable land
between solemnity and daftness, was characterised not so much by first-rate
mock-epic as by superb mock-elegy in the Standard Habbie mode. When
we read Fergusson's earliest student poetry, we are aware of an expansive
Scots fluency but also, as when he elegises 'Mr David Gregory, late Professor
of Mathematics in the University of St Andrews', of a tonal balance that is at
once intellectually ambitious, regretful and snook-cocking, so that it is often
impressively impossible to tell where the one tone begins and the other
ends:

> He could, by *Euclid*, prove lang sine
> A ganging *point* compos'd a line;
> By numbers too he cou'd divine,
>   Whan he did read,
> That *three* times *three* just made up nine;
>   But now he's dead.
>
>   (F, II, 1)

Fergusson had inherited this verse form and this tonal balance from Allan Ramsay, who, like its apparent inventor Robert Sempil, had used it to fuse high and low tones, mixing fun and solemnity. More than that, since as a young poet he enjoyed trying out Standard Habbie, we may regard Fergusson as in part formed *by* the tonal mix, not simply as choosing to inhabit it. So the tonal balance of Standard Habbie played its part in forming the young Robert Fergusson, as much as he played his part in developing this poetic mode, one so eagerly taken up by Robert Burns that its modern name has become the 'Burns stanza'. It's important to realise that this Standard Habbie/Burns stanza is more than a metrical or acoustic pattern: it is also a splicing of tones and emotions, a mixture that we would call parodic if it were not also serious, that we would characterise as regretful if it were not also playfully daft. This is a particularly Scottish-vernacular kind of mock-heroic, one that exploits the connections already being made at the time of the 1707 Union of Parliaments between the Scots language and a dying culture: elegy-fodder, and yet at the same time ludically, vulgarly vital.

The odd tonal mix of Standard Habbie articulates a culture, and it was the poets most attuned to that culture who were most at ease in Standard Habbie. In admiring Fergusson, Burns followed a poet who had used a verse form which he would gleefully inherit; but with that inheritance went wider cultural assumptions, often implicit but percolating with no less insinuating power for that. At times, Fergusson would inhabit the originally elegiac music of Standard Habbie to celebrate the vitality of the living, as in 'Caller Oysters'. Elsewhere, as in his celebration of vernacular, eating-and-drinking St Andrews student culture in his 'Elegy on John Hogg, late Porter to the University of St Andrews', he allowed a note of (perhaps slightly bitter) regret to come closer to the jaunty surface:

> Say ye, *red gowns*! that aften here
> Hae toasted bakes to *Kattie*'s beer,
> Gin 'ere thir days hae had their peer,
>   Sae blyth, sae daft;
> You'll ne'er again in life's career
>   Sit ha'f sae saft.
>
> (F, II, 193)

Fergusson's talent and tonal balance seem to have owed much to his time as a student. He was encouraged to write by William Wilkie, the well-known, scruffy author of *The Epigoniad* and, more interestingly, the poet of the Scots verses 'The Partan and the Hare'. But Wilkie's Scots, solemnly footnoted, was presented as a dead language, and, though Fergusson paid tribute to Wilkie as mentor, it is principally in his reaction against the official culture of the university that Fergusson developed as the poet who would attract and serve as exemplar for the Burns whose best work would synthesise the vernacular in patterns whose tonal balance is often enliveningly wobbly.

Fergusson's most impressive direct reaction against the culture of his education comes in the poem which he wrote in response to Dr Johnson's visit to St Andrews and his reception there by the academics. The poem 'To the Principal and Professors of the University of St Andrews, on their Superb Treat to Dr Samuel Johnson' is a minor classic of Scottish literature, and a crucial text for those interested in that contesting of cultural authority in which Fergusson and his follower Burns would engage. Rob Fergusson addresses his former teachers and their guest in a strategically-deployed vernacular. The lexicographer is 'Samy' and his hosts 'lads' and 'billy boys':

> ST ANDREWS town may look right gawsy,
> Nae GRASS will grow upon her cawsey,
> Nor wa'-flowers of a yellow dye,
> Glour dowy o'er her RUINS high,
> Sin SAMY'S head weel pang'd wi'lear,
> Has seen the ALMA MATER there:
> Regents, my winsome billy boys!
> 'Bout him you've made an unco noise;
> Nae doubt for him your bells wad clink
> To find him upon EDEN'S brink . . .
>
> (F, II, 182–3)

It is tempting here just to relish the reductive use of Scots, but the use of the technically correct 'Regents' and the Latin 'ALMA MATER' reminds us that the language-range of this poem is wide and that it deploys an insider's as well as an outsider's vocabulary and perceptions. Fergusson writes in and from the standpoint of the vernacular, but takes from the language of high culture and literary decorum what he needs in order to play these back to his Principal and Professors in a way that outflanks and mocks them. It is their language, not the vernacular, which leads Fergusson to begin his verse paragraphs with '*Imprimis*' and '*Secundo*', as if delivering the headings for a lecture. It is he, not the Professors, who presents a text for discussion. After ridiculing the foreign delicacies, all 'snails and puddocks', which the 'college kitchen' provides for Johnson, Fergusson goes on to give the profs a real good talking-to:

> But hear me lads! gin I'd been there,
> How I wad trimm'd the bill o' fare!
> For ne'er sic surly wight as he

Had met wi' sic respect frae me.
Mind ye what SAM, the lying loun!
Has in his Dictionar laid down?
That AITS in England are a feast
To cow an' horse an sican beast,
While in Scots ground this growth was common
To gust the gab o' MAN and WOMAN.

(F, II, 183)

Of course, what Fergusson is focusing on here is Johnson's now notorious definition of oats in his *Dictionary*: 'A grain, which in England is generally given to horses, but in Scotland supports the people', but he's not simply attacking that; he is doing something cheekier. By first of all translating Johnson's words into Scots, Fergusson successfully robs the great *Dictionary* of all of its supposed cultural authority as arbiter of the English language, and leaves it as exposed to attack as any other piece of gabbing. What Fergusson is about here is levelling the cultural playing field. That is why he chooses to write about the academics when they are at table, for at that moment (however elaborate their culinary preparations) they are in an obvious way just like everybody else: they eat and drink. But, with a submerged pun on such ideas as 'food for thought' and being made to 'eat one's words', Fergusson suggests an alternative menu whose components are not imported but thoroughly native:

Imprimis, then, a haggis fat,
Weel tottl'd in a seything pat,
Wi' *spice* and *ingans* weel ca'd thro',
Had help'd to gust the stirrah's mow,
And plac'd itsel in truncher clean
Before the gilpy's glowrin een.
Secundo, then a gude sheep's head
Whase hide was singit, never flead,
And four black trotters cled wi' girsle,
Bedown his throat had learn'd to hirsle.
What think ye neist, o' gude fat brose
To clag his ribs? a dainty dose!
And white and bloody puddins routh,
To gar the Doctor skirl, O Drouth!

(F, II, 183–4)

If Johnson's *Dictionary* is made to talk Scots, then the conversion process goes so far that the Doctor himself is made to emit the most Scottish of sounds when he 'skirl[s]'. The foods which effect this change are not just superbly and distinctively Caledonian – 'haggis' and 'sheep's heid' – but also rich in the aforementioned oats, whether in the haggis or in the white and black puddings. Fergusson upends Johnson's Anglocentrism in a feast-poem which celebrates vernacular culture by contesting authority through the politics of oatmeal. This is just where Burns follows Fergusson in his celebrated feast-poem, 'To a Haggis', written just before the poems addressed to Fergusson, and again celebrating vernacular culture by contrasting its cooking with the foreign cuisine of the 'French *ragout,*/Or *olio* that wad staw a sow,/Or *fricassee* wad mak her spew' (*Poems and Songs*, 251). As in Fergusson's menu-poem, there is in Burns's a sense that the bill of fare may appear joyfully outrageous, but this is relished as part of its appeal.

When Burns apostrophises Fergusson as 'Heaven-taught', then, he is celebrating in him a natural poetic virtue, but also a potent vernacular resistance to Anglocentric, high, academic literary culture. Henry Mackenzie, whose work Fergusson had mocked, remembered that poet as 'dissipated and drunken' (a charge that would dog Burns also); but, in complaining to Edinburgh's worthies that they had neglected Fergusson, Burns is slyly adopting Mackenzie's position in his review of Burns's first book, and adopting it in such a way that it rebounds on Mackenzie.[8] For that gentleman had concluded his review of Burns by mentioning hints of that poet's 'misfortunes' and pointing out that

> To repair the wrongs of suffering or neglected merit; to call forth genius from the obscurity in which it had pined indignant, and place it where it might profit or delight the world; these are exertions which give to wealth an enviable superiority, to greatness and to patronage a laudable pride.[9]

In one sense, when he writes about Fergusson to the Bailies of the Canongate, Burns is following Mackenzie's injunctions exactly, restoring to view the suffering poet who had died pining in an Edinburgh madhouse at the age of 24 some thirteen years earlier; yet in so doing, Burns is also exposing the size of the failure of Edinburgh's great and proud patrons to nurture native, vernacular talent. If Burns's 'misfortune' was noticed by Mackenzie, then Burns at this time felt himself all the closer to the Fergusson whom he called just months after Mackenzie's review 'O thou, my elder brother in Misfortune/By far my elder Brother in the muse.' (*Poems and Songs*, 258). The phrase 'Brother in the muse' seems based on the expression 'brother in Christ' and suggests a particularly important poetic kinship. In the same months as he wrote his poems to Fergusson stressing his fraternal bond with the dead poet, Burns wrote a Standard Habbie mock-elegy for 'Robert Ruisseaux' (French for Burns), imagining himself gabbling in poverty on his own death-bed. If Fergusson quickened and reinforced in Burns a sense of the ability of vernacular life to contest the cultural authority of Anglocentric high culture, then he also fed in Burns a vein of despair. With no other poet in the Scottish tradition did Burns identify so closely. He was not so much preceded by Fergusson as haunted by him.

It was Fergusson's 'The Farmer's Ingle' that formed the model for one of Burns's early big set-pieces, 'The Cotter's Saturday Night', and, as is a just commonplace of students' essays, Fergusson's remains in many ways the better poem because its fidelity to its subject matter prevents it from condescending to the people and ethos which it describes, whereas Burns has too much of an eye and ear on the lawyer to whom his sometimes grandiosely pious poem is addressed. As has often been remarked, and as is thoroughly documented by Matthew McDiarmid and James Kinsley in their splendid editions of the two poets, other Fergusson poems also underpin works by Burns. Fergusson's dialogue between 'Plainstanes and Cawsey' relates to Burns's 'The Twa Dogs'. But probably more important than any of these particular points of correspondence is the way that, in poems from 'Leith Races' and 'Auld Reekie' to 'Caller Oysters', Fergusson celebrates the street and, not least, pub life of Scots vernacular culture without sacrificing an intellectual and linguistic reach that can go beyond these when needed. Fergusson's skills and techniques were already in evidence in his days as student rioter and serious/mock precentor as well as in the poems relating to his university experience, but these skills were honed and developed in the fraternal world of the Edinburgh clubs which Burns would frequent in the next decade.

Often thought of as literary and intellectual, the Scottish clubs of the eighteenth century have been rather sanitised by history.[10] I think it is time that we reviewed the nature and importance of these institutions which are closely related to some of the most valuable literature of the time, not least the vernacular poetry of Fergusson and later Burns. Though there was a tiny number of female clubs, the vast majority were all-male and may be seen as institutions which were crucial for the circulation and maintaining of the cultural codes which characterised eighteenth-century Scotland. In particular, these clubs functioned as part of the articulation of eighteenth-century Scottish masculinity through their rituals and use of literary texts, drink, male bonding and initiations. Intellectual historians have tended to see these fraternities as significant, but have also concentrated on narrow aspects of their behaviour. If, before looking at several clubs in more detail, we see them in relation to other core institutions, we may gain a better understanding of their place in the culture, and the way in which they nourished and were nourished by the work of both Fergusson and Burns.

To begin with the obvious, the controlling institutions of this society were male, and were themselves closer to the world of male clubs than would be the case today. In such a cultural climate, it was possible, for instance, for

Dr Johnson to speculate about staffing the faculties of the University of St Andrews entirely by members of his own London club.[11] Particularly in a small country like Scotland, many of the legal, ecclesiastical and academic leaders knew one another well, and these worlds of church, law and academia frequently overlapped. So Hugh Blair, for instance, was both a Church of Scotland minister and Professor of Rhetoric and Belles Lettres at the University of Edinburgh. His voice spoke with and conducted ecclesiastical as well as literary-academic authority. But beyond these close, interlocking professional coteries were formal all-male groupings whose construction was bound up with the power structure of the society and the social regulation of masculinity. Foremost among these were the freemasons, a movement whose Scottish origins and whose remarkable power in Enlightenment Edinburgh have been documented by David Stevenson.[12] As another modern scholar has written, fraternities such as those involved in freemasonry, by means of elaborate rituals, promoted an ideal of brotherhood through which 'Self-conscious dissociation from women and the family, the rituals of initiation and testing, and the articulation of a hierarchical social order' were reinforced by 'fraternal association' which 'provided an institutional means by which men, as agents between households, were able to dominate the religious, political, economic, and social networks that were understood to define the culture and unify society'.[13] Burns, eager to escape from woman trouble through 'all kinds of dissipation and riot, Mason-meetings, drinking matches, and other mischief', was an ardent freemason before he arrived in Edinburgh, and his career was certainly thoroughly assisted by masonic networks (*Letters*, I, 39).[14] At the time that the Edinburgh edition of his *Poems* was in press in early 1787 (the period of his poems to Fergusson), he was pleased to hear the Grand Master propose a toast to 'Caledonia, & Caledonia's Bard, brother Burns' when Burns attended a meeting of the Canongate Kilwinning masonic lodge in the capital (*Letters*, I, 83). I wish to return to Burns and freemasonry soon, but first of all to recall that the freemasons, whose rituals in some ways paralleled those of the Christian church, were only the most prominent of many Scottish male associations and clubs of this period, all of whom played their part in the social articulation and regulation of masculinity.

The most scandalous of these clubs was certainly the Beggar's Benison of Anstruther, later translated to Edinburgh. This club was named after the blessing supposed to have been bestowed by a female beggar on King James V of Scotland. The records of the club have it that, after carrying the King over the Dreel Burn in Anstruther, the 'buxom gaberlunzie lass' was rewarded with a gold sovereign and said to the King 'May your purse naer be toom / And your horn aye in bloom'. The club's modern historian, Alan Bold, records that from 1732 the Beggar's Benison met as a society at Dreel Castle, Anstruther, on Candlemas (2 February) and St Andrew's Day (30

November). Anstruther, as its architecture still attests, was strong masonic territory, and some of the rituals of the club seem like parodies of masonry. Members were known as Knights and were initiated in a rite involving a Bible whose flyleaves were scribbled over with erotica. The club made use of toasts and of regalia involving drinking cups, platters, medals, seals, certificates and a horn. One of the club's main practices was masturbation and phallic exhibitionism. A local girl was engaged to strip or pose naked for meetings, but otherwise played no part in the proceedings. She was present simply as a sexual object. A nineteenth-century history of the club's meetings records the traditional format:

> The Fee for Initiation, Test, and Diploma was £3 3s. 0d., and £1 1s. 0d. additional was charged for the Medal (silver-gilt) which every Member had to wear at the Head Quarters, Anstruther, on St Andrews' [*sic*] Day. The annual Subscription was £1 1s. 0d. In initiation every Member was necessitated to go through the Test, once for all, on St Andrew's Day, at Anstruther, at the Council before the annual Banquet. The Sovereign presided over the Members wearing their sashes and silver-gilt medals. The Remembrancer produced the Testing-Platter which was placed on a high Stool or Altar in the centre of the room. The Recorder and two Remembrances prepared the Novice in a closet, by causing him to propel his Penis until full erection. When thus ready he was escorted with four puffs of the Breath-Horn before the Brethren or Knighthood, and was ordered by the Sovereign to place his genitals upon the Testing-Platter, which was covered with a folded white napkin. The Members and Knights two and two came round in a state of erection and touched the Novice Penis to Penis. Thereafter the special Glass, with the Society's Insignia thereon and medal attached, was filled with Port Wine, when the new Brother's health was heartily and humorously drunk. He was told to select an amorous passage from the Song of Solomon and to read it aloud with comments; after which he was arrayed with Sash and Medal by the Sovereign, repeating the words along with the others, '*May Prick nor Purse never fail you . . .*'. The Banquet followed, when were shown Curiosities; Songs were sung composed for the occasion; Sentiments and Toasts were given, with Recitations and Classical Bon Mots . . .[15]

Literary texts were now 'spouted' and these would eventually include works as diverse as Ovid's *Ars Amatoria*, *Fanny Hill* and the poetry of Byron. Original compositions and gathered songs played their part alongside such literary texts. This was a ritualised bawdy club founded on wordplay among other things, and celebrating the potency of its 'members' through masculine rites that asserted the dominance of the male.

We know that there was some overlap between the membership of the Beggar's Benison and the St Andrews professoriate, and it has even been suggested that Fergusson may have visited this club, but that is sheer speculation.[16] The Beggar's Benison was certainly not the norm for eighteenth-century Scottish clubs, but nor was it in all ways exceptional. There was, for instance, an Edinburgh society called the Wig Club whose regalia included a wig made from the pubic hair of Charles II's mistresses. Even the most innocent-seeming of eighteenth-century associations tended to celebrate male potency and to depend on male exclusivity and dominance. So the title of Burns's Tarbolton Bachelors' Club is as significant as the stipulation in its constitution (for which Burns may have been responsible) that its members must be 'a professed lover of one or more of the female sex'. Meetings ended with convivial drinking and 'a general toast to the mistresses of the club'.[17] This was essentially a debating society, but it was also one clearly formed according to rituals of masculinity. Nor should its rituals be seen as at the opposite pole from those of the all-male masons' meetings with their toasts, constitutions and regalia. The Tarbolton Bachelors' Club even met in the same room as that used by Burns's local masonic lodge. This was a pub room, owned by a mason mentioned in Burns's verse. The pub setting, focus of so many eighteenth-century Scottish clubs, reminds us of the key role played by drinking in their procedures.

Edwin Morgan has suggested recently that Fergusson's poetry may contain a homoerotic element; if this is true, that might seem to set it apart from the work of Burns, the celebrant of heterosexual love.[18] Yet Burns rejoiced in belonging to the masculine world of fraternities; and, once again, Fergusson had preceded Burns as his 'brother' poet involved in this milieu. Fergusson's club was the Cape in Edinburgh, which he joined in 1772. This organisation met in various Edinburgh pubs, and had as its regalia pokers and a cape for its principal dignitary, its Sovereign. Like the members of the Beggar's Benison, its ordinary members were called Knights, and each took the title Sir, followed by a name suggestive of some scrape or adventure which had befallen him. So Fergusson became Sir Precenter. Details of the club's initiation rite survive:

The novice, on making his appearance in Cape Hall, was led up to the Sovereign by two knightly sponsors, and, having made his obeisance, was required to grasp the large poker with his left hand, and laying his right hand on his breast, the oath *de fideli*, was administered to him by the Sovereign – the knights present all standing uncovered, – in the following words: –

I swear devoutly by this light,
To be a true and faithful Knight,

> With all my might
> Both day and night.
> So help me Poker!

Having then reverentially kissed the larger poker, and continuing to grasp it, the Sovereign raised the smaller poker with both his royal fists, and aiming three successive blows at the novice's head, he pronounced, with each, one of the initial letters of the motto of the Club, C. F. D., explaining their import to be *Concordia Fratrum Decus*.[19]

Perhaps some of this may parallel masonic ritual, but what matters is that it is again a ritual peculiar to this all-male club, one involving an ideal of fraternity, a rite in which the name of God is replaced by the phallic poker. The Cape's liquors were beer and porter; members entertained each other with songs. It was not a rich man's club, nor a particularly uproarious one, though its members were involved in at least one recorded 'riot' (F, I, 52). Fergusson loved it. His poem 'Auld Reekie', celebrating the vernacular life of Edinburgh, and its nocturnal epicurean pleasures, hymns the Cape:

> BUT chief, O CAPE, we crave thy Aid,
> To get our Cares and Poortith laid:
> Sincerity, and Genius true,
> Of Knights have ever been the due:
> Mirth, Music, Porter deepest dy'd,
> Are never here to Worth deny'd:
> And Health, o' Happiness the Queen,
> Blinks bonny, wi' her Smile serene.
>
> (F, II, 113–14)

In this club world, pub world, Fergusson was fully at home, and he celebrates its fraternal ideals. Some of Edinburgh's clubs were more decorous than the Cape, others were less so; but the pattern of blending song, ritual, regalia and drinking in a masculine-charged atmosphere was repeated across the city, and across the clubs of Scotland.

In Edinburgh, Burns, who got to know several Cape members and friends of the late Robert Fergusson, was not only an active mason but also a member of a club very similar to the Cape. This was the Crochallan Fencibles, called Crochallan after a favourite Gaelic song of the landlord in whose pub they met, and called Fencibles because they were a mock-regiment. This latter fact emphasises the 'manliness' of this brotherhood, all of whom took military titles. Burns spoke of a meeting of this 'corps' as a 'field-day', and some of the members, including the man responsible for 'drilling' new recruits, were phenomenal drinkers, even by eighteenth-century standards

(*Letters*, II, 79, 458). Burns's printer and friend William Smellie, one of the originators of the *Encyclopaedia Britannica*, appears to have founded the Fencibles and introduced the poet to it. What we know about the Fencibles shows that they celebrated not simply conviviality but also maleness and masculinity. The title page of *The Merry Muses of Caledonia*, Burns's posthumously-published collection of bawdry, gives as the work's subtitle *A Collection of Favourite Scots Songs, Ancient and Modern; Selected for use of the Crochallan Fencibles.*[20]

Even if we cannot be certain how many of these songs were written by Burns, we know that he collected bawdy material for the club. As a song-collector, Burns often altered earthy verses for polite consumption, but we know that he and many of his associates relished the bawdy. Those works from *The Merry Muses* which are authenticated by James Kinsley, editor of the authoritative Oxford *Poems and Songs of Robert Burns*, are quite sufficient to show that the Crochallan Fencibles were close to the Beggar's Benison in their literary tastes. So we have the fraternal address of 'The Fornicator' which urges 'jovial boys' to 'welcome in a Frater,/For I've lately been on quarantine,/A proven Fornicator' (*Poems and Songs*, 79), or the hairy cunts and arses of 'Bonie Mary', or the ithyphallic romp 'Come rede me, dame' with its 'carlin' who

> clew her wanton tail,
> Her wanton tail sae ready –
> I learn'd a sang in Annandale,
> Nine inch will please a lady. –
> (*Poems and Songs*, 363)

Even if we restrict ourselves to the material certainly in the Burns canon, the verses of *The Merry Muses* give us access to the world of initiated club fraternities of which Burns, like Fergusson before him, was part. One of the effects of this is to make us review Burns's many celebrations of fraternity. For the fraternity which he knew was not simply that of *liberté, égalité, fraternité*; it was also the fraternity of the various brotherhoods to which he belonged – whether that of the freemasons or of the Crochallan Fencibles. What this means is that when we read works such as Burns's 'Song – For a' that and a' that', we can admire its revolutionary fervour, the democratic impulse in those last lines:

> For a' that, and a' that,
> It's comin' yet for a' that,
> That Man to Man the warld o'er,
> Shall brothers be for a' that. –
> (*Poems and Songs*, 603)

Yet, in our own century, when issues of gender and democracy have been closely linked, we should be wary about simply translating Burns's 'brothers' into the more universal 'people' so as to include females as well as males. Burns was not unaware of pressures for female emancipation, but his poem 'The Rights of Woman', whose title draws on Mary Wollstonecraft's 1792 *Vindication of the Rights of Woman*, seems artificial, contorted and unconvincing. Its plea for the 'protection' of women hardly matches the radicalism of the 1795 'Song – For a' that and a' that'. The reasons are not hard to find. The song is the product of a fraternal, masculine culture in which Burns was far more deeply rooted. It is a work of poetry which uses male imagery throughout and is the product in part at least of exclusively gendered ideals of fraternity. As if to demonstrate this, he also wrote a companion song to the same tune, beginning:

> THO' women's minds, like winter winds,
>   May shift, and turn an' a' that,
> The noblest breast adores them maist,
>   A consequence I draw that.
>
> Chorus
>
> For a' that, an' a' that,
>   An' twice as meikle 's a' that,
> My dearest bluid to do them guid,
>   They're welcome till 't for a' that.
>
> (*Poems and Songs*, 430)

This is clearly a celebration of male power; in its use of the phrase 'The noblest breast' and in its use of the word 'blood' it is also subtly democratic, moving nobility from rank to sentiment, and blood from aristocracy to semen. It is like a politer version of one of the songs for the fraternity of the Crochallan Fencibles. Yet the ideal of 'Man to Man the warld o'er,/Shall brothers be for a' that' also subtly partakes of that world in its making fun of rank, its suggestion of alternative rankings, and its resolute emphasis on masculinity.

To say this is not to claim that Burns was unable to write credibly from a female perspective, as he does in 'John Anderson my Jo', or that he was unable to match coarseness with delicate eroticism; the latter quality is in evidence not just in works like 'Mary Morison' but throughout the corpus of his songs. Yet appreciating how much Burns's work is informed by the vernacular club-world of masculinity in which, like Fergusson before him, he was so at home, is an essential task for a modern audience. To view Burns in this light is to make possible important recalibrations of our understanding of the cultural authority of his poetry, and of his wider legacy. I shall take as a test-case Burns's acknowledged later masterpiece, 'Tam o' Shanter. A Tale'.

It is significant that this mock-heroic work of 1790 was written for Captain Francis Grose, and some knowledge of that man helps to contextualise the poem. An Englishman whom Burns called his 'kind funny friend' and for whom he wrote several poems, Grose was a connoisseur of vernacular language, and author of *A Classical Dictionary of the Vulgar Tongue* (1785) in which, among many other things, the expression 'beggar's benison' is explained. Described as a sort of antiquarian Falstaff, Grose was a 'man's man' whose military title was not an assumed one, like those of the Crochallan Fencibles, but came from his time in the Hampshire militia. He was an artist, author of *An Essay on Comic Painting* which celebrated energetic scenes like those found in Hogarth or Burns, and works of 'laughable contrast' such as

> that vulgarly styled *a Woman and her Husband*, this is a large masculine woman, and a small effeminate man; but the ridicule here chiefly arises from the incompatible; the man seeming more likely to receive protection from the woman, than to be able to afford it to her.[21]

Like the Burns of 'The Rights of Woman', Grose knows that the female is there to be protected by the male, and that any reversal of this situation would be ridiculous. Again, like Burns, Grose relishes the world of masculine literary bawdy, as is plain in his satirical *Advice to Officers of the British Army* (1782), which suggests to young officers:

> If you have a turn for reading, or find it necessary, to kill in that manner the tedious hours in camp or garrison, let it be such books as warm the imagination and inspire to military atchievements, as, *The Woman of Pleasure, Crazy Tales, Rochester's Poems* . . .[22]

The volumes mentioned here are Cleland's *Fanny Hill: Memoirs of a Woman of Pleasure* (a work enjoyed by the Beggar's Benison), John Hall Stevenson's 1762 *Crazy Tales* (a book based on a Rabelaisian satanic sect), and Rochester's notoriously sexually explicit poetry. Grose's library contents also indicate that he had a taste for the supernatural; he was a celebrated antiquary, and it was while he was compiling his *Antiquities of Scotland*, that he met Burns, whose supernatural romp 'Halloween' he thought 'excellent'.[23] Burns shared Grose's relish for the vernacular; and he warned his own 'brither Scots' that 'A chield's amang ye, taking notes, / And, faith he'll prent it'. Burns delighted in Grose's taste for odd ritual objects and secret, unholy rites:

> Ilk ghaist that haunts auld ha' or chamer,
> Ye gipsy-gang that deal in glamor,
> And you, deep-read in hell's black grammar,
>   Warlocks and witches;
> Ye'll quake at his conjuring hammer,
>   Ye midnight b—es.

Most of all, though, it seems that Burns (who gave Grose considerable advice about his volume on Scottish antiquities) admired the captain's gift for masculine sociability:

> But wad ye see him in his glee,
> For meikle glee and fun has he,
> Then set him down, and twa or three
>   Gude fellows wi' him;
> And *port, O port!* shine thou a wee,
> And THEN ye'll see him!
>
> (*Poems and Songs*, 392–3)

It is just such masculine sociability that 'Tam o' Shanter' (*Poems and Songs*, 443–9) begins by celebrating; for the 'we' who 'sit bousing at the nappy' are taken for granted as male, emphatically close to the male protagonist at this point, and set apart by all those 'lang Scots miles,/The mosses, waters, slaps, and styles' from the home where sits 'our sulky sullen dame'. Whatever else it is, this is a poem about gender, gender roles and sexuality, and Francis Grose was alert to the fact. He wrote to Burns about the poem as 'The pleasant Tale of the Grey mare's Tail' (*Letters*, II, 63). His words show that the lexicographer of 'the vulgar tongue' was quite aware of the sense of Burns's subtitle to the poem, 'A Tale'. For 'tale' is not just story; it is also (in a way that reinforces J. C. Bittenbender's Bakhtinian view of Burns) 'tail' – the lower body, the buttocks, the penis or the female genitalia.[24] Tam will be punished for his glimpse of tail, and it is his horse's tail which will be exacted as a penalty. While critics have speculated that the removal of Maggie's tail is a symbolic castration, they tend to miss the mark a little. The significance of the subtitle and the nature of the man for whom the poem was written, not to mention that of the author, make it clear that this is a tale all about tail, gender roles and masculinity.

Though the poem's narrative voice shifts, it remains one which mocks the feminine. Its mimicry of Tam's wife's haranguing him – 'She tauld thee weel thou wast a skellum,/A blethering, blustering, drunken blellum' – wins over our sympathies for Tam, not least because Kate's 'bl . . . , bl . . . , bl . . .' is the characteristic noise of blabber. At first glance, Kate may be correct when

> She prophesied that late or soon,
> Thou would be found deep drown'd in Doon;
> Or catch'd wi' warlocks in the mirk,
> By *Alloway's* auld haunted kirk.

But Kate is wrong, for, though Tam almost gets drowned and caught, in the end he suffers neither fate, so that his victory is not only over his female-led pursuers, but also over his wife's vatic powers. Burns follows with lines that, perhaps unexpectedly, seem addressed directly to a female audience:

> Ah, gentle dames! it gars me greet,
> To think how mony counsels sweet,
> How mony lengthen'd sage advices,
> The husband frae the wife despises!

These lines are clearly mocking, obviously designed at least as much to delight the male audience as to speak to the female. Moreover, since Kate's prediction turns out to be proved wrong (if only just), this passage is all the more mischevious; the phrase 'gentle dames' rings rather mischievously hollow coming so soon after the impressively long account of Tam's 'sulky sullen dame'. What Burns is doing here is keeping the female and the feminine in their rightful subject place.

To emphasise that, he goes on to sweep aside this address to the ladies with the abrupt words 'But to our tale'. The vulgar 'tale' replaces the supposedly refined 'gentle dames', and Burns proceeds to emphasise the pub not so much as the place where Tam grows 'gracious' with the landlady as the snug zone where, as Souter Johnny tells 'his queerest stories', as the landlord laughs and the drink flows, the male bonding of true brotherhood is achieved. This is the protected place of fraternity:

> But to our tale: Ae market-night,
> *Tam* had got planted unco right;
> Fast by an ingle, bleezing finely,
> Wi' reaming swats, that drank divinely;
> And at his elbow, Souter *Johnny*,
> His ancient, trusty, drouthy crony;
> *Tam* lo'd him like a vera brither;
> They had been fou for weeks thegither.

It is this male-dominated space of fou fraternity which Tam must leave to go to his hame and dame. 'Weel mounted on his gray mare, *Meg*', 'heroic' Tam is in control of (but, it transpires, dependent on) the female and feminine; moving from the 'bleezing' ingle to the 'bleeze' of Kirk Alloway, he is moving into more and more frightening, hellish and eventually danger-ously female territory. The 'mirth and dancing' which he now sees are things secret and forbidden; he becomes an onlooker at a secret ritual with its own satanic regalia – murderers' bones on the communion table, tomahawks, scimitars, knives and other horrors:

> Wi' mair o' horrible and awefu',
> Which even to name wad be unlawfu'.

Here the narrator trades on a sense of forbidden, secret rituals with their regalia and dreadful rites. From the fraternity of the pub, Tam has come to find himself a spectator at the arcane goings-on of another group of which he is certainly not a member; moreover, this is not just a satanic group but also one scandalously female, a coven not just of warlocks but of semi-naked witches too.

At first Tam is 'amaz'd and curious' rather than simply scared. He watches voyeuristically as 'ilka carlin swat an reekit,/And coost her duddies to the wark,/And linket at it in her sark!' Excitement mounts, so much so that the poet imagines himself entering the action. There follows a passage which, in its vision of a trouserless narrator watching beautiful young near-naked women dancing, hints at the kind of pleasures relished by the Beggar's Benison and celebrated by clubs like the Crochallan Fencibles:

> Now, *Tam, O Tam*! had thae been queans,
> A' plump and strapping in their teens,
> Their sarks instead o' creeshie flannen,
> Been snaw-white seventeen hunder linnen!
> Thir breeks o' mine, my only pair,
> That ance were plush, o' gude blue hair,
> I wad hae gi'en them off my hurdies,
> For ae blink o' the bonie burdies!

But the narrator keeps his breeks on, because this passage is a male sexual fantasy which the poem refuses to realise in full. What is disturbing for Tam and the narrator is that the female dancers reveal not the sort of feminine sexual attractiveness desired by the male gaze but an 'auld and droll' female sexuality of a kind normally taboo for men to see. 'I wonder didna turn thy stomach', girns the narrator, speaking to Tam; but Tam is as yet in control of the situation, for he remains the silent spectator and even manages to find one of the witches whose physique is 'winsome . . . and wawlie'. Yet this leads him towards danger, towards a loss of male control as, like even the Satan who fidg'd fu' fain' and gets sexually excited at the sight of this female body, so Tam grows 'like ane bewitch'd' to the extent where 'he tint his reason a' thegither'. Yelling out to this creature 'Weel done, Cutty-sark!', Tam turns her from his voyeur's sexual object into his active pursuer as she, Nannie, becomes the foremost of the hellish legion of witches chasing Tam. What Tam risks is a loss of male and masculine power – a loss of rationality not just to the powers of drink and the devil but to a threatening female who is literally bewitching.

Tam seems now at the mercy of the female in two ways. It's not just that he risks being caught by Nannie; it is also that the only way he can be rescued is if his mare Meg can save him. He is nominally still Meg's 'master', but it is her 'mettle' rather than anything else which saves him. Tam becomes a little ridiculous in several senses, one of which is that he has to rely on his mare for protection. He turns, for a moment at least, from the male as sly voyeur to the male who is made absurd by having to seek protection from the female. That moment, the climax of the poem, is a moment of parodic sexual climax when Maggie's

> Ae spring brought off her master hale,
> But left behind her ain grey tail:
> The carlin claucht her by the rump,
> And left poor Maggie scarce a stump.

This isn't really a castration, for it marks the reassertion of male power: Tam is saved; but it is a kind of joke-castration visited on the female who for a moment took the dominant part and became the active protector of her supposed 'master'. Tam triumphs over his wife's prophecies and over Nannie's hellish pursuit. The taboo female sexuality of the witches is banished, thanks to the 'mettle' of Maggie, and it's Maggie who has to pay for it: 'Remember Tam o' Shanter's mare', intones the mock-moral. It is the female who is punished in the end, not the brotherly Tam. This is a poem which plays a game involving a female challenge to the male, but makes it clear that (even if he needs a little help from his mare) it's the male who wins. That male is a boozing, fraternal male of the sort that Burns knew and liked from his masculine clubs. His poem hints at the kinds of sexual licence relished in song (and otherwise) by these clubs' members; it also makes fun of secret rituals, satanic parodies of Christian forms, and bawdy wordplay; yet it does so for wide public consumption, drawing its strength from the values of the fraternal subculture, yet presenting a mischievous public face which almost – but not quite – subverts decorum. It is a teasing triumph of masculinity.

I say this not to inveigh against the poem from the anachronistic stand-point of late twentieth-century gender politics, but to attempt to define and characterise more closely its ludically masculine values. It is a poem whose jokiness will give it an afterlife far longer than that of many more solemnly phallocentric works. We can relish it without fully believing in its value system. Indeed, like Standard Habbie and much of Burns's work, 'Tam o' Shanter' is a poem which encourages a complicated, part-serious, part laughing response; or, at least, it delivers a not-to-be-dismissed message about male and masculine superiority even as it makes a joke of the whole thing. It may be that for later ages the joke will more and more gobble up the celebration of masculine triumph; but each element, in whatever proportion, is likely to persist.

Finally, it was of course Burns clubs themselves which did most to continue the spirit of Robert Fergusson's Robert Burns and of the clubs discussed in this essay. Over the years they may have become more and more proper, but their fetishising of regalia, their toasts and fraternal conviviality, and their predominantly masculine character all continue the fraternal club spirit so beloved by the Burns who followed in so many of Fergusson's footsteps. Though often the tone of the clubs may have been masculine or masculinist in a way that lacks the sophistication of Burns's best poetry, it did resolutely continue an aspect of that poetry, not least of 'Tam o' Shanter'. A rare instance of women being admitted to a nineteenth-century Scottish Burns Supper came in 1859 when at the Exchange Rooms in Paisley 270 gentlemen (many in full masonic costume) celebrated the centenary of the Bard's birth. All the toasts were addressed to 'gentlemen', but towards the end of the proceedings 'a goodly selection' of about 100 ladies were admitted to the gallery.[25] They sat there confronted by a large transparency of 'Tam o' Shanter crossing the Brig of Doon, and his mare's tail in the clutch of the vindictive witch'. They had been put in their place.

NOTES

1. William Wordsworth, 'Preface' to the 1805 edition of *Lyrical Ballads*, repr. and ed. Derek Roper, 2nd edn (London: MacDonald and Evans, 1976), p. 21.
2. Burns hails Fergusson as 'brother' in the poem '[On Fergusson]'; see James Kinsley's one-volume edition of Burns, *Poems and Songs* (Oxford: Oxford University Press, 1969), 258. All references in the body of my text are keyed to this edition, using the abbreviation *Poems and Songs*. See also Fergusson's signature in the University of St Andrews Matriculation Roll for 1764–5 (University of St Andrews); this entry is printed in James Maitland Anderson (ed.), *The Matriculation Roll of the University of St Andrews, 1747–1897* (Edinburgh: Blackwood, 1905), p. 15.
3. *The Letters of Robert Burns*, ed. J. De Lancey Ferguson, 2nd edn ed. G. Ross Roy 2 vols (Oxford: Clarendon Press, 1985), I, p. 90. All other references to Burns's letters in the body of my text are keyed to this edition, using the abbreviation *Letters*.
4. Henry Mackenzie, unsigned essay in *The Lounger* (9 December 1786), repr. in

Donald A. Low (ed.), *Robert Burns: The Critical Heritage* (London: Routledge and Kegan Paul, 1974), pp. 70–1.

5. René Rapin, *The Whole Critical Works of Monsieur Rapin, in two Volumes* (London: Bonwick et al., 1706), II, p. 54.

6. R. W. Chapman (ed.), *Johnson's Journey to the Western Islands of Scotland and Boswell's Journal of a Tour to the Hebrides with Samuel Johnson, LL.D.* (Oxford University Press, 1970), p. 201. (Boswell, 19 August 1773).

7. Charles Webster cited in Matthew P. McDiarmid (ed.), *The Poems of Robert Fergusson* (Edinburgh: Blackwood for the Scottish Text Society, 1954–6), 2 vols, I, p. 18; other biographical information and the poems quoted in my essay are taken from this splendid edition (hereafter cited in my text as F), which should be reprinted.

8. Henry Mackenzie cited in F, I, p. 47.

9. Henry Mackenzie, art. cit. (see note 4 above), p. 71.

10. The standard work is still Davis D. McElroy, *Scotland's Age of Improvement: A Survey of Eighteenth-Century Literary Clubs and Societies* (Washington WA: Washington State University Press, 1969).

11. Chapman, ed. cit. (see note 6 above), p. 228 (Boswell, 25 August 1773).

12. David Stevenson, *The First Freemasons: Scotland's Early Lodges and their Members* (Aberdeen: Aberdeen University Press, 1988); Professor Stevenson demonstrated the centrality of freemasonry to the culture of Enlightenment Edinburgh in his as yet unpublished 1993 inaugural lecture as Professor of Scottish History at the University of St Andrews.

13. Mary Ann Clawson, *Constructing Brotherhood: Class, Gender, and Fraternalism* (Princeton: Princeton University Press, 1989), p. 51.

14. There is a considerable but disappointing account of Burns and freemasonry in Marie Roberts, *British Poets and Secret Societies* (London: Croom Helm, 1986), pp. 52–87.

15. Alan Bold (ed.), *Records of the Ancient and Puissant Order of the Beggar's Benison and Merryland, Anstruther* (Edinburgh: Paul Harris, 1982), pp. 8–10. Other details about the Beggar's Benison come from this work. I am grateful to Dr Christine Crow for lending me a copy. Whether or not all its details are accurate does not alter my argument.

16. Edwin Morgan, 'A Scottish Trawl' in Christopher Whyte (ed.), *Gendering the Nation: Studies in Modern Scottish Literature* (Edinburgh: Edinburgh University Press, 1995), pp. 209–10.

17. For these and other details about the Tarbolton Bachelors' Club, see James Mackay, *Burns: A Biography* (Edinburgh: Mainstream, 1992), pp. 82–3 and 119.

18. Morgan, art. cit. in note 16 above, pp. 208–9.

19. Daniel Wilson cited in F, I, pp. 50–1.

20. This extremely rare title page is helpfully reproduced in the modern edition of *The Merry Muses of Caledonia*, ed. James Barke and Sydney Goodsir Smith, with a Prefatory Note and some authentic Burns Texts by J. De Lancey Ferguson (Edinburgh: Macdonald, 1982), frontispiece.

21. Francis Grose, *Rules for Drawing Caricatures and An Essay on Comic Painting* (London: Hooper, 1788), pp. 27–8.

22. Francis Grose, *Advice to Officers of the British Army: A Satire* (n. p. [?1782]), pp. 66–7.

23. *A Catalogue of the Genuine Library . . . belonging to the late Francis Grose, Esq.
     . . .* (1791), repr, in Stuart Piggott (ed.), *Sale Catalogues of Libraries of Eminent
     Persons, Vol. 10, Antiquaries* (London: Mansell, 1974), pp. 479–80; Grose's
     library contents also indicate his interest in such volumes as *The Secret History of
     Clubs* (p. 480); he calls Burns's 'Halloween' 'excellent' in Francis Grose, *The
     Antiquities of Scotland, Second Volume* (London: Hooper, 1791), p. 210. 'Tam o'
     Shanter' appears in this work.
24. See J. C. Bittenbender, 'Bakhtinian Carnival in the Poetry of Robert Burns',
     Scottish Literary Journal, 21:2 (November 1994), 23–38.
25. Robert Brown, *Paisley Burns Clubs, 1805–1893* (Paisley: Alexander Gardner,
     1893), pp. 192 and 243–4.

LOVE COMPOSITION:
THE SOLITARY VICE

A. L. Kennedy

I hope I may impose upon your patience by beginning with a mild digression. I am not equipped with a convincing academic training, I have no ability to write any kind of poetry and I was almost entirely unacquainted with the works of Robert Burns before I reached the age of 18. I feel that a little mental leeway granted now may allow me to approach my subject with even the smallest degree of confidence.

I shall, therefore, tell you the story of my first encounter with Henry Mackenzie's 'Heaven-taught ploughman' – the same ploughman and Bard of Caledonia who was never mentioned during my schooling without the ponderous wag of a moral finger, exhortations towards a good and healthy life and muttered threats against ill-considered straying from standard English.

At 18, I was a student of Drama and Theatre Studies in what is accurately, if overly romantically, described as the Heart of England. A chain of coincidence too tedious to unravel here led me to spend a surreal evening in our local Burns club – a beleaguered but not unpleasant building which I remember being lost in a warren of concrete underpasses. The club boasted a great many features and facilities of note, including a bar which allegedly supplied every possible brand of Scotch, and The Howff.

As a young and delicate lady caught in the company of older, expatriate Scots, I was treated with extreme gallantry; and, whenever The Howff was referred to, shins were kicked, throats cleared and our conversation steered back to the nobility and international fame of the great bard Burns. Naturally, the whisky gantry ultimately caused a certain relaxation of social standards, and I found myself and my companion ushered ceremoniously into The Howff. The door having been opened, our escorts fell back, eyes glistening, and a curiously respectful silence descended. Somewhere a light was turned on.

And I saw 'our painting' – a mural of such monstrous proportions and gothic execution that it did effectively deprive me of breath. There across the wall – as I was gently told – rode Tam o' Shanter on his faithful steed Maggie, galloping over the keystone of the bridge to escape the pursuing Cutty Sark. Tam and Maggie might well have alarmed any physicians or veterinarians attending, but the anonymous muralist's efforts had undoubtedly been focused most disturbingly on the witch. Her sark was indeed 'sorely scanty' in longitude and was also fashioned out of fabric bearing an unlikely resemblance to chiffon. This negligéed creature was so monumentally well endowed that her vividly desperate lunge at Maggie's tail seemed not an attempt to trap Tam, but a last vain effort to prevent herself from being toppled forwards by her staggering mammary exuberance.

My hosts grinned with bashful pride as I nodded some kind of numb consent to the ghastly scene before me. Perhaps today I would have taken more vocal offence. Perhaps I would not, because I still believe I was shown something which was more than the group erotic fantasy of twenty or thirty fading Scottish men. The picture contained a terrible melancholy – a longing for a home and culture slowly descending into memory and imperfect reinvention. I feel I may also have witnessed a pictorial attempt to give Burns his female sexual equivalent in the eyes of men who loved him. That fitting rival, eyes aflame and breasts like missiles in free-minded pursuit, could only be what they had made her – a kind of intercontinental ballistic witch.

Thus Burns and sex both reared their heads together in my thinking, and thus I was first introduced to the heady blend of fiction, aspiration, hope and hero-worship that has now swirled around the memory of the man and his works for slightly more than 200 years.

Rather than present you with a Burns Sexual Almanac – the recorded liaisons, the locations of rendezvous, the resulting verse – I choose to take my themes from my encounter with that memorable mural. I will examine the harnessing and channelling of sexual energy for literary ends and the relationship between Burns's use of sex in his work and in his life. A poet does not necessarily choose his inspirations – sexual or otherwise – but he can choose how deeply they interact with his identity and his writing. In hypothesising on these interactions, I will also touch upon the Burns sex myth as an influence still at work in Scottish writing and wider culture today.

In choosing to step a small distance aside from the facts of Burns's life, I realise the risks I run, and I will state very clearly that I abhor the tendency in modern criticism to ignore the writer's craft, the writer's work and even the existence of such a thing as imagination. I have no appetite for amateur psychology, gossip and downright nonsense which seeks to confuse the writer and the writing and then to abandon both in favour of theorising which manages both to patronise the 'ploughman' and to mythologise away the labour inherent in being whatever 'Heaven-taught' might imply. I fully acknowledge that every guess I make at Burns's motivations and working methods will probably tell you far more about me than it does about him. What follows will, at least, be harmless and will leave his work largely unscathed for your later enjoyment.

First steps into sexuality, or indeed poetry, can establish patterns; systems of reinforcement and reward that can last for life. We know that Burns began his career as man and poet by producing – among other things – a barrage of paper serenades to almost every woman who crossed his path. A young man of an artistic turn of mind, brought up on Shakespeare and the classics of his day, a man brought up with Betty Davidson's story *telling*, Sunday sermonising and the power of the living word, might be expected to do little else. I would argue that the implications of these early actions quickly brought Burns into touch with a massive source of energy and inspiration for his work which moves beyond the simple fact that a little over half the population could be relied upon to provide him with easy subject matter.

What does the young Burns actually do when he sets out to celebrate the likes of Peggy Thomson? He turns his object of desire under the eye of imagination, examining her, dwelling on her in his mind – a not unpleasant process with which most of us would probably be familiar. Who can say whether, when Burns caught sight of a likely lady, he saw an ideal subject for a verse, or an ideal subject for a less literary exploration? I would suspect that both could often have been true, almost simultaneously. Writing would have presented the excitements of learning a new craft and of massaging libidinous reflection. Less socially acceptable expressions of lust might have been avoided by the exorcising effect of a line or two, but a vast field in which passions could be cultivated may also have been set under the plough. Burns's first Commonplace Book describes the effect of his writing and thinking of Miss Thomson as having 'battered [him]self into a very warm affection for her . . .'.[1]

I would be unsurprised to learn that a young man, living in a number of small and morally restricting communities, might find it both pleasantly relieving and wonderfully stimulating to devote a fair percentage of his writing time to his opposite sex.

Burns clearly had a desire to write against which he was willingly defence-less, but the sexual element of his work could have presented further powerful inducements towards the exercise of his abilities. Writing has been described as a solitary vice, and this can be one of its blessings; Burns's fixed and rewarding focus on the objects of his verses would naturally have lent a certain passion and clarity to his work. It would also have given him, very early in his career, the positive impetus which writing for a specified audience can provide. He was writing for the sake of writing, but also to exercise his will in the creation of a fitting gift, if not the first volley in a seduction.

Burns, very early, put his writing under public pressure and relied on it to perform, a risky but highly educational course of action. He also rapidly learned that eloquence could gain him almost, if not absolutely, everything. The power of his thought to change inspiration into a finished form within the absolute freedom of his thinking may well have seemed to continue into the realities of his life. In 1784, at the age of 25, he was certainly not unaware of the force in sexual energy which could be tapped for a poet's less hazardous private purposes. Before offering some of his own work, he speaks in his Commonplace Book of the disciplines and commitment which he feels are demanded by 'Love composition'.

> I have often thought that no man can be a proper critic of Love com-position, except he himself, in one or more instances, have been a warm votary of this passion. As I have been all along a miserable dupe to Love, and have been led into a thousand weaknesses and follies by it, for that reason I put more confidence in my critical skill in distinguishing *foppery* and *conceit* from real *passion* and *nature*.[2]

Burns's initial passions may well have been innocent, but – as we all know – the enthusiasms which he could batter himself into soon grew into liaisons, gossip and the repeated spectre of inadvertent impregnation. By 25, if not before, Burns was almost undoubtedly attempting to contain a number of mammoth tensions. In the area of sex, his passionate delight in sensuality battled his awareness of physical decay and death, morality fought sin, total power in imagination met total responsibility after the satisfaction of his imagined desires, and his expectations continually robbed or distorted his reality.

I generally feel that interior conflict can be hugely helpful in a creative process. Anger and frustrations can produce huge reserves of strength and a desire to build and triumph in what is sometimes the one area left open to an artist – the art. In Burns's case, I have the benefit of enough hindsight to say that such an array of unresolved conflict might well have offered an explosive impetus in his early years, but may have also been able to conduct a campaign of attrition that would ultimately tear him apart. He nourished appetites which grew with feeding and which had the potential to consume him. Having taken Amor Vincit Omnia for his personal battle-cry, Burns certainly came to understand that all really does mean all.

But first he could be beguiled by the generosity of his own temperament and surroundings. Burns's invention not only produced the writing, it also produced the writer; and a man of his intelligence and creative instinct could not have been unaware of the potentials which he contained. He had at his disposal, among other driving forces, the sexual tensions which I have suggested above and will now deal with in slightly more depth.

Like any writer of quality, Burns could be utterly overtaken by an element of the world or the life about him; whether that might be Jacobitism, outrage at cruelty to an animal, or – of course – attraction to a woman. A man who could be obsessed by the mere sight of Agnes Craig; by the taking of Miss Lindsay's arm; who could be bewitched by the picking of thorns from Nelly Kirkpatrick's hands, the feel of her skin, their exchange of little pains – would have an immediate access into the key details and the emotional vocabulary that could nourish great work. This sensual intensity would be all the more burning and poignant when set against the poet's fear of extinction and death. Increasingly this was mingled, if not replaced, by a fear of the Judgement to come beyond death, the final line drawn under a rising catalogue of sins. Burns knew his Bible and the rewards of the Just, and was also educated in the effects of poverty and hard labour: he watched them kill his father, the man who tried to ensure Burns's moral education. Burns's nocturnal cold baths to wash away night terrors – if not nocturnal lusts – his presentiments of mortality at every bout of ill-health and the grind of rural life all about him may have helped to convince him that the godly win nothing but a dubious prize in Heaven and that all flesh is indeed grass. Meanwhile, his discovery that a great many examples of flesh are also delightful seemed to give rise to a desperate need to both experience and immortalise a poet's vigour and his pleasures while they lasted. It is not surprising that Burns blazes into creative life with mingled prayers, bawdry and love songs.

While the Kirk and convention preached against fornication – and other smaller comforts – Burns could slip his pen into uncommitted sin, making the most of appetite's unblinking observations. As we know, appetite, once encouraged, did not confine itself to the page. Burns in writing, had the amoral author's right to examine, savour and penetrate just as he wished, and then walk away free. Burns in reality – always honing his craft, his words remarkable and sweet – could, for much of his life, be almost exactly as sexually successful as he wished.

What he could not rewrite later were the scandals attendant on his amorous forays; the social ostracism and the unplanned but hardly unpredictable pregnancies. Burns, the man who loved the simple company of women, would ultimately know that his presence alone could be enough to blacken a lady's name. I am loath to agree with my old English teachers, to say nothing of the Rev. George Gilfillan, but a more chaste Burns would quite possibly have lived longer. Freed from Jean Armour and what I must say I find her almost imbecilic tolerance, freed from the demands of their children and Mrs Hyslop's little addition to the brood, he might not have been forced to work in the Excise and struggle with his hapless farms. His politics might have proclaimed themselves more fully without a family to protect. Burns could have been permanently installed in Edinburgh, or made the move to London; he could have had time and new opportunities to write. Whether he would have been arrested for treason, or simply found his inspiration drained away for lack of stimulation, we will never know. Would we want a long-lived, healthy Burns if he wrote only insipid verses or nothing at all?

Certainly, there was nothing insipid about the young Robert, perched on the brink of publication and about to charm Edinburgh's interpretation of literary society. Dwelling morbidly on sex, as my subject compels me to, I will ignore the many other factors propelling Burns towards the next phase of his career and look at the final sexual tension listed above, that which lies between imagination and actuality. Burns was not a stay-at-home scribbler, nursing impossible dreams of passionate conquest. My interest lies in what he might have found to be his literal embarrassment of sexual riches.

Take Anne Merry – Burns did. No harm to her, but like many of his early loves she was not regarded as any kind of local beauty. The rigours of rural existence would hardly preserve delicate complexions and dainty bearings, but, even by the standard of the day, Burns's tastes often seemed to run from the plain to the ugly. I might argue that the poetic soul that could dedicate 'The Riggs of Barley' to a singularly muscular girl from the sticks, after one night in the mud together, could soar above such considerations as physical beauty. Perhaps he was a connoisseur of character. This kind of supposition would, of course, run against the massive evidence of Burns's hugely sensitive and romantic visual sense. A man who fell in love with the purely spiritual might well be disinclined to spend the nights in fields and hedges and on riverbanks, indulging in the semi-anaesthetised, one-night tumbles of which Burns seemed so enamoured.

So what was Burns doing? I can only guess, but I feel that at least part of him was triumphing in the fact that he could elevate any woman into a Beatrice, simply by an act of imagination. Darkness and spirituous liquor could have helped to make the actual woman concerned almost irrelevant at a certain level. I am not implying that Burns was a cold man, that he was at all snobbish in relations, or not genuinely delicately disposed towards womankind, but when the gloves – or rather, the britches – were off I think Burns could have been in love with *a* woman and in love with *every* woman, in love with love and in love with his own unstoppable abilities, all in a stroke of the same familiar motion.

As Burns's abilities flourished, however, his appetite for a less casual communion might well have grown. I do not mean by this that he experienced moral qualms at his behaviour which led him away from the flesh, although he does – of course – express regrets for his failings. Whether he found it consistently comfortable or not, Burns's sexually rapacious nature was with him to stay. As the forbidden unions repeated and repeated until they became commonplace, they quite probably prickled less and less with the excitement of sin, but I believe that Burns began to seek an additional satisfaction in his liaisons. He would always tend to return to the more purely animal act, but he seems also to have started a search for intellectual as well as sexual compatibility, a search in which he was never truly satisfied.

Seducing a farmer's daughter with pretty phrases was pleasant in itself, but it must have been a hollow victory if Burns knew she was impressed by the idea of a poet, by the simple existence of the poem rather than its technical perfection. At a very intimate level, he had outgrown his chosen audience.

I will emphasise again that I do not intend to imply that Burns was much of an intellectual snob. He was simply moving on. The young poet, unable to resist the desire to write, focused his art with the aid of another irresistible desire. His abilities were measured against – among other things – an urgent need to impress. Now he was moving towards women who would test his mettle further and help him to push himself towards better and better performances. The possible reward? To put it bluntly, a head-fuck – the ultimate trip for a man who could often live so intensely inside the walls of his own mind.

I am, after all, speaking of the young man who allegedly impressed the Misses Biggar with a plagiarised witticism from L'Estrange's 'Ruins of Quevedo'. Having been upbraided for looking at the ground as he passed them, he is supposed to have answered with: 'Madam, it is a natural and right thing for man to contemplate the ground from which he was taken, and for woman to look upon and observe man from whom she was taken'.[3] Whether this is true or not, I would guess it has survived as an anecdote because it is the kind of thing that Burns *would* have said – Burns, the same man who trained his dog to follow him devotedly so that he could wish aloud that a woman could love him as well. He was, in short, a seduction waiting to happen, but a seduction with a massive intellectual topspin which must very often have gone unappreciated. His early, stagey ploys are minor in themselves, but point to a stumbling level at which Burns would not be content to rest. In speech, in thought and in writing, he would move towards a confident presentation of both sinuous and subtle language, towards inspired improvisation and towards sharpening his attacks on stronger defences.

In this context, Burns's strong attraction to the quite attractive and well-educated Ellison Begbie makes sense. Here he can woo a mind, he can seek to capture the essence of a real physical and personal beauty, rather than seeking to paste a ready-made pattern on the next available woman on his list.

Jean Armour again offered a number of appetising challenges: a relatively well-off family, a certain respectability and education. Her subsequent pregnancy and Burns's abandonment of her would suggest that Jean's challenge proved slightly less demanding or interesting than Burns might have guessed. Burns's tendency to love them and leave them – no matter their condition – is hardly a state secret, and he may well have been a sexually compulsive blackguard. I cannot in any way condone his behaviour, but I'm afraid that I may understand it. Burns's poems and his women were largely treated in the same way. The sexual and creative drives going hand in hand would lock into action to produce a finished piece or pieces of work. Leaving aside a completed poem is very different from turning your back on a woman expecting your child, but to Burns the actions may well have felt very much the same.

Naturally, if Burns really wanted to scale the heights of education and good breeding, body and mind, Edinburgh society was the perfect hunting ground. It's not hard to imagine him in his blue coat and snug leather britches, positively steaming with rural vigour, pronouncing wit and wisdom with a teasingly unlikely accent and all the while looking brazenly about with those preternaturally bright blue eyes. He was the ultimate bit of rough: straight from a culture which might as well have existed on the dark side of the moon with all the delicious threats that that implied; and yet he was remarkably gallant, intelligent and – most aphrodisiac of all – a rising star.

We know that Burns detested fawning and was consistently revolted by the fact that he could dine with the likes of the Lord Monboddo only because he was a poet, when anyone else of his class would have been rejected out of hand. Of course, he enjoyed being hailed as the Bard of Caledonia by the Grand Lodge, and the thrill of publication and fame; but he must on occasion have felt himself being trotted out like a performing bear, fêted and then packed off back to his Lawnmarket lodgings.

Writers and artists have always been and are still being treated in much the same ways. There is always an uneasy line between the meritocracy and the aristocracy. Judging by my own experience and observations of this social phenomenon, I would say that Burns responded to it with admirable restraint. He may have been filled with righteous indignation, if not disgust, and may have been seared with sudden glimpses of his own soaring powers, but he did not strike out at what might arguably have been his hosts' weakest point. He did not give in to the pleading eyes and nervous mouths of all those wives and daughters, he didn't submit to the urge to bring pretence and condescension sweating down into honest humanity, even animality, with the simple application of skin against skin.

Obviously, I can only read between the lines of letters and the Commonplace books and then edge towards how frustrated Burns may actually have felt in Edinburgh. I can only assure you that I myself – a thoroughly mild-mannered and apologetically heterosexual woman – have never felt more inclined to commit indecent assault than after a literary luncheon. In occasionally comparing notes with male colleagues in similar situations, something of a common theme has begun to emerge. The worm longs to turn and to leave behind it a lasting chaos of emotional turmoil and hopelessly naked failures of politesse. Perhaps we might attribute some of Burns's later eloquence on the subject of man's essential equality to the sting of those patronising, prick-teasing Edinburgh evenings.

Whatever Burns's thoughts on his surroundings were, in Edinburgh he seems to have moved on to a hair trigger which had remained unexplored hitherto. Enter Agnes Craig: educated, a small-time versifier, voluptuously lovely, married to an estranged husband James MacLehose and cousin of a Lord. Burns couldn't have hoped for better; and, after one brief evening, he plunges into what becomes the 'Clarinda and Sylvander' correspondence. The rest, as they say, is history.

The letters preserved between Burns and Mrs MacLehose are a remarkable mix of studious passion, false modesty, saccharine mutual appreciation and frustrated lust. I suppose that the experience of reading strangers' love letters will generally prove to be much the same – oddly dull, oddly frustrating and ultimately slightly grubby. I would say that the Clarinda/Sylvander letters differ from the average in their lack of unguarded moments. For all the authors' protestations of hurry, interruption, rising passion and drunkenness, their sentences are almost always on their best behaviour and positively invite the voyeur.

'My great constituent elements are *pride* and *passion*', writes Burns.[4] Yet, two letters later, he will apparently interrupt his paper seduction to point out 'a slight inaccuracy in your rhyme' to his beloved.[5] There is much talk of hearts, but also of brains, of intelligence and stupidity and the ability of the lover to proof-read especially effectively. Of course, what might be seen as jarringly intellectual notes in another correspondence only underline the thrilling depths which this particular course of intercourse could have opened to Burns. And, no doubt, to Mrs MacLehose – the relationship would not have worked, had they not been temperamentally quite similar and equally frustrated in their personal desires. Here we find two people, beguilingly safe from a physical consummation, but able to enjoy every possible mental portrait of love. Burns has found his ultimate head-fuck.

Here we see Burns playing up to the idea of a receptive and attentive reader, making much of disclosed and undisclosed information. Thus we find that Burns, having written the word 'love' with relation to Agnes, then draws her attention to his error by suggesting that she insert a less explicit verb, so absolving himself from any guilt and still managing to let the ideal rabbit out of the hat. Burns was always a careful correspondent, crossing out a word in a casual business letter in an automatic improvement of scansion; but here Clarinda's undoubted concentration on his every comma adds the cream to his strawberries, and Burns can revel in the 'peculiar deliciousness' of the result.[6]

Burns polishes his craft and, while his life changes rapidly about him, has an opportunity to invent and immortalise his preferred identity. The man he presents to Clarinda can write of a teasingly anonymous love:

> Her name is indelibly written in my heart's core – but I dare not look in on it – a degree of agony would be the consequence. Oh! thou perfidious, cruel, mischief-making demon, who presidest o'er that frantic passion – thou mayest, thou dost poison my peace, but shalt not taint my honour! I would not for a single moment, give asylum to the most distant imagination that would shadow the faintest outline of a selfish gratification, at the expense of *her* whose happiness is twisted with the threads of my existence.[7]

What a man of honour. Even the fact that a reader today might initially think twice as to whether Burns meant Clarinda, Jean, Ellison, Mary, or yet another, only detracts a little from his portrait of barely suppressed longing.

Burns as Sylvander was the master poet, generous with the knowledge of his craft; he was the well-read admirer of Milton's romantic Satan; witty, devout, tender, gentlemanly and yet superbly insistent in his eloquently unspoken demands.[8]

Both parties having battered themselves to a fever-pitch, these demands did escalate. Despite Burns' injured knee, social convention and Agnes's vividly moral recollection of her absent husband, the pair do seem to have explored the border of the possible, although not as extensively as Burns wished. For Burns, this seems to have released and redefined many of the old tensions. While Clarinda writes of their relationship, 'Something in my soul whispers that it approaches criminality',[9] Burns again fights the religion that binds Agnes, even to an estranged husband, and that leaves him 'one who is haunted with conscious guilt, and trembling under the idea of dreaded vengeance!'[10] Between them they have built the bottle and the genie and the bottle-opener, but the last thing that either of them can afford is a full-blown affair.

So Burns writes through the few winter months that turn 1787 into 1788. Sending letters on a daily – sometimes hourly – basis, confined by an injury and sexual convention, he spends the dark days and darker nights exercising his ability to express passion as never before. He has found a melancholy, forbidden love that would only be damaged by consummation, but that can raise a remarkable literary energy.

I would not seek to make any comment on Burns's sincerity when he writes to Clarinda. I feel that he may well have believed the unbelievable as he wrote it to her, that he aspired to become and in some ways did become the man he described to her. If the fiery emotions which he expressed were not as eternally enduring as he suggested, I believe that his commitment to their expression was.

We know that the correspondence dwindled when Burns left Edinburgh. Clarinda's tone becomes very realistically petulant and distraught, while Burns grows increasingly, though gently, evasive. Sylvander's final surviving letter to Clarinda, written after Burns's return to the capital for one more meeting, is charged with convincing grief and seems to suggest some degree of physical accommodation and a compromise in solitary pursuits. Burns writes:

> I call over your idea as a miser counts over his treasure! Tell me, were you studious to please me last night? I am sure you did it to transport. How rich am I who have such a treasure as you! You know me; you know how to make me happy and you do it most effectively.[11]

No more high-flown declarations are necessary; this has the simplicity of real intimacy. Free and amoral as it is, though, this affair between minds has advanced to its furthest possible conclusion, in spite – or perhaps because – of Burns's recent marriage to Jean.

Burns had effectively written himself into an impossible corner: his actual relations with Agnes could not advance further, and, bluntly, the strength of Burns's memory and imagination could make the real Agnes almost irrelevant; the couple's frequent separations had allowed them both to become each other's figure of fantasy. Nevertheless, Burns almost undoubtedly left Agnes at a mutual peak of frustration and desire and then plunged himself into a period of intense poetic productivity.

The year 1789 sees the first in a small series of tense, sporadic letters between the formally-addressed M. Robert Burns and Mrs MacLehose. Although Burns did abandon Agnes physically in their hour of need, he was never entirely free of her mentally. Burns was cavalier with his loves, but his mind also had a strange kind of loyalty to its more absorbing objects of affection. Burns's later letters to Mrs MacLehose have a familiar precision, along with a wounded, mature tenderness. In one way or another, their mutual actions have almost always belied their words, but at the level of their greatest intimacy their imaginations seem to have remained true and to be following a script established with their very first letters. Throughout the rest of his literary career, Burns could rely on missives from Agnes to appear without warning and open their old, lyrical wound.

In their later letters, Burns may also have been revisiting a time when his mind and its labours seemed capable of anything and when the exercise of his passions had not left him with little more than regrets, isolation and a family to support.

This may chime in with his return to Mary Campbell – at the time, three years dead – as a subject for a loving lament. Jean, by then finally his wife, seems to have smiled indulgently on his sloping off to lie in the Ellisland straw and moon over an impossible love. Presumably this was less stressful for her than forays towards rather warmer flesh and blood; and perhaps, like me, she was moved towards compassion for the poet. It's not hard to imagine him, slightly under the weather, caught by a sudden quality of the light and seduced by the heat of his own past. Rather than a man barely containing his energies, anxious to conquer and shine and confident that all will eventually fall before his gifts, we begin to catch sight of someone paying the price for his choice of a combustible life and beginning to feel his isolation from the necessary fuel for his fire. With 'To Mary in Heaven' he dips into grief as an inspiration, but it lends a chilling, almost self-destructive light. Not the best company for Burns as he moves towards times of financial pressure, increasing work and failing health.

Burns's muse did not run solely on sexual energy, but it is interesting to consider how he adjusted to the circumstances of his final years, bearing in mind the part that sex and 'Love composition' played in his work. As a married man with growing responsibilities, a hard-pressed Exciseman and farmer, Burns still found bursts of creative passion to keep him producing a veritable flood of letters, songs, laments and, of course, what he thought of as his best piece, 'Tam o' Shanter'.

I mention 'Tam o' Shanter' by name, not only in memory of the Howff mural, but also because it can be used to suggest a development in Burns's behaviour and sexual inspiration.

'Tam o' Shanter' is not a young man's poem. Technically, it shows Burns's mature confidence and experience; but, for the purposes of this essay, I would point out that it does not reflect a young man's passion. The poem has a sexual charge, but it is non-participative; sex at one or two removes. Here, Burns deals with the sensuality of evil, of the unnatural, of cold flesh. We are not overwhelmed by the discovery of new love or fresh lust, but by a late, hard burst of strangely isolated passion and the guilty kick of voyeurism. Tam's scantily-clad witch can be ogled with impunity because she is so much less alive and so much more immoral than the observer. She is more than asking for it. Cutty Sark begins to seem very much like the wishful middle-aged male fantasy which my muralist portrayed.

A point can always be pressed too far, but is it any coincidence that this undoubtedly fine work coincides with a time when Burns's sensual stimulation must surely have been sorely limited? He is married to a woman whose passivity seems occasionally to border on the cataleptic, burdens of work and an increasingly ugly reputation limit his opportunities to stray, while for a man so careful to shape his own identity as he wished and so aware of morality, the possible door-to-door philanderings of a married Exciseman could not have appeared solely as a charmingly roguish indulgence.

But the poet still had consoling flames remaining. For Burns, the naturally sociable soul, there were boys' nights out a-plenty to keep him cheery, if not actually paralytic with drink. Whether Burns was an alcoholic I will not argue here. I have read highly plausible evidence to suggest that he suffered from an altogether different illness, and we can all pick through the anecdotes that describes him lying in the street, incapable in his Volunteer uniform, or living a life of exemplary chemical prudence and continence. I think I might be safe in saying that Burns was a sensual drinker, that he thoroughly embraced the effects of alcoholic intoxication, just as he did those of libidinous inebriation. I might also suggest that, from the time he moved to Dumfries, if not earlier, Burns seems to have become rather more of a drinker and rather less of a fornicator. Obviously – setting aside the possible effects of venereal disease – Burns's poetic output would suffer rather more after a night spent drinking a systematic poison than it would after a night of clandestine sweat with a barmaid from The Globe. His turning from one sensuality to another may well have hindered the muse, to say nothing of wearing down his health and reputation.

A slightly less perilous beacon in Burns's interior life was, of course, provided by his voluminous and varied correspondence. I would particularly pick out here his relationships with Mrs Dunlop – after whom Burns named one of his children – and Mrs Riddell. In his letters and meetings with these women, Burns may again have been able to enjoy the pursuit of compatible minds, the Edinburgh pleasures of being lionised by another class and the frisson of literate intimacy with women.

Mrs Dunlop was, I think, as he described her – his 'dearest' and 'much valued friend'.[12] Burns was warm in his affections, and in this case I think he was primarily enjoying simple affection, intellectual stimulation and some of the benefits of patronage, benefits which may well have felt less humiliating when dispensed by a woman. Close friendship may also have been aided by the fact that Mrs Dunlop was firmly married and out of Burns's social reach. This may have been enough to apply the brakes, even to Burns's sexual aspirations, and to give him confidence to proceed, safe in the knowledge that no moral line would be crossed. In writing to a woman for whom he had great fondness and respect, a person of education and good standing, Burns was placing himself under a familiar pressure to shine. Thoughts and verses offered were not traded casually, they were part of a process which kept the poet's critical and creative faculties alive.

We also find in Burns's correspondence with Mrs Dunlop characteristic expressions of his dangerous political enthusiasms. He can hardly be held responsible for the course that history would take about him, and seems always to have held to what one might call Libertarian and Nationalist beliefs, but some of his more personal frustrations may well have mingled with fellow feelings for his brother man. Much of the fire in his later pieces like 'Scots Wha Hae' comes from political, universal themes, rather than the subsiding personal or sexual inspirations. Outside Burns's writing, seditious club nights gave him one outlet for expression in daring toasts, but there may well have been a particular pleasure in trusting delicate political opinions in his own hand to a lady correspondent. And Mrs Dunlop did prove trustworthy, a friend when Burns's Excise job was threatened by his political activity; she apparently also destroyed more incriminating sections of Burns's letters.

Matters of intimacy and trust took on an additional intensity with Mrs Maria Riddell. Again, Mrs Riddell was far out of Burns's social and financial league, and was married; and in reading Burns's correspondence with Maria I cannot help being reminded of the Clarinda correspondence. As ever with Burns, phrases are elegantly turned, high hurdles are jumped and self-deprecation flows. What is added is a familiar urgency, that extra bite of sexual awareness. Burns can tease his 'first of friends, and most accomplished of women! Even with all thy little caprices!' and place himself willingly under her close observation, all the while trying to pick her like a lock, perhaps simply out of habit.[13]

Mrs Riddell is the lady of the manor who, if we believe Burns, could freeze his blood with a heartless look and set him padding round the door of her theatre box like a hungry dog.[14] He certainly seemed keen that Mrs Riddell should believe that this was the case. The descriptions which he gives her of their meetings and not-meetings echo the tone of his narrations of snatched or chaperoned rendezvous with Agnes Craig.

During the summer of 1793, Burns was deprived of Mrs Riddell's company for some time. On her return to the Riddells' Woodley Park mansion, Burns was still largely denied Maria's company because of her husband's absence. Warm letters were sent and a few meetings managed before Mr Riddell's return meant that more regularised calling could recommence. What happened next can only be guessed at; perhaps a pleasing enthusiasm rehearsed once too often in Burns's mind began to take on a life of its own beyond his imagination, perhaps – in the heat of a moment – a mark was overstepped, perhaps the ploughman simply forgot his place. We only know that the Burns/Riddell correspondence suddenly becomes decidedly frosty. The friendship is shattered and Burns loses one of the lights from his mind.

Until recently, Mrs Riddell's break with Burns was firmly linked with the most unmentionable, not to say inexplicable incident of his sexual career. Legend had it that Burns suggested a re-enactment of the Rape of the Sabine women while attending a small social gathering which included Mrs Riddell. Burns was supposed to have embraced this jolly scenario to such an extent that his relations with Mrs Riddell remained damaged for the rest of his life. Well, it would have been just like him, wouldn't it?

In fact, modern evidence seems to prove that the lady involved in the Roman amateur dramatics was Elizabeth Kennedy Riddell, another Mrs Riddell altogether.[15] Nevertheless, this remnant of salacious gossip has provided centuries of pleasantly prurient entertainment for the justified and just, and now raises a number of unanswerable questions. Why the two Mrs Riddells? Coincidence? Or did Burns want a more accessible version of the particular Pandora's Box which he could never open? Lovers have been known to fixate on brand names rather than personalities. And where and when exactly did the confusion of Riddells begin? Did the poet or his patron feed the already hungry literary gossip machine to create in fantasy what could not exist in fact, or were they torn apart by a chance configuration of rumour – that coincidence of names?

I can only suggest that the heat of Burns's friendship with Mrs Riddell would always be both a teasing inspiration and a social, personal and professional risk. We do, after all, tend to expect more and better of our close friends than we do of our acquaintances. An offence taken on either side could hardly fail to be grievous. With Mrs Riddell, Burns knows both the delight of a union of minds and the pain of being rejected by a woman and of losing an important friend.

It is significant that Burns's next letter in reply to one of Clarinda's infrequent communications contains satirical verses aimed at Mrs Maria Riddell.[16] Burns knew just the satisfaction that his old love would gain at the expense of the new, and could once again feel himself on sexually confident, safe ground. Burns expended a good deal of energy on attacking Mrs Riddell in writing, just as he had once courted her attentions. She was the woman who spurned his *mind*, something which may never have happened to him before. Needless to say, he not only aims his scorn at her, but also at her writing. The pieces against Mrs Riddell are hardly great art, or indeed great insults; they show too much hurt and anger on the part of the author. Her closure of their intimacy robbed him of a friend, of escape into a like mind, of an ego-flattering pseudo-relationship and of fuel for his work. Bear in mind that Mrs Riddell had also acted – like many of his correspondents – as a kind of surrogate editor.

It is this editorial role that Burns is careful to re-establish when their relations heal enough for correspondence to recommence. Once again recalling the Clarinda letters, Burns is carefully formal in his terms of address, carefully packing the space between the lines with wounded dignity and painstakingly repressed friendship. Soon verses and books are exchanged, and some semblance of a former source of nourishment returns. By the time it does, Burns's health and finances are precarious, and every God-fearing head in Dumfries could nod in stern agreement that his candle had burned at both wicked ends, given a bright but demonic light, and would sputter out directly, destroyed by its own appetites.

It makes a neat end to the story: Burns thought that he could get away with doing what lesser mortals wouldn't dare, but in the end his comeuppance comes up. Our national poet provides an apparently perfect example to shore up a plethora of theories on the nature of genius and the roots of creativity. He was a Great Man, therefore he suffered. He was a Great Artist, therefore he could behave quite abominably but was frequently forgiven because genius would be much too frightening to consider if it weren't terribly flawed, particularly if it is manifest in one of the lower classes. He was a Great Writer, therefore he ate himself alive in a series of pyrotechnically sensual episodes, thus allowing us to criticise him from a distance and perhaps overlook the less comfortable parts of his work. I could extend the list, but I'm sure you get the general idea.

And I'm not denying that some of the poetic myths have a basis in actuality. For example, it would hardly be surprising of someone who works mainly with their brain should sometimes seek mindless and/or highly physical recreations. Equally, there is no law that dictates that those pursuits need be either utterly immoral or completely inane. I have hoped to indicate that the interaction between the interior and exterior lives of Burns, or any other writer, is much more delicate, complex and wonderful than some critics and many journalists might suppose.

A writer moves in the grip of a great many higher powers. The baseline desire to write, the opportunity and ability to practise the necessary craft, the outlet to any kind of audience – all these are in some degree beyond the writer's control. Quite possibly, before he was even aware of these forces working in his life, Burns had moved to the next level of imponderables – the individual, specific inspirations for coming work and the larger forces which would propel the writer through a life which demanded writing: fresh writing, live writing, better and better writing.

I hope that I have been able to show in some degree that sex and sensuality provided a massive impetus as a major and a specific inspiration for Burns's work. He submitted himself and his actions to the intimate alchemy of writing and found himself balancing thought and action, possibility and actuality, intellectual devotion and play. In working so greatly with his own sex drive, he gained himself considerable force and eloquence, but may also have unleashed a sexually compulsive side which came to conflict with his work, if not his life.

As a role model for yet another generation of Scottish writers, Burns still lays a warm and shaky hand across any number of shoulders. The boozing, fornicating, self-destructive caricature is alive and well in lounge bars across the country, some would-be authors choosing to cut out the tedious processes of creation and publication and going straight for the wet brain and divorce. For every promiscuous and alcoholic poet, there are dozens of quiet men who go about the business of writing poems, flaming with different passions; but they don't make good copy. Even the male writers who are portrayed as the Oliver Reeds of literate Scotland may in fact comport themselves like Christian gentlemen and would rather be productive than dead, but rumour and the press often seem to prefer that this went unsung.

As part of a general intellectual devaluation, we now live in a country where the writer is reviewed instead of the writing. The production of literature is not in itself thrilling, and so the writer's life must be spiced up; and what better model that the Burns/Behan/Thomas tortured-Celtic-genius priapic drunk?

You may have noticed that women do not fit into this picture at any point. I am sad to say that women writers remain somehow imperfectly realised. A woman, mad with drink, is not a stout fellow having fun. A sexually overactive woman is not an admirable stud, laved with the musky scent of success. A woman writer can write, but will still be on shaky ground when it comes to *being a writer*. Our archetypes are held to be 110 per cent male, and malest of them all is Burns. The tenderness of his love lyrics, his liking of, his reliance on and his passion for women are apparently forgotten – as is the variety of his celebration of the interplay between the sexes.

As a woman, I might well have found Burns the man charming but ultimately repellent. As a writer, I can admire Burns the poet, above all for his ability to make passion articulate, to let love speak. His sins were largely those of a writer, and for those I can only forgive him. I have writer's sins of my own.

NOTES

1. 'Burns' First Common-Place Book', in *The National Burns*, ed. Rev. George Gilfillan, 4 vols (London, Glasgow, Edinburgh: William Mackenzie, [1879?]), IV, p. 316 [September 1784].
2. Ibid., IV, p. 314 [April 1784].
3. Cited by Gilfillan, 'Life of Burns', ibid., I, viii
4. J. De Lancey Ferguson (ed.), *The Letters of Robert Burns* (1931), 2nd edn ed. G. Ross Roy, 2 vols (Oxford: Clarendon Press, 1985), I, pp. 189–90 [28 December 1787].
5. Ibid., I, p. 196 [4 January 1788].
6. Ibid., I, p. 189 [28 December 1787].
7. Ibid., I, p. 202 [8 January 1788].
8. Ibid., I, p. 198 [5 January 1788].
9. 'The Clarinda Correspondence', in *The National Burns*, ed. cit., IV, pp. 270–312 (p. 297) [6 February 1788].
10. *The Letters of Robert Burns*, ed. cit., I, p. 225 [3 February 1788].
11. Ibid., I, p. 262 [14 March 1788].
12. Ibid., II, p. 170 [31 December 1792]; Ibid., II, p. 155 [October 1792].
13. Ibid., II, p. 267 [December 1793].
14. Ibid., II, p. 272 [January 1794].
15. Ibid., II, p. 473.
16. Ibid., II, pp. 298–300 [25 June? 1794].

BURNS, WOMEN, AND SONG

Kirsteen McCue

Even now, 200 years after Burns's death, the largest single body of his work – his songs – is still underrated and often misunderstood. As they do with his poetry, most Burnsites remember and hold dear a handful of his songs. Like his poems, many of the songs have been translated, and some – 'Auld Lang Syne' (Low, 105) being the supreme example – are performed almost every day somewhere in the world. But, until the twentieth century, Burns's songs have been virtually ignored by scholars. James C. Dick's volume of the songs was produced at the beginning of this century together with informative notes, and James Kinsley's definitive edition of the works also did much to emphasise the importance of the songs.[1] Cedric Thorpe Davie and Caterina Ericson-Roos examined them in more detail in the 1970s.[2] Most recently, Donald Low's bringing together of the 373 songs in his impressive *The Songs of Robert Burns* has set them on a new platform for discussion in the 1990s.[3]

There seems, on the face of it, little reason for this gap in scholarship, especially as the songs themselves have been published incessantly since their first appearance in James Johnson's *Scots Musical Museum* (1787–1803) and George Thomson's *Select Collection of Original Scottish Airs* (1793–1846).[4] Burns's songs have been included, almost without exception, in every general and/or specific volume of Scots songs published since the end of the eighteenth century. Thomson's volumes introduced the songs to European composers,[5] and the lyrics alone inspired some of the most famous nineteenth-century composers, including Schumann and Brahms.[6] Moreover, nearly all Scottish composers have set the lyrics with their original tunes, or with newly-composed tunes, at some point in their careers. But, as Donald Low has pointed out, the unrivalled popularity of a tiny number of Burns's songs has made it even more difficult to persuade the public at large that this area of the poet's work has been almost completely ignored.[7]

It has not simply been Burns's songs which have been neglected. Any examination of song publications produced in the eighteenth and nineteenth centuries shows that the lyrics of well over 100 Scottish writers were in print, and most of them have long since been forgotten. With the sole exception of Thomas Crawford's invaluable study of eighteenth-century Scottish song culture, *Society and the Lyric* (1979),[8] their work has not been examined by scholars in this century. There is clearly a reluctance to deal with song, in either musicological or literary terms, and there is apparently an equal aversion to recognising its popularity with the public during the period.

The title of this essay, 'Burns, Women, and Song', sounds like an appropriate title for an exploration of Burns's presentation of women in the large body of his work which falls under the heading 'songs'. But the aim is to examine briefly the work of a small number of Burns's fellow women writers who were equally fascinated by this literary and musical medium, and to determine the similarities between several of their songs and those of Burns. About thirty of the Scottish songwriters published during the period were women. Some, like Joanna Baillie, Anne Grant and Elizabeth Hamilton, were professional writers, but most were women of the upper classes, married to clerics, lawyers, doctors and military men. I have chosen to focus on only three of these women in this essay. Two, Jean Glover and Isobel Pagan, were working women who also came from Ayrshire, and whose lyrics influenced Burns, or became entwined with his. The other was Lady (or Baroness) Nairne, the most popular of the women songwriters of the time. But before examining some of the songs and their so-called 'creators', I want to pause a little and give some potentially useful background information.

Song benefited from the exciting developments in the publishing industry in Scotland during the early 1700s. There was a general interest in volumes of national songs and tunes elsewhere in Britain, but the number of publications of this sort in Scotland far outnumbered those produced in England, Ireland or Wales at this time.[9] The reason for the popularity of such collections during the eighteenth century has never really been explained. In Scotland it may well have been a natural consequence of the Union of the Parliaments of 1707, which applied some pressure to the Scots to collect their national heritage and protect it for future generations. In the eighteenth century, the Scots were passionate about the antiquity of this rich tradition of tunes and lyrics, and many surveys and essays were produced discussing the similarities between the ancient musical heritage of the Scots and that of the Greeks, for example.[10] Collections appeared in their hundreds, presenting many of Scotland's ancient songs and poems for the first time. Song lyrics which apparently hailed from past battles such as Flodden ('The Flowers of the Forest'[11]) or Bannockburn ('Scots Wha Hae' (Low, 246)) were very popular for their antiquity and for the obvious national importance of the occasion mourned or celebrated.[12] But we now know that most of these lyrics were written in the 1700s, a fact purposely ignored by the contemporary audience. These songs were nearly always inspired by a tune or an older song which did have its roots in an oral tradition. So, while the editors and writers played a game of old and new, they also dabbled in the game called fantasy and reality. Examination of the work undertaken by editors in the eighteenth and nineteenth centuries becomes a labyrinth filled with men and women of contradictory tastes and morals. In this case, songs were no different from other Scottish artistic media of the period, which displayed the same 'multiplicity of voice and complexity of personality', now commonly regarded as a national characteristic.[13]

The main issue to accept here is that published songs of the period were certainly not exact oral transcriptions, even if they posed as such. These songs were, as the German musicologist, Carl Dalhaus, has stated, 'written by composers [writers, editors] and presented to the populace for the purpose of educating it'.[14] Little, if any, fieldwork was carried out by the major song-editors. The collecting of the songs was done by individuals who often noted them down in manuscript.[15] The adaptation of the songs for publication was carried out either by the songwriters or by the editors of the collection. William Tytler's 'Dissertation on the Scottish Music' of 1792 stated quite clearly: 'it is well known, that many of our old songs have changed their original names, by being adapted to more modern words'.[16] Any survey will illustrate that the majority of the Scottish song collections of the period included the same material, copied from one publication to the next with variations which were ultimately the responsibility of the editor.

Burns collected tunes and lyrics from performances, but was influenced, like most other songwriters, primarily by collections. His inspiration came directly from *The Lark: Being a Select Collection of the Most Celebrated and Newest Songs, Scots and English* (1765), and from the volumes edited by Allan Ramsay, another whose work is greatly underestimated.[17] He was also inspired by the wealth of fiddle tunes presented in James Oswald's volumes entitled the *Caledonian Pocket Companion*, published throughout the 1740s, and he was certainly excited to get his hands on Oswald's collection, as he explained to James Johnson:

> I have besides many other Songs [on] the stocks, so you need not fear a want of materials – I w[as] so lucky lately as to pick an entire copy of Oswald's Scots [Music,] & I think I shall make glorious work out of it. – I want m[uch] Anderson's Collection of [s]trathspeys &c., & then I think I will [have] all the Music of th[e cou]ntry.[18]

Just as Burns was inspired by his forerunners, few songwriters, after the publication of his work in 1786 and 1787,[19] and the appearance of the first volume of Johnson's *Scots Musical Museum*, could fail to be impressed by Burns's songs. These publications inspired some women to write about

Burns.[20] Others, including Carolina Oliphant (Lady Nairne), began to write their own songs after seeing the fruits of Burns's efforts. As far as the Victorians were concerned, Burns quickly became the hero of Scottish song. The prolific Charles Rogers, a minister who produced numerous literary volumes and also edited many collections of sacred and secular songs throughout the nineteenth century, wrote in 1870:

> Scottish song reached its climax on the appearance of Robert Burns. He so struck the chord of the Scottish lyre, that its vibrations were felt in every bosom. The songs of Caledonia, under the influence of his matchless power, became celebrated throughout the world. He purified the elder minstrelsy, and by a few gentle, but effective touches, renovated its fading aspects.[21]

While sadly little personal correspondence exists for the women songwriters of the time, we can easily assume that most of them were equally influenced by contemporary volumes. After all, Ramsay dedicated his popular *Tea-Table Miscellany* (first published in 1724) to 'ilka lovely British lass', and George Thomson regarded himself as a 'Song-Broker for the ladies'.[22] Many song collections were produced specifically with young women in mind. Singing or learning a musical instrument such as the fortepiano, guitar or German flute became just as important a social skill as drawing, sewing or dancing.

While Burns's influence on others should not be underestimated, neither should their influence on him. Burns did collect some of his songs from performers, many of whom were women. His mother and his wife, Jean Armour, were fine singers. He also noted that an 'old Maid of my Mother's' had 'the largest collection in the country of tales and songs concerning devils, ghosts, fairies, brownies, witches, warlocks . . .', which, he confidently stated, 'cultivated the latent seeds of Poesy; but had so strong an effect on my imagination, that to this hour, in my nocturnal rambles, I sometimes keep a look-out in suspicious places'.[23] Moreover, it was the beauty of Nelly Kilpatrick's singing which caused him to write his first song at the age of 15, a moment which he vividly described in the same letter. He remembered how 'the tones of her voice made my heartstrings thrill like an Eolian harp', and continued: 'Among her other love-inspiring qualifications, she sung sweetly; and 'twas her favorite reel to which I attempted giving an embodied vehicle in rhyme'.[24]

Editors such as James Paterson and John MacIntosh later produced volumes including work by Ayrshire poets, claiming that while Burns did much for the area and encouraged many, his fame also overpowered other writers working there.[25] Two of the writers featured in Paterson's volume were women whose work influenced or impressed Burns. Jean Glover

(1758–1801), daughter of a weaver from Kilmarnock, performed the song 'O'er the moor amang the heather', a jaunty pastoral love lyric in which Burns understandably recognised certain qualities. He was impressed by her singing, but interestingly he was only too keen to note that Glover had failed to follow social conventions in marriage:

> This song is the composition of a Jean Glover, a girl who was not only a whore, but also a thief; and in one or other character has visited most of the Correction Houses in the West. She was born, I believe, in Kilmarnock. I took down the song from her singing as she was strolling through the country, with a slight-of-hand blackguard.[26]

Glover's name is associated with only one song, a common characteristic of other songwriters of the time. In the case of Glover, this fact allows room for suspicion. There is no evidence to prove that Glover wrote the lyric; we only have written proof that she performed it. It is a simple song filled with repetition and carried by a foot-tapping 'tick-tocking' melody. The subject matter of the lyric is also memorable. The hero of the song ends up in love with the shepherdess, encouraged, like Burns and Nelly Kilpatrick, by the sweet tones of her singing, and he announces:

> She charm'd my heart, an' aye sin syne,
>   I couldna think on ony ither:
> By sea and sky she shall be mine!
>   The bonnie lass amang the heather.

Certainly this lyric is not descriptively in the same league as Burns's song for Nelly Kilpatrick – 'O once I lov'd a bonnie lass' (Low, 1) – but Glover's lyric displays the same rhythmic power as 'Corn Riggs' (Low, 7), which was also one of Burns's early creations.[27] The refrains of the two songs follow an almost identical format, dictated by the shape of their respective melodies:

Burns:

> Corn rigs, an' barley rigs,
>   An' corn rigs are bonie:
> I'll ne'er forget that happy night,
>   Amang the rigs wi' Annie.

Glover:

> O'er the moor amang the heather,
> O'er the moor amang the heather,
> There I met a bonnie lassie
> Keeping a' her yowes thegether.

It seems rather ironic for Burns to comment so crudely on Glover's immorality, but he obviously appreciated the song which she performed, alerting Johnson and ensuring that it became famous through publication in the *Scots Musical Museum* (no. 328, 1792).

'Ca' the yowes', attributed to both Isobel Pagan (1741–1821) and Burns, illustrates how complex the development of lyrics can be. Pagan was also termed a 'peasant poet', though unlike Glover she apparently did see the publication of a small book of her poems.[28] Burns made no reference to Pagan, though she was based in Muirkirk and was well known locally, primarily because she ran a 'kind of low tippling house'.[29] Burns presented two versions of the song. The first (Low, 64) was for Johnson's *Museum*, and Burns noted that it was 'a beautiful song in the true old Scotch taste, yet I do not know that ever either air or words, were in print before'.[30] It begins:

> As I gaed down the water-side,
> There I met my shepherd-lad,
> He row'd me sweetly in his plaid,
> And he ca'd me his dearie.

This version of the song is almost identical to that supposedly created by Isobel Pagan and included in several nineteenth-century volumes. The difference between the Burns and Pagan versions lies in the omission of only one verse, which Burns included in his version for Johnson (*Scots Musical Museum*, no. 264, 1790). The song begins with the meeting of the lovers and their walk along the water-side. Then Burns includes the following verse:

> I was brought up at nae sic school,
> My shepherd-lad, to play the fool,
> And a' the day to sit in dool,
> And nae body to see me.

In reply to the above verse, the shepherd promises to give his girl 'gowns and ribbons' and 'cauf-leather shoon' and pledges to love her. She decides that if he stands by his word she will agree to be his. It seems strange that this potent verse, in which the girl shows her strength of mind, should be omitted for Pagan's published version but included in Burns's. However, as can be seen when examining many of the songs of the period, editors could often make changes if they felt that the sentiment of a piece was too challenging for their clientele.

Burns sent his second version to George Thomson in 1794 and stated confidently that he was indeed the first to bring the song to public notice:

I am flattered at your adopting, 'Ca', the yowes to the knowes', as it was owing to me that it ever saw the light. – About seven years ago, I was well acquainted with a worthy little fellow of a Clergyman, a Mr Clunzie [sic], who sung it charmingly; & at my request, Mr Clarke took it down from his singing. – When I gave it to Johnson, I added some Stanzas to the song & mended others, but still it will not do for *you*.[31]

He denied all knowledge of Isobel Pagan and referred instead to Mr Clunzie's rendition as the source of his song. In his *Illustrations of the Lyric Poetry and Music of Scotland*, published in 1853, William Stenhouse made reference to the song on two occasions. Pagan's name is not mentioned in connection with Burns's lyrics,[32] but, when Stenhouse discussed the song a second time, he noted that Allan Cunningham, who produced a four-volume collection of Scots songs in 1825, described 'Ca' the yowes' as being 'partly old and partly new; what is old is very old, what is new was written by a gentleman of the name of Pagan'.[33] At this point, Stenhouse admitted that 'In Ayrshire . . . the song has been assigned to a different person, named Isabel [sic] Pagan'.[34] There is much similarity between the versions, but suffice it to say that, there is no way of proving that the song was originally Pagan's, or that Burns was indeed the first to find it. In his *Illustrations*, Stenhouse also quoted the 'old verses' which were obviously the direct ancestor of the lyrics attributed to Burns and to Pagan. Unfortunately he gave no source for the 'old verses', which adds to the confusion.[35] It is possible to surmise that the lyric was a popular one, which inspired others to dabble with its essence and create new songs. There has been little controversy surrounding Burns's later version beginning 'Hark! the mavis' evening sang,/ Sounding Clouden's woods amang', which is now the best known of the different versions (Low, 260).

Confusion with the 'ownership' of lyrics also played a major part in Burns's relationship with the most important and prolific of the women songwriters, namely Carolina Oliphant, or Lady or Baroness Nairne (1766–1845). Sadly, the two poets never met, nor did Burns know Nairne's work, as none of her lyrics were published before the early 1820s.[36] But William Stenhouse was to make the rather grand declaration that Burns and Nairne were 'the two most beloved personalities in all Scottish Literature'.[37] Though almost unheard of in the 1990s, Nairne's songs were very popular during the late nineteenth century, when they appeared in numerous editions.[38] Charles Rogers believed that Nairne 'proved a noble coadjutor and successor to the rustic bard [Burns] in renovating the national minstrelsy'.[39]

So great was the influence of Burns on Nairne that one song in particular was believed to be Burns's creation for many years after her death, until her biographer found proof of Nairne's authorship. 'The Land o' the Leal' has been the subject of heated controversy. Charles Rogers's testament that

Nairne composed the lyrics to the famous martial tune known as 'Hey tutti taiti' (the same tune matched with Burns's 'Scots Wha Hae') was made in his *Life and Songs of the Baroness Nairne* published in the 1890s.[40] Rogers insisted that she had written the song on the death of the baby daughter of Mrs Campbell Colquhoun of Killermont, a close friend of Carolina Nairne:

> I'm wearin' awa', John,
> Like snaw-wreaths in thaw, John,
> I'm wearin' awa'
>   To the land o' the leal.
> There's nae sorrow there, John,
> There's neither cauld nor care, John,
> The day is aye fair
>   In the land o' the leal.
>
> Our bonnie bairn's there, John,
> She was baith gude and fair, John,
> And oh! we grudged her sair
>   To the land o' the leal.
> But sorrow's sel' wears past, John,
> And joy's a-comin' fast, John,
> The joy that's aye to last
>   In the land o' the leal.

Rogers gave a long and involved history of the writing of the song, and quoted from a letter in which Carolina Nairne stated: 'I wrote it merely because I liked the air so much, and I put these words to it, never fearing questions as to the authorship'.[41] Nairne's insistence on anonymity, here and on many other occasions, resulted in public ignorance of her work for many years, but it was an activity shared by several women writers of the period, who feared family backlash or public disdain through publication. Lady Ann Barnard (1750–1825), creator of the famous 'Auld Robin Gray', likewise hoped that no-one would recognise her as the author.[42] 'Mrs Colquhoun was entreated not to divulge the authorship' of 'The Land o' the Leal',[43] and consequently the song was ascribed to Robert Burns 'by the universal consent of his countrymen',[44] who concluded that the song must be Burns's 'deathbed valediction'. Alexander Crichton believed that Rogers was a 'scheming inventor' who was only interested in a good story.[45] but it is a little unsettling that William Stenhouse supported Crichton's theory.

To summarise a long and complex debate, Crichton believed that Burns's illness and death, and the hunger of his family, were undoubtedly the subject of the song. He argued that when the name 'John' was changed to 'Jean', then it referred, of course, to Burns's wife Jean Armour, and that this version of the song was far superior to the 'John' version. The song was indeed published in several collections in its 'Jean' version, most notably in George Farquhar Graham's *Songs of Scotland* of 1848.[46] Crichton also made reference to the death of Burns's daughter in October 1787, and cited the apparent memory of Jessie Lewars, a friend of Burns, claiming that she remembered Burns presenting her with the lyric scribbled on the back of a 'menagerie bill'. Finally, he tried to prove that the words included in the song could only be the choice of Burns, arguing avidly that 'fain' and 'leal' were favourite words of the poet, and stating categorically that the song was so similar to 'John Anderson my Jo' that it could only be the work of Burns.

In contrast, Crichton had few good words to say about Nairne, dismissing all possibility of her as the author since she spent so much time posing as a 'Tinkerer of Songs'.[47] He claimed that Rogers had got much of his information from discussions with a friend of Nairne's, Miss Helen Walker of Dalry, whom he described as 'an eccentric who attended tea parties with a black bag which she filled of the eatables to treat cab men on her way home'.[48] In Crichton's opinion, Nairne's refusal to have her name published with the song was proof that she had stolen Burns's verses. In fact, Nairne hardly ever gave her own name with the songs which she published, and she created the memorable pseudonym of 'Mrs Bogan of Bogan' for the first publication of her songs in Robert Purdie's *The Scottish Minstrel* which appeared in several volumes between 1821 and 1824.[49] The debate over the authorship of the song continued until the 1920s, but the three major scholars of Burns's songs – Dick, Kinsley and Low – make no reference to the song and clearly agree with Nairne. She had apparently questioned the absence of the song in earlier editions of Burns's collected works.[50]

There is, however, little doubt that Burns cast a major influence on Nairne in her early years. Rogers explained the motivation for Nairne's writing:

> Robert Burns had just appeared on the horizon. Carolina Oliphant was charmed with his verses; she was among the first to recognise his genius. When the poet proceeded to Edinburgh in 1786, and announced a subscription edition of his poems, she induced her brother Laurence to enter his name on the list of subscribers. During the following year Burns became a contributor to *The Scots Musical Museum*, a work designed by James Johnson, engraver in Edinburgh. In the pages of this publication Carolina remarked the successful efforts of the Ayrshire poet in adapting new words to tunes which had heretofore been linked to verses degrading and impure. With renewed interest she watched his labours, when, in 1792, he appeared more systematically engaged as a purifier of the elder minstrelsy, in the elegant collection of Mr George Thomson.[51]

Nairne's other biographers, George Henderson and her great-niece Margaret Stewart Simpson,[52] also laid much emphasis on the purification of lyrics as Nairne's major inspiration. It would be incorrect to suggest that this was Burns's primary motive in collecting and writing songs. He did much 'cleaning' of songs for Thomson's *Select Collection* to ensure that Thomson's volumes included 'delicate', 'suitable' or 'proper' verses, and in doing so created some of his finest songs: 'John Anderson my Jo' (Low, 142), 'Duncan Gray' (Low, 222), 'O let me in this ae night' (Low, 279), 'Dainty Davie' (Low, 245) and 'Comin' thro' the Rye' (Low, 312), to name a few. However, his personal song collection now known as *The Merry Muses of Caledonia* shows that Burns's interest was in all songs, not only 'acceptable' ones.[53]

The history of one of Nairne's best-known lyrics, 'The Laird o' Cockpen', illustrates the process of purification which she undertook. The lyric was composed to match the bouncy tune entitled 'When she cam ben she bobbit', which appeared in Johnson's *Scots Musical Museum* in 1792 (no. 353).[54] The lyric printed by Johnson was also concerned with the Laird of Cockpen, a friend of Charles II, but it told the story of his extra-marital affair:

> O when she cam ben she bobbit fu' law,
> O when she cam ben she bobbit fu' law,
> And when she cam ben she kiss'd Cockpen,
> And syne deny'd she did it at a'.
>
> And was na Cockpen richt saucy witha',
> And was na Cockpen richt saucy witha',
> In kissing the dochter of a Lord,
> And kissin' a collier lassie an a'.
>
> O never look down, my lassie at a',
> O never look down, my lassie at a',
> Thy lips are as sweet and thy figure compleat,
> As the finest dame in castle or ha'.
>
> Tho' thou has nae silk and holland sae sma',
> Tho' thou has nae silk and holland sae sma',
> Thy coat and thy sark are thy ain handywark
> And lady Jean was never sae braw.

This lyric was clearly too improper for Nairne's liking. Again fantasy meets reality to some extent, for even though it is often thought that the peasantry of the period were far more promiscuous than the middle and upper classes, Lawrence Stone explains that 'freedom of sexual expression was one of the many by-products of the eighteenth-century pursuit of happiness'.[55] There was consequently an 'easy-going attitude to sexual promiscuity among the higher aristocracy'[56] and the professional classes, at least until the last decades of the century. This lyric is particularly interesting because it also presents the distinct roles of women: as wife and mother (Lady Jean), whose chief role was to produce the heir; and as mistress (the collier lassie), who was there for 'companionship and sexual pleasure'[57] alone. Furthermore, the lyric describes the facility of the crossing of social barriers for men – from the aristocratic Lady Jean to the common collier lassie. That Cockpen, and many others, were highly promiscuous was still no reason to present this story as an approved code of conduct, but the tune was particularly attractive.

Nairne's version was clearly linked to the above lyric. In her song, the Laird decides to find himself a wife and settles on a neighbour's daughter. He dresses in his Sunday best and calls upon her, but her answer to his proposal of marriage is unexpected:

> The laird o' Cockpen, he's proud and he's great
> His mind is ta'en up wi' the things o' the State;
> He wanted a wife, his braw house to keep,
> But favour wi' wooin' was fashious to seek.
>
> Down by the dyke-side a lady did dwell,
> At his table head he thought she'd look well,
> McClish's ae daughter o' Clavers-ha' Lee,
> A penniless lass wi' a lang pedigree.
>
> His wig was weel pouther'd and as gude as new,
> His waistcoat was white, his coat it was blue;
> He put on a ring, a sword, and cock'd hat,
> And wha could refuse the laird wi' a' that?
>
> He took his grey mare and he rade cannily,
> An' rapp'd at the yett o' Clavers-ha' Lee;
> 'Gae tell Mistress Jean to come speedily ben, –
> She's wanted to speak to the Laird o' Cockpen'.
>
> Mistress Jean was makin' the elderflower wine;
> 'An' what brings the laird at sic a like time?'
> She put aff her apron, and on her silk gown,
> Her mutch wi' red ribbons, and gaed awa' down.

An' when she cam' ben he bowed fu' low,
An' what was his errand he soon let her know;
Amazed was the laird when the lady said 'Na',
And wi' a laigh curtsie she turned awa'.

Dumfounder'd was he, nae sigh did he gie,
He mounted his mare – he rade cannily;
An' aften he thought, as he gaed through the glen,
She's daft to refuse the laird o' Cockpen.

Nairne's lyric is quietly ironic when one considers the version published by Johnson. She keeps a close association by using the same names, and by incorporating the first line of the earlier song, 'When she cam ben she bob-bit fu' low', with a subtle difference – 'An' when she cam' ben he bowed fu' low'. But Cockpen's arrogance is rather crudely undermined by Nairne in Miss McCleish's refusal, when in the middle of the dignified meeting she gives the answer 'Na' to rhyme with 'awa'. This process of purification was similar to that followed by Burns, as can be seen when comparing the final effusion of love, or the comic songs of wooing which were inspired by his bawdy originals. Like Nairne, Burns often maintained the names of charac-ters in the original songs – Duncan and Maggie in 'Duncan Gray', or John Anderson in 'John Anderson my Jo', or Davie in 'Dainty Davie' – but he concentrated on removing the sexual connotations of the bawdy lyric, and focused instead on the zest of the personalities or the presentation of sound morals for his new version.

Miss McCleish in Nairne's 'Laird o' Cockpen' displays the same strength of will as many of the heroines in Burns's songs; indeed, this feminine independence of mind was something of a characteristic of songs of the period. Burns's Maggie in 'Duncan Gray' almost ruins her chances of future happiness because of her determination to refuse Duncan's approaches. Likewise, his young heroine in 'What can a young lassie do wi' an auld man?' (Low, 176) is stubborn and angry about her lot, and 'Last May a braw wooer cam' down the lang glen' (Low, 293) and 'I'm ower young to marry yet' (Low, 69) involve other young women who are more than capable of controlling their own destinies. But few lyrics escaped the hands of editors, who felt they could be even better.

'The Laird o' Cockpen' was first printed in the above form in George Thomson's 1825 octavo collection entitled *Thomson's Collection of the Songs of Burns, Sir Walter Scott Bart. and other Eminent Lyric Poets . . .*[58] But in later editions Nairne's tightly-knit proposal-scene was completely transformed by adding two verses in which Mistress Jean recognised her error and ultimately agreed to marry the Laird. When Thomson printed the song in 1843 in the fifth volume of his *Select Collection of Original Scottish*

Airs (no. 250), he added two stanzas written by himself. He apologised to the unknown author by stating that the song was frequently made more respectable by this false coda: 'The Editor hopes the Author will pardon him for thus terminating the courtship, to which he was induced by having observed that the song, as generally sung, rarely escapes without some sort of postscript matrimonial'. Two simple and rather unadventurous verses transformed the whole story, and the characteristics which made it so dynamic, into a rather common love song, for the Laird gets everything and the girl's gesture of independence is shown to be a foolish mistake on her part. If the song managed to avoid Thomson's coda, then it was just as often printed with two extra verses telling the same story attributed to 'Miss Ferrier'.[59]

Another similarity between Burns and Nairne was the importance of the melody and an ear for attractive tunes. Burns noted that 'untill I am compleat master of a tune, in my own singing, (such as it is) I never can compose for it'.[60] And Nairne explained in a letter of 1782, in reply to her uncle:

As May is at present very busy playing some favourite tunes of mine, I hope you won't expect a very correct epistle; for to hear agreeable music, and at the same time employ my mind about anything else, is what I can hardly do . . . I do think fine music engrosses all the senses, and leaves not one faculty of the mind unemployed.[61]

Several of Nairne's songs were inspired by tunes which had also encouraged Burns: 'The lea-rig', 'Down the Burn Davie', 'Comin' 'thro' the Rye', 'Here's a health to and I lo'e dear'. The lyrics are often very different, and Nairne did display a leaning towards nostalgia and sentimentality, almost stretching into the expression of the Kailyard writers at the beginning of the twentieth century. But her best songs, including 'The Laird o' Cockpen', 'Caller Herrin' ' and her famous Jacobite lyrics – 'Charlie is my Darling', 'Wha will be King but Charlie?', 'A Hundred Pipers', 'Will ye no come back again?', etc. – are comparable with any of Burns's best lyrics.[62]

What becomes clear is this sharing of common material. Any comparisons of women's lyrics with those of Burns – and, to my knowledge, those of male lyricists follow the same pattern – home in on the same melodies, or the same sources. Ironically, it was not necessary to be musically literate to be able to write songs. It was possible for a writer to pose as a songwriter by following the structure of any set of lyrics, and ignoring the tune for which the lyrics were written. This activity was positively encouraged by the large number of the song-collections produced without music. Such volumes were the continuation of a much older Scottish tradition stretching back to the sixteenth century and possibly earlier. The popularity of broadsides and songsheets was surely based on the circulation of new words to well-known tunes. The most important Scottish volumes of the eighteenth century – including James Watson's *Choice Collection of Comic and Serious Poems both Ancient and Modern* (1706, 1709 and 1711), most of Allan Ramsay's volumes, and David Herd's *Ancient and Modern Scots Songs* (1769) – presented lyrics alone, even though the title of the tune to which the lyrics were meant to be sung was also given. This process continued throughout the nineteenth century, and Allan Cunningham's *Songs of Scotland, Ancient and Modern* of 1825 and the numerous collections edited by Charles Rogers – *The Modern Scottish Minstrel* (1845), *The Sacred Minstrel* (1859) and *The Scottish Minstrel: The Songs of Scotland subsequent to Burns* (1870) – likewise included biographies and lyrics but no music. Cedric Thorpe Davie rightly stated, in discussing Burns's songs, that 'but for the tunes, the words would never have come into existence, and it is absurd to regard the latter as poetry to be read or spoken aloud'.[63] But in reality, because of such published collections, songs were too often regarded as 'poetry to be read or spoken aloud'. It should therefore be little surprise that many these songs had died by the twentieth century, limping on without their tunes. Without performance, later generations had no way of learning the tunes, unless they actively sought out the lost melodies in older collections. And even then, many different melodies could be set to one lyric, and vice versa.

Working with songs of the period is therefore always problematic. This uncomfortable blend of materials has probably been one of the reasons for avoiding major academic discussion of songs in general.[64] All published Scottish song of the eighteenth and, to a large extent, the nineteenth centuries was inextricably linked to an oral tradition. It is often impossible, as the above discussion shows, to account for the development of a song. Just when a pattern seems to be clear, another version of the tune or the lyric, or reference to the song, will be found in a hitherto undiscovered manuscript or published volume, which changes everything. Of course, ultimately it is this mysterious blend, and the excitement of the unknown history, which makes these pieces so rich. Hidden in a new song, which is coded with moral messages for today, are secrets from 100 years ago, and these messages are commonly conveyed by means of an instrumental or vocal melody which carries in it the musical history of a people. Whether noted directly from performance, or altered for publication in a collection; whether created by men or by women, these pieces still represent a huge section of our national heritage. We tend to scoff at Victorian opinions; but perhaps Eliza Cook, writing in 1852, had it just about right:

It may be truly averred that the *heart* of the Scotch people is written in their songs. They are the vehicle of deepest emotion, of playfulest humour, and of most passionate love.[65]

NOTES

1. James C. Dick, *The Songs of Robert Burns* (London, Edinburgh, Glasgow and New York, 1903). Dick subtitled the book 'A Study in Tone Poetry' and presented invaluable notes about each of the songs; there are 361 songs printed. Kinsley's is the standard reference text of the poet's work, which included the songs with their tunes: James Kinsley, *Burns: Poems and Songs* (Oxford, 1969).

2. Cedric Thorpe Davie published his article entitled 'Burns, Writer of Songs' in *Critical Essays on Robert Burns*, ed. D. A. Low (London, 1975), pp. 157–85. Caterina Ericson-Roos produced a doctoral thesis examining the unity of the poetry and music in the songs: *The Songs of Robert Burns: A Study of the Unity of Poetry and Music* (Uppsala, 1977).

3. Donald A. Low, *The Songs of Robert Burns* (London, 1993).

4. Thomson also included Burns lyrics in his *Select Collection of Welsh Airs*, 3 vols (Edinburgh and London, 1809–17), and his *Select Collection of Irish Airs*, 2 vols (Edinburgh and London, 1814–16), though by far the majority of his lyrics appeared in the larger 'Scottish Collection', 6 vols (Edinburgh and London, [1793–1846]).

5. Pleyel, Kozeluch, Haydn, Beethoven, Weber and Hummel.

6. For further information, see R. Fiske, *Scotland in Music: A European Enthusiasm* (Cambridge, 1983), pp. 156–86.

7. Low, *Songs*, p. 1. Low states: 'It is remarkable that after two hundred years a dozen or so of Burns's songs are widely known through live performances and records. But the sometimes hackneyed favourites of Burns Suppers and recording companies are only a tiny number of a large and impressive body of work.' Many biographers, including David Daiches, James Mackay, Hans Hecht and Ian McIntyre, discuss the songs, but their examinations are a tiny proportion of their overall study. See also Thomas Crawford, *Burns: A Study of the Poems and Songs* (Edinburgh, 1960), and Carol McGuirk, *Robert Burns and the Sentimental Era* (Athens GA, 1985).

8. Crawford concentrates most closely on individual manuscript collections of song, and not on published collections.

9. With the exception of famous collections like Durfey's *Wit and Mirth, or Pills to Purge Melancholy* (1719–20) and Thomas Percy's *Reliques of Ancient English Poetry* (1765), the English were not interested in their traditional songs. The Welsh produced few musical publications before the late 1820s, and the Irish song publications came later than the Welsh.

10. See William Tytler, 'Dissertation on the Scottish Music', *Transactions of the Society of the Antiquaries of Scotland* (Edinburgh and London, 1792), p. 470: 'from their artless simplicity, it is evident, that the Scottish melodies are derived from very remote antiquity'. See also James Beattie, *An Essay on Poetry and Music as they effect the Mind* (Edinburgh, 1776); Joseph Riston, *An Historical Essay on Scottish Song*; Allan Cunningham, *The Songs of Scotland Ancient and Modern* (London, 1825), p. i. Cunningham presents a long 'Introduction to Scottish Song'.

11. The two versions of the lyrics printed with this song were both written by women in the eighteenth century: Jean Elliot (1727–1805), 'I've heard the lilting at our yowe-milking', and Alison Rutherford (Mrs Cockburn) (1712–94), 'I've seen the smiling of fortune beguiling'.

12. David Daiches, *The Paradox of Scottish Culture* (Oxford, 1964), p. 27. As Daiches

has noted, 'Scottish nationalism in the eighteenth century inevitably became associated with antiquarianism'.

13. Kenneth Simpson, *The Protean Scot: The Crisis of Identity in Eighteenth Century Scottish Literature* (Aberdeen, 1988), p. 2.

14. Carl Dalhaus, *Nineteenth Century Music*, tr. J. Bradford Robinson (Berkeley and Los Angeles, 1989), p. 108.

15. Tom Crawford examines some of the most important manuscript sources of the period in *Society and the Lyric*, pp. 4–5.

16. Tyler's 'Dissertation', p. 471.

17. Ramsay's collections included his *Scots Songs* of 1718, *The Evergreen* of 1719 and several editions of his *Tea-Table Miscellany* from 1724.

18. [Robert Burns,] *The Letters of Robert Burns*, ed. J. De Lancey Ferguson, 2nd edn, ed. G. Ross Roy, 2 vols (Oxford, 1985), II, p. 91 (452), hereafter referred to as Ross Roy, *Letters*.

19. The Kilmarnock edition of 1786 and the London and Edinburgh editions of 1787 did include some of the songs, though without tunes attached.

20. Helen Maria Williams (c. 1761–1827), the radical London-based writer, who was actually brought up in Berwick-upon-Tweed, wrote a 'Sonnet on Reading the Poem upon the Mountain Daisy, by Mr Burns' in 1787, and the underrated Ayrshire milkmaid, Janet Little, also wrote an epistle to him, published in her own collection, *The Poetical Works of Janet Little, The Scotch Milkmaid* (Ayr, 1792). See also Valentina Bold, 'Janet Little "the Scotch Milkmaid" and "Peasant Poetry"', *Scottish Literary Journal*, 20:2 (1993), 21–30.

21. *The Scottish Minstrel: The Songs of Scotland subsequent to Burns with Memoirs of the Poets*, ed. Charles Rogers (Edinburgh, 1873), p. v. This is the second edition; the volume was first published in 1870.

22. George Thomson's letter to David Vedder, 21 December 1829. British Library, Add. MS 35269, fos 9–10.

23. Ross Roy, *Letters*, I, p. 135 (125).

24. Ibid., p. 137. Also Low, *Songs*, p. 5.

25. See *The Contemporaries of Burns, and the more Recent Poets of Ayrshire with selections from their Writings*, ed. James Paterson (Edinburgh, 1840), and *The Poets of Ayrshire*, ed. John MacIntosh (Dumfries, 1910).

26. From Burns's manuscript noted in an interleaved copy of the first volumes of the *Scots Musical Museum. Notes on Scottish Songs by Robert Burns*, ed. James C. Dick (London and Edinburgh, 1908), p. 57.

27. See Low, *Songs*, p. 62. Burns claimed that he wrote it before his twenty-third birthday after finding the chorus of an old song and also seeing the tune in Ramsay's *The Gentle Shepherd* with the lyric 'My Patie is a lover gay'. Ramsay's cantata was written in 1725.

28. Noted in *The Poets of Ayrshire*, ed. John MacIntosh (Dumfries, 1910), p. 29. No title or publication date is given. The lyrics for the songs are also published here.

29. William Stenhouse, *Illustrations of the Lyric Poetry and Music of Scotland* (Edinburgh and London, 1853), pp. 315–16. Many visited her to taste her whisky and to listen to her beautiful singing.

30. *Notes on Scottish Song by Robert Burns*, ed. James C. Dick (London and Edinburgh), 1908, p. 49.

31. Ross Roy, *Letters*, II, pp. 305–6 (637).

32. Stenhouse, *Illustrations*, pp. 248–9.
33. See Allan Cunningham, *The Songs of Scotland Ancient and Modern* (London, 1825), p. 249.
34. Stenhouse, *Illustrations*, p. 316*. The asterisk denotes the unusual pagination of Stenhouse's 'Illustrations'. The pages marked with the asterisk were extra pages, added when Stenhouse had more information to give about particular songs. Note that there is also an ordinary p. 316, not to be confused with the above.
35. Ibid., pp. 248–9.
36. Nairne's songs first appeared in *The Scottish Minstrel: A Selection from the Vocal Melodies of Scotland Ancient and Modern, Arranged for voice and pianoforte by R. A. Smith*, ed. Robert Purdie, 6 vols (Edinburgh, [1821–4]). Like many collections, including Thomson's *Select Collection*, there is a complex bibliography, as numerous volumes appeared in different editions.
37. A. Crichton, *The Land o' the Leal: Irrefutably proved from a searching investigation to be The Deathbed Valediction of Robert Burns* (Peterhead, 1919), p. 7. This is the third edition 'Containing the latest Discoveries, including a very vital disclaimer by Baroness Nairne' and with an introduction by William Stenhouse from which this quote is taken. Crichton had already written a series of articles on the subject for the *Glasgow Weekly Herald*.
38. Nairne's songs were published posthumously with musical arrangements by Finlay Dun in *Lays of Strathearn* (Edinburgh, 1846). Alan Reid arranged twenty-four of her songs as partsongs in *Lady Carolina Nairne and her Songs* (London and Glasgow, n.d.). Her works also appeared in the series entitled *The Lighthouse Library of Great Poets* (London, 1902), and as *The Songs of the Baroness Nairne: Calendar for the Year 1911* (Edinburgh and London, 1911). Her biography by George Henderson, entitled *Lady Nairne and her Songs* (Paisley and London), appeared in three editions: n.d., 1901 and 1905.
39. Charles Rogers, *The Scottish Minstrel: The Songs of Scotland subsequent to Burns* (Edinburgh, 1873), pp. v–vi.
40. Charles Rogers, *Life and Songs of the Baroness Nairne* (Edinburgh, 1896), pp. 35, 163 and 279–82.
41. Ibid., p. 281. Rogers's account is the only published source, but his work is not trustworthy, as he never cites his sources. He had access to Nairne's manuscripts before publishing this volume. Several of the songs are now kept in the National Library of Scotland (Oliphant of Gask papers, MSS 8,211–8,219; songs, used by Rogers for his edition, are found in MS 82.9.10 (ii)).
42. See her account in *Lays of the Lindsays; being Poems by the Ladies of the House of Balcarres* (Edinburgh, 1824), p. 4.
43. Rogers, *Life and Songs*, p. 281.
44. Crichton, p. 7.
45. Ibid., p. 77.
46. *The Songs of Scotland adapted to their appropriate Melodies*, ed. George Farquhar Graham, p. 78. Graham comments in a long note: 'The excellent verses here given were published about the year 1800 – the author is still unknown. The words were originally "I'm wearin' awa', John"; they seem to have been altered with the intention of making the song appear to be the parting address of Burns. There are many versions of it, and as one is not of more authority than another, we have selected what we conceive to be the best.'

47. Crichton, p. 17.
48. Ibid., p. 85.
49. S. Tytler and J. L. Watson, *The Songstresses of Scotland*, 2 vols (London, 1871), pp. 134–6. Tytler and Watson described Nairne's extreme measures to ensure the anonymity of her lyrics: 'she [Nairne] ventured, however, on personal interviews with Mr Purdie, at his place of business, as Mrs Bogan of Bogan. On these occasions she was carefully got up for the occasion as an old country lady of a former generation.'
50. Rogers, *Life and Songs*, p. 281. Rogers quoted a passage from Nairne's letter: 'but the parties could not decide why it never appeared in his works, as his last song should have done. I never answered.'
51. Charles Rogers, *Life and Songs of the Baroness Nairne* (Edinburgh, 1896), p. 32.
52. See George Henderson, *Lady Nairne and her Songs* (Paisley and London, 1901); also Margaret Stewart Simpson, *The Scottish Songstress – Carolina Baroness Nairne* (Edinburgh and London, 1894).
53. [Robert Burns,] *The Merry Muses of Caledonia*, ed. James Barke and Sydney Goodsir Smith (Edinburgh, 1982).
54. A lyric to this tune also appeared in Ramsay's *Tea-Table Miscellany*, but it was a drinking song beginning 'Come fill me a bumper, my jolly brave boys'.
55. L. Stone, *The Family, Sex and Marriage in England 1500–1800* (London, 1979), p. 328. Stone also describes the development of pornographic publications in England during the second half of the eighteenth century. There is as yet no evidence to prove that Scottish customs differed substantially.
56. Stone, p. 330.
57. Ibid., p. 338.
58. The song appears in the sixth volume of Thomson's octavo edition of 1825 as no. 49. Thomson noted that the song had been presented to him in manuscript by Sir Adam Ferguson.
59. Rogers, *Life and Songs*, p. 284. Rogers gives no other information, and only entitles the author 'Miss Ferrier'. He notes that the song was sometimes attributed to Sir Alexander Boswell, but this was perhaps due to the fact that he wrote a lyric of similar content entitled 'I'll hae my coat o' gude snuff-brown', in which the laird also decides to propose to a 'tocher'd quean', but is advised, by his servant Meg, to stay at home (Thomson, *Select Collection of Original Scottish Airs*, vol. III, p. 147).
60. Ross Roy, *Letters*, II, p. 242 (586).
61. Rogers, *Life and Songs*, p. 21.
62. For the history of the Oliphants' Jacobite activities, see E. Maxtone Graham, *The Oliphants of Gask: Records of a Jacobite Family* (London, 1910).
63. Cedric Thorpe Davie, 'Robert Burns, Writer of Songs', in *Critical Essays on Robert Burns* Donald A. Low (ed.), (London, 1975), p. 157.
64. Not all academics have avoided the complexities of this mixture of traditions in Burns's songs. See discussions presented by Mary Ellen Brown in *Burns and Tradition* (London, 1984) and more especially in her essay entitled '"That Bards are second-sighted is nae joke": The Orality of Burns's World and Work', *Studies in Scottish Literature*, 16 (1981), 208–17. See also the ninth chapter of Carol McGuirk, *Robert Burns and the Sentimental Era* (Georgia, 1985), pp. 120–48.
65. *Eliza Cook's Journal*, ed. E. Cook, London, no. 174, vii (1852), pp. 275–8.

'A VERY SCOTTISH KIND OF DASH': BURNS'S NATIVE METRIC

Douglas Dunn

In trying to describe Burns's artistry as a poet, I've appropriated the term 'metric' from T. S. Eliot's *Ezra Pound: His Metric and Poetry*.[1] In some ways the source is less than apt, although its modernity could encourage a different kind of approach to Burns's artistry than is customary. Therefore, following Eliot, I intend the idea of 'metric' to include more than versification; instead, it involves the poet's entire system of resonance, his acoustic and voice, as these are at the centre of his meaning. As well as inviting a critic to attend to poetic forms, prosody and the technical aspects of poetry, in the performance of which we can appreciate the extent, and kind, of a poet's artistry, the idea of 'metric' demands that close attention be paid to the significance of formal choices and accomplishments. How a poet exploits verse – its alms to artistry, and also at times its extortionate demands – might not be undertaken simply for the sake of the more superficial or showy impressions of performance (although these are always part of a poem's entertainment, in both the profound and more immediate meanings of that word). Verse, by itself, by the identity which a poet invests in it, can be a gestural revelation of meaning, transcending the mechanics of verse to become an inescapable part of poetry. At best, Burns's artistry is taken for granted. Praised, perhaps, as technically dazzling, or seen as 'rude, often awkward metre' (by Carlyle, for example), it is usually relegated to a relatively undervalued place in the overall assessment of Burns's work and his identity as a poet. It is rare to see the term 'artistry' used of Burns, probably a consequence of his prestige as a darling of the casual reader, as perhaps the most 'popular' of all poets. His work gives the appearance of being undemanding. How Burns is read, and what he is read for, encourage the neglect of the possibility that a remarkable poetic intelligence inheres in, inhabits, his masterly command of a range of stanzas, the fecundity and the tirelessness of his rhyme. Critical endeavours which seek to identify him as 'the poet of Humanity', a libertarian and democratic voice in the traditions of poetry, a patriotic, republican hero of

Scotland, the representative of the voice of the Scottish people, an amorist and lyricist, a dismisser of humbug and cant, especially of the religious variety, and the champion of Scottish song, are of undoubted importance. He is all of these; but he would be none of them were it not that his poetry is written with tremendous technical dash, and a 'very Scottish kind of dash' at that, to use a line of a poem of George MacBeth's.

As a guide to his own artistry, Burns is reliably and self-consciously full of mock self-deprecatory shyness of a kind which it would be a mistake to take at face value. Whatever else Burns was – gifted, courteous, feckless, rampant, harassed – shy he undoubtedly wasn't. He began his Preface to the Kilmarnock edition of 1786 by saying:

> The following trifles are not the production of the Poet, who, with all the advantages of learned art, and perhaps amid the elegancies and idlenesses of upper life, looks down for a rural theme, with an eye to Theocritus or Virgil. To the Author of this, these and other celebrated names (their countrymen) are, in their original languages, 'a fountain shut up and a book sealed'. Unacquainted with the necessary requisites for commencing Poet by rule, he sings the sentiments and manners he felt and saw in himself and his rustic compeers around him, in his and their native language.

Simultaneously defiant, pretending to be an excuse-me note, making it clear that he knows his station in poetry and in society, and in that extract not even declaring his disavowals and justifications in the first person, it is also the beginning of Burns's self-controlled myth. He describes himself as a self-taught rustic who amuses himself 'with the little creations of his own fancy, amid the toil and fatigues of a laborious life', even if, unlike many of his readers then, and especially now, he is familiar with Theocritus and Virgil in translation, and they aren't. He quotes Shentone's remark that 'Humility has depressed many a genius to a hermit, but never raised one to fame'. In doing so, he authorises a tentative assertion that he is publishing his book because he 'looks upon himself as possest of some poetic abilities'. That seems as far as he will go; but it is in keeping with the calculatedly elegant, the wilfully good-mannered, practically deferential tone of the Preface, that his reader is invited to accept what Burns says and then alter it according to how the poems which follow will justify, or not, the poet's deeply bowing reverence towards others and to the art of poetry in general: 'but to the genius of a Ramsay, or the glorious dawnings of the poor, unfortunate Ferguson [sic], he, with equal unaffected sincerity, declares that, even in his highest pulse of vanity, he has not the most distant pretensions'.

It is not the language of the poems. However else we might want to describe Burns's prose in the Preface to the Kilmarnock edition, 'Ayrshire' is not the epithet that comes to mind, unless it be the Ayrshire of fine and leisured country houses (and they certainly existed) but not the county of small farms dedicated to back-breaking toil. Burns's contemporary reader, having gone through the poems of the Kilmarnock volume – such poems as 'The Holy Fair', 'Address to the Deil', 'The Vision', 'Halloween', 'To a Mouse', 'To a Louse', and the Epistles to Lapraik, Simson and Rankine – might then have returned to the Preface and suspected a strong dose of eighteenth-century *English* tongue-in-cheekiness being made to work in the service of an Ayrshire small farmer's apologetics tested against sub-Augustan principles of propriety. Once the irony of the Preface has been attended to, the extent to which Burns identifies himself there can be seen as robust. It offers us an insight into his mind at the moment of his first appearance in print and which can illuminate what he says about poetry in the poems themselves, as well as what can be interpreted as his views on poetic style and choices of forms and stanzas. He *knew* that they were remarkable poems and not just as good as he could make them. He *knew* that they were at least as good as those of Ramsay and Fergusson, and probably superior, which is what I think we can infer from his respects paid to his immediate prede- cessors, even taking into account the acknowledgement to Fergusson in particular, who caused Burns 'to string anew his wildly-sounding rustic lyre with emulating vigour'. As a possibility (at the very least), it does not detract from Burns's honest, invaluable submission to their influence, and which indicates, too, the passion which he devoted to sustaining what they had begun or revived. He knew, too, that he had better not make too many claims for himself in as many words but that it would be a better tactic to disguise his awareness of his own highly gifted artistry.

Most of Burns's best poetry is in stanzas, with the major exception of his most popular poem 'Tam o'Shanter', although its iambic tetrameter couplets have a long history in Scottish verse, from Barbour's *The Bruce* through Sir David Lindsay's *Squyer Meldrum* (and much of *The Threi Estaitis*) to Ramsay and Fergusson. Almost all of these stanzas and lines have an ancestral root in Scottish poetic tradition, including the stanzas sometimes called after Burns but known in Scotland as Standard Habbie after Robert Sempill of Beltrees's jaunty, mock, perhaps even condescending elegiac poem for Habbie Simson, the Piper of Kilbarchan, which was written in the mid seventeenth century but unpublished until some fifty years later. Other stan- zas occur as well, notably the Spenserian stanza of 'The Cotter's Saturday Night' – the verse of Spenser's *The Faerie Queen*, which had a vogue in the eighteenth century (and it was used by Robert Fergusson, too) before its revival once more by Byron in *Childe Harold's Pilgrimage*, by Keats in 'The Eve of St Agnes' and by Shelley in 'Adonais'. However, the stanzas which I want to be concerned with most are Standard Habbie, or Burns's Stanza, or 'the Scottish stanza', the stave of 'Holy Willie's Prayer' and many others of

Burns's poems. Also important is the verse of such poems as 'Halloween', 'The Holy Fair', 'A Dream' and 'The Ordination', which stems from a tradition either initiated or summarised by the late fifteenth-century poem *Christ's Kirk on the Green*.[2] A third native stanza is that of Montgomerie's *The Cherrie and the Slae* (1597), which is the verse form of 'Epistle to Davie, a Brother Poet'. There is also the eight-line Ballad Royal, beloved of King James VI, and its variants. Given Burns's interest in the English poetry of the eighteenth century and earlier, we can expect it to have been a modifying and enriching source of stimulus and example, and hence his excursions in the Spenserian Stanza, or in pentameter couplets, the dominant poetic mode of a century which is, however, distinguished by more variety than the legendary approach to literary history would have us believe. Clearly, though, native, vernacular forms engaged Burns more fully. They were essential to his aspirations as a Scottish poet, as hinted at in the Preface to the Kilmarnock Edition, under the seven veils of irony. Also, there is the presence, at virtually every turn, of traditions of song and balladry, of melody and story, so rooted in the national psyche and in Burns's own as to be pervasive.

Standard Habbie is a six-line stanza with two rhymes. The first three lines are iambic tetrameters rhyming *a a a*, followed by a dimeter, rhyming *b*, another tetrameter rhyming *a*, and a dimeter rhyming *b*. More often than not, the stanza is occupied by a single sentence, and it appears to have been an artistic requirement that there be no running on of the grammar from one stanza to another. Or its design encourages (as often in Burns's use of the stanza) two sentences, the second short and incisive. A notionally perfect example of the stanza would therefore show forty syllables. Two rhymes in six lines, however, insist on an ingenuity that will include feminine rhymes, which the Scots language encourages in any case, so in terms of syllables Burns's practice often extends to forty-six or more, as in the last verse of 'Epistle to J. Lapraik' where, however, the feminine rhymes are full ones. Full rhymes were standard in Burns's day, whether mono- or disyllabic, and, in the Scottish tradition of verse, perhaps even more of an insistence:

> But, to conclude my lang epistle,
> As my auld pen's worn to the grissle,
> Twa lines frae you wad gar me fissle,
>   Who am most fervent,
> While I can either sing or whistle,
>   Your friend and servant.

The stanza's origins are ancient and not Scottish at all. Since the 1880s at least, it has been known to have been first devised by Troubadour poets whose fascinations for intricate verses of varying but regular line lengths and rhyme schemes were a highly-developed aspect of their virtuosity. T. F. Henderson's note to 'Address to the Deil' in the Centenary Edition[3] is the pioneering statement on the topic, to which can be added Allan H. MacLaine's 'New Light on the Genesis of the Burns Stanza'.[4] Henderson suggests that the first signed example of this six-line stave of *rime couée* is by William IX, Count of Poitiers and Duke of Guienne (1071–1127). By the thirteenth century, the form begins to occur in English verse, and Henderson speculates that it could have been brought to England by Eleanor of Poitou, the grandchild of the Troubadour poet Bernard de Ventadour. Henderson's first example of its use by a Scottish poet is a snatch from Part 1 of Lindsay's *Ane Pleasant Satire of the Threi Estaitis*:

> There is ane thing that I wald speir,
> Quhat sall I do quhen scho cume heir?
> For I knaw nocht the craft perqueir
>   Of lufferis gyn;
> Thairfoir, at lenth, ye mou me leir
>   How to begin.

Ten more examples from sixteenth-century Scottish poetry are given by Henderson. Professor MacLaine, though, found two earlier ones in the Makculloch Manuscript, which confirms Henderson's scholarly guess that it was used in Scotland in the century before.

'Eminently aristocratic in its inception,' Henderson wrote, 'it presently became a rhythmus for the people, with which artists in prosody, as Chaucer and Henryson, in the end disdained to deal'.[5] MacLaine confirms this to an extent when he points out an echo in Sempill's 'The Life and Death of Habbie Simson . . .' of a lyric in *The Gude and Godlie Balladis* in the same metre. As a lyrical assembly of the early Reformation, in its Lutheran pre-Calvinist phase, put together by the Wedderburn brothers as a means of introducing new religious sentiment to a wide social range of auditors and readers, *The Gude and Godlie Balladis* relied on the forms of popular poetry and common song as part of a proselytising tactic. The presence there of what has come to be known as Standard Habbie suggests therefore that it was sufficiently current for the users of that Reformation anthology to have recognised it. There would have been little point otherwise in its inclusion. Aristocratic, and Troubadour, in its origin, then, that six-line verse had established itself in popular Scottish consciousness as much as the verse of *Christ's Kirk on the Green* or *Peblis to the Play*. There is nice, expressive significance to the fact that an aristocratic measure was appropriated and demoticised by Scottish poetry. It tells us much about the psychology of Scottish literature. However, perhaps we ought not to be too surprised, for the origin of the villanelle, one of the most precious of poetic forms, is supposed to lie in improvised Tuscan folk poetry.

In its original design, the *Christ's Kirk on the Green* stanza goes like this:

> Was never in Scotland hard nor sene
> Sic dansing nor deray,
> Nother in Falkland on the grene,
> Nor Peblis to the play,
> As was of wooeris as I wene
> At Chrystis Kirk on ane day.
> Thair come our Kittie weschen clene
> In hir new kirtill of gray,
> > Full gay,
> At Chrystis kirk on the grene.[6]

That is, it is a ten-line stanza, in which the ninth line is a bob, or abrupt line, usually of two syllables, but sometimes one, or three, and the tenth line is repeated as the same and last line of every stanza. There are only two rhymes. Lines being alternately of four and three stresses (with the exception of the truncated bob line), then the rhymes are disclosed very quickly. As a result, the effect is one of speed, a tempo which informs the ear of both authorial virtuosity and the rapid happenings of narrative neatly and conclusively ended with the bob and refrain. Neither listener nor reader is left in any doubt as to what the poem is concerned to show and tell. Indeed, it seems a form devised peculiarly for recitation, like the bob-and-wheel stanzas of near-contemporary late medieval poems such as *The Book of the Howlat* and *The Taill of Rauf Coilyear*. Listeners to the poem are given a chance to follow what is being said or sung through the intrinsic mnemonics of the form, and to be entertained by the high spirits implicated in the carnivalesque subjects associated with this stanza, while the *performer* is given an opportunity for a display of virtuosity. Also, as a ritualisation of speech, which all poetry is, it is a kind of verse which invites a full-throated, sociable range of sounds. Like Standard Habbie, the in-built tempo is too quick for meditation.

Burns inherited the revival of both Standard Habbie measure and the *Christ's Kirk* metre from Allan Ramsay and Robert Fergusson. To say that Ramsay's collection of older Scottish poetry *The Ever Green* is one of the most important collections in Scottish literature is not to put the matter too strongly. Its title, too, attested to his own opinion (and perhaps appealed to a latent consensus) that the styles and forms of these earlier poems represented, or should be claimed to represent, an indigenous standard, that there was something usefully permanent about them, something distinctively national. Their 'moving parts', as it were, articulate a psyche; they satisfy the anticipations of a people. Ramsay wrote a continuation of *Christ's Kirk*, as well as the spirited 'Lucky Spence's Last Advice', in Standard Habbie, and, in 'The Vision', an imitation of antique manner in the stanza of Montgomerie's *The Cherrie and the Slae*. Although familiar with Ramsay's poetry and the poems in *The Ever Green*, Burns had his eye on Fergusson's variation of the *Christ's Kirk* verse (which had, however, been around since before Fergusson's time). It is Fergusson's measure in 'Hallow-Fair', 'Leith Races' and 'The Election'. By then the two-rhyme foundation of the stanza was no longer an insistence, and the repeated last line was dropped, so that the verse was now one of nine lines, not ten, with the last a bob doubling as a variable refrain, not necessarily rhyming. Fergusson's 'Hallow-Fair' begins:

> At Hallowmas, whan nights grow lang,
>   And starnies shine fu' clear,
> Whan fock, the nippin cald to bang,
>   Their winter hap-warms wear.
> Near Edinbrough a fair there hads,
>   I wat there's nane whase name is,
> For strappin dames and sturdy lads,
>   And cap and stoup, mair famous
>   Than it that day.[7]

With four rhymes, the stanza is easier to manage, although some stanzas have three, as in 'Leith Races' as well, while three is the norm in 'The Election':

> Rejoice, ye Burghers, ane an' a',
>   Lang look't for's come at last;
> Sair war your backs held to the wa'
>   Wi' poortith an' wi' fast:
> Now ye may clap your wings an' craw,
>   And gayly busk ilk' feather,
> For Deacon Cocks hae pass'd a law
>   To rax an' weet your leather
>   Wi' drink thir days.[8]

Burns's 'The Holy Fair' opens:

> Upon a simmer *Sunday morn*,
>   When Nature's face is fair,
> I walked forth to view the corn,
>   An' snuff the callor air;
> The rising sun, owre GALSTON muirs,

Wi' glorious light was glintan;
The hares were hirplan down the furrs,
The lav'rocks they were chantan
Fu' sweet that day.

As lightsomely I glowr'd abroad,
To see a scene sae gay,
Three *hizzies*, early at the road,
Cam skelpan up the way.
Twa had manteeles o' dolefu' black,
But ane wi' lyart lining;
The *third*, that gaed a wee aback,
Was in the fashion shining
Fu' gay that day.

The *twa* appear'd like sisters twin,
In feature, form an' claes;
Their visage – wither'd, lang an' thin,
An' sour as onie slaes:
The *third* cam up, hap-step-an'-loup,
As light as onie lambie, –
An' wi' a curchie low did stoop,
As soon as e'er she saw me,
Fu' kind that day.

Clearly, this is a kind of verse (like Standard Habbie) in which the author takes it for granted that his readers (or listeners) will be predisposed to appreciate the naturalness and inventiveness of rhyme as well as the triumphant pursuit of an awkward stanzaic shape. As in the much earlier poems of this kind, in the stanza from which Burns's derives, the poet is more than a describer of misrule, but in his depiction of it an approver, a participant, like the speakers in the earlier poems in this stanza; the technical sorcery of the verse is a counterpart of the gaiety and animation of the scenes which it brings to life. It proves that the poet is 'one of us', or even 'one of them' (out of sorts with established social behaviour, at least temporarily, or for the purpose of the poem), perhaps even with the prestige of a commemorating master-of-ceremonies, the poet as a lord of misrule. Another expectation was the directness of a speaking voice embedded in the intricacies and difficulties of a stanza without them getting in the way of plain-spoken address. The same is true of the larger, even more awkward *The Cherrie and the Slae* stanza, which Burns chose for 'Epistle to Davie, a Brother Poet', two of the Recitativo passages of 'Love and Liberty', and, in English, in two of his least attractive poems, 'To Ruin' and 'Despondency, an Ode'. Both are technically accomplished, but their resonance feels incomplete, as if diminished by the absence of Scottish diction.

Montgomerie's Stanza, as I think it ought to be called, first appeared in a poem called 'The Bankis of Helicon' and can be identified with an up-tempo tune of the same name.[9] When first printed in 1597, *The Cherrie and the Slae* was described as 'composed into Scottish Meeter, by Alexander Montgomerie'.[10] Mention of 'Scottish Meeter' is as interesting to my subsequent argument as the probability that the stanza was composed to a tune, and it could even be likely that the two were considered synonymous. Although *The Cherrie and the Slae* is a poem of high culture in which the cherry = Catholicism and the sloe = Protestantism, through its stanza, its general principles of composition, it has strong links with the demotic impulse which marks so much of Scottish literature, past and present, especially at moments when it seeks to renew itself or defend its priorities from the linguistic and social as well as literary influences of English literature. It is not the only road that a Scottish writer can take, nor is it Burns's singular manner. Part of the subsequent complications of Scottish writing, to which Burns's legacy contributes, is a fraudulent cultural and critical demand on demotic and vernacular styles and *bona fides* long after the option of a Scots language makes complete sense except as an ongoing succession of revivals and regression dependent on a gestural philology more than an instinctively contemporary poetic impulse. A poetry can only become predictable when grounded on a few major stanzas, directness of manner, and head-on encounters with its subject matter. Similarly, when a literature insists that its true identity must be demotic, then it excludes as much of human experience as it takes on board.

Montgomerie's Stanza is one of the most intriguing ever devised. It has fourteen lines, but, as a quatorzain, that need not indicate a connection with the sonnet, although it could be suspected that such a link would have existed in Montgomerie's mind, perhaps as a way of suggesting through form itself that his was a poem of divine as opposed to profane love. Montgomerie's writing, too, is capable of moments of contemplative pace. This is the first stanza of Burns's 'Epistle to Davie':

> While winds frae off BEN-LOMOND blaw,
> And bar the doors wi' driving snaw,
>   And hing us owre the ingle,
> I set me down, to pass the time,
> And spin a verse or twa o' rhyme,
>   In hamely, *westlin* jingle.
> While frosty winds blaw in the drift,
>   Ben to the chimla lug,

> I grudge a wee the *Great-folk's* gift
>   That live sae bien an' snug:
>   I tent less, and want less
>   Their roomy fire-side;
>   But hanker, and canker,
>   To see their cursed pride.

The fourteen lines of Montgomerie's Stanza divide cleanly into ten and four. In the first part of the stave, the lines vary regularly between tetrameters and trimeters on a rhyme scheme of *a, a, b, c, c, b, d, e, d, e*, while the phrasing in the longer line almost always seems to divide neatly into two equal parts. Tetrameters rhyme with tetrameters, trimeters with trimeters: the impression, therefore, is one of symmetry, a degree of balance which might remind us of the etymological origin of metre in the Greek for 'measure'. Also, the first nine lines are almost always grouped into units of three by both syntax and statement. Considered as sound, wordless, without diction, ignoring what Burns is saying, then this elaborate structure looks more like the vehicle of High Culture (the property of 'Great-folk', indignantly criticised in these lines) where 'hamely, *westlin* jingle' should look distinctly out of place. The architecture of the poem is at odds with what it expresses. Misrule, in the sense of disorder between the gestural effects of what is being said and the form in which the meaning is being conveyed, is at work here. It is an ironic contrast between form and statement, and it is supported by the peculiar quatrain which concludes each stanza. In each set of the last four lines, there is a change of tempo and rhythm to which the probable response is a metrical shock in the form of a disconcerting uplift, or a backward lilt to the notional tune of the verse. In the first (or eleventh) and third (or thirteenth) lines, the disyllabic rhymes unsettle the iambic cadence of the first ten lines of the stanza and introduce a jolt to the sonic system which has been established in the preceding lines. It could be scanned in three ways: as a fundamentally trochaic intrusion on the preceding iambic measure of the poem, a blow to what has been carefully set up as what the ear anticipates, or as a weak stress followed by a spondee, or as two trisyllabic feet, known as Anti-Bacchic – a short followed by two long stresses, described by Saintsbury as 'Of very doubtful occurrence anywhere in English verse'.[11]

All three of these stanzas so far are of Scottish provenance or inheritance, with very considerable longevity. So, too, is a fourth stanza used by Burns, the eight-line Ballad Royal of 'The Lament', or 'Address to Edinburgh', which has three rhymes *a b a b b c b c*. Burns also used an eight-line stanza in a number of his poems and songs, such as 'Epistle to a Young Friend', 'Mary Morison', 'Man was Made to Mourn', and 'For a' that and a' that'. Although they do not follow the rhyme scheme of Ballad Royal, they have in common a four-beat tetrameter line, suggesting that Scottish versification as traditionally conceived preferred a shorter line than its English counterpart, especially in the eighteenth century, and that Burns was well aware of it, even if it might have been instinctive in the manner of poets if not in the retrospective analytic gaze of critics. Ample pentameters exist in Burns's poetry (and in Ramsay's and Fergusson's), but in their longer, narrative works the impression is that these poets were happier, more comfortable and more convincing when writing in iambic tetrameter couplets, such as Fergusson's 'Auld Reekie' and 'To my Auld Breeks', or Burns's 'Tam o' Shanter'. In these, too, the neo-classical associations of *English* tetrameter couplets (Milton's, for example, in 'L' Allegro' and 'Il Penseroso') are subverted by a Scottish preference for the demotic, the ostensibly 'low' subject and the language and psychology that go with it. In the eleven stanzas of 'Epistle to Davie, a Brother Poet', the fancy sonics and metrical structure are devices, the *artifice* of a poet who pretended that he had none, who pretended to be free of the need for them, who claimed, indeed, to be incapable of such dexterity, who associated them with the poets of an allegedly loftier and more 'learned' tradition, and who in 'Epistle to Davie' vaunts the *natural* inspiration of friendship, love and local poetry – 'All hail! ye tender feelings dear! . . . The sympathetic glow!' – above the products of High Culture.

To invent or perfect a poetic stanza is the equivalent of inventing a musical instrument or of being among its instigating virtuosi. Very few invent a significant or acceptable noise, and not many poets invent a stanza which enters the repertoire and is named after them. Robert Burns's stanzas are all retrievals and perpetuations from the recent and distant past, which can make his practice of verse seem like a revival of sackbuts. In his best poems, though, it ought to be conspicuous that his choices of stanza or measure are Scottish ones. It is possible to think of stanzas, metre, rhyme, the whole business of versification and prosody, as visions – but of the ear and mind and not of the eye. To use the old idea of verse as 'numbers', then perhaps we can hear these stanzas (so obviously devised for spokennness as they are) as audible arithmetic, and, in Burns's case, as local and national arithmetic, peculiarly audible. The mention of locality is not entirely risible. Alexander Montgomerie's family roots were in northern Ayrshire and southern Renfrewshire, and Sempill of Beltrees, he of the tripping elegy for Habbie Simson, the Piper of Kilbarchan, was from Lochwinnoch in southern Renfrewshire close to the Ayrshire border. Shorter distances are involved between the places associated with Burns and his eminent poetical ancestors than, for example, between those in Provence associated with the Troubadours. One way of looking at this geographically finite source of poetic inventions is to see Scottish poetry are astoundingly intense, and, in the longevity of these forms, determined on the preservation of its identity.[12]

Among his other achievements, Burns is a poet of the virtues of excess, the comforts of going over the score, the satisfactions of plain speaking and, indeed, the solace of outspokenness. Such a literary temperament demanded of itself kinds of verse in which propulsion was of the very essence. In a real sense, that is how it was fated to be, and for a number of reasons. First, it does not seem too far-fetched to understand Burns as having been one of those men destined to have discovered within himself characteristics of feeling, thought, belief and behaviour, a full force of *being*, which were typical of his countrymen as well as displayed in greater variety and at greater extremes than can be considered ordinary. How else are we to explain the phenomenon of Burns? Edwin Muir put it very clearly when he said that 'For a Scotsman to see Burns simply as a poet is almost impossible'. However, that is the purpose at hand. At the same time, there is something like an obligation to acknowledge Muir's perhaps irritable or bewildered survey of the problems which Burns poses for a Scottish critic or poet or an intelligent reader unwilling to put up with an unacceptable front-loading of mythology.

> He is more a personage to us than a poet, more a figurehead than a personage, and more a myth than a figurehead. To those who have heard of Dunbar he is a figure, of course, comparable to Dunbar; but he is also a figure comparable to Prince Charlie, about whom everyone has heard. He is a myth evolved by the popular imagination, a communal poetic creation, a Protean figure; we can all shape him to our own likeness, for a myth is endlessly adaptable.[13]

Muir's sagacity is, I feel, too reasonable. He seems to have been unable to take seriously the possibility that a man could also embody within himself and present through his work and life a range of typical declarations and activities which would *recommend* him as comprehensive, as somehow complete in his prestige as a representative of the best and worst of the masculine life of his time and place, as, in a way, not so much a life as a national psychology. Muir comes close to saying exactly that. Or, rather, he says it, but appears to do so in a state of disbelief, when he admits that the Protean Burns is, to the respectable, a decent man, 'to the Rabelaisian, bawdy; to the sentimentalist, sentimental; to the Socialist, a revolutionary; to the Nationalist, a patriot; to the religious, pious; to the self-made man, self-made; to the drinker, a drinker'. Burns, however, is more than a poet whose *reputation* has been evolved *by* the popular imagination. Despite his frequent attempts at poetry in the correct idioms and metres of the English/North British high culture of his time, the concentration in his best work on indigenous poetic forms (and the use of local language, albeit in the midst of eighteenth-century English poetic diction) should suggest the pronounced extent to which Burns's poetry as well as his subsequent reputation evolved *through* popular imagination and its forms. He *was* a 'communal poetic creation' in that he wrote his best poems in forms and metres which were rooted profoundly in usage and tradition even if part of the creative reason for doing so was the recovery or preservation of technical priorities and preferences reintroduced by Ramsay and Fergusson because it was felt to be of national importance to do so. That, too, seems to have been a choice that was not a choice, but was destined. Literary history can sometimes appear to present us with what can look like inevitabilities. There had been Ramsay, and there had been Fergusson, and it needed a third, more varied poet, who would revere his predecessors but then set the seal on the national revival of verse which they had done more than just initiate. Burns could therefore establish himself instinctively within a historical and present community of authorship, and 'authorship', we should remember, contains the medieval notion of 'auctoritas', authority: in a literature as rooted as Scottish poetry at least until Burns's time, that older ideal still seems to have been built into the practice of writing. He addresses himself frequently to other, lesser, con-temporary poets, and he memorialises Fergusson and Ramsay (deferring to them, indeed, in the Preface to his first appearance in print), and he honours an entire tradition of verse through the forms which he used. His awareness of the past, his erudition in verse, was what gave Burns his confidence as well as a store of examples. Addresses to other poets can be seen as an instinctive assertion of the existence of a community of writers: even when his addressees are second-rate poets, the idea of fraternity, of a down-home 'Castalian Band', is used too often to be seen as conventional or insignificant. A common stock of forms and poetic procedures is surely part of this sociable but also mutually protective syndrome. It served to enlarge the confidence of its participants, but chiefly that of Burns himself. He might even have used others by enlisting them into a self-identifying strategy to strengthen a vul-nerable 'local poetry' in the face of potential sneers from the metropolises of Edinburgh and London. There are moments in literary history when local poetry is the best on offer and when it serves the cause of a national literature. Wordsworth is a clear example; Thomas Hardy is another.

Burns wrote a good deal about his own concept of poetry, its aspirations and its position within contemporary letters. In his 'Epistle to J. Lapraik', for example,

> I've scarce heard ought describ'd sae weel,
> What gen'rous, manly bosoms feel;
> Thought I, 'Can this be *Pope*, or *Steele*,
>   Or *Beattie*'s wark?';
> They tald me 'twas an odd kind chiel
>   About *Muirkirk*.

Although amusing, it also serves a serious purpose and has general meaning.
It is part of Burns's intellectual strategy. In detecting local literary merit, he
is saying: 'It happens here, and it is happening now'. The apparently sly
irony of his defence of the local and contemporary is complicated by the
subjective ironies of a passage from later in the same poem:

> I am nae *Poet*, in a sense,
> But just a *Rhymer* like by chance,
> An' hae to Learning nae pretence,
>   Yet, what the matter?
> Whene'er my Muse does on me glance,
>   I jingle at her.
>
> Your Critic-folk may cock their nose,
> And say, 'How can you e'er propose,
> 'You wha ken hardly *verse* frae *prose*,
>   'To mak a *sang*?'
> But by your leaves, my learned foes,
>   Ye're maybe wrang.

That verse cancels the self-effacement of the one before. It suggests, too, that
part of Burns's resonance, informing his preferred stanzas and how he
handles them, is an ironically subsumed indignation. What follows can be
read as a conventional exploitation of eighteenth-century estimates of
spontaneity and sentiment; but at the same time it asserts Burns's aggressive
self-definition and a self-conscious knowledge of where his power and
distinctiveness came from.

> What's a' the jargon o' your Schools,
> Your Latin names for horns an' stools;
> If honest Nature made you *fools*,
>   What sairs your Grammars?
> Ye'd better taen up *spades* and *shools*,
>   Or *knappin-hammers*.
>
> A set o' dull, conceited Hashes,
> Confuse their brains in *Colledge-classes*!
> They *gang in* stirks and *come out* Asses,
>   Plain truth to speak;
> An' syne they think to climb Parnassus
>   By dint o' Greek!
>
> Gie me ae spark o' Nature's fire,
> That's a' the learning I desire;

> Then tho' I drudge thro' dub an' mire
>   At pleugh or cart,
> My Muse, tho' hamely in attire,
>   May touch the heart.

Burns's kittling up of his *'rustic reed'* ('To William Simpson, Ochiltree', 29) is both actual and part of a sophisticated piece of myth-making and literary space-clearing. It is part of a whole series of complicatedly ironic, protective manoeuvres, the function of which is instinctively aggressive. Burns, after all, is a poet who could state the following in a letter with no hint of self-pity or appearance of loss of dignity:

> I do not say this in the ridiculous idea of seeming self-abasement, and affected modesty. I have long studied myself, and I think I know pretty exactly what ground I occupy, both as a man, & a Poet; and however the world, or a friend, may sometimes differ from me in that particular, I stand for it, in silent resolve, with all the tenaciousness of Property. – I am willing to believe that my abilities deserved a better fate than the veriest shades of life; . . .

He was well aware that a hospitable climate of opinion could turn hostile very quickly were he to disobey too flagrantly the conventions which tied him to his station in life. Sexual scandal, episodes of behaviour fuelled by alcohol, could be contained, or fed into the myth. Not just the high-born, however, but all-comers, would have found more serious grounds for scandal or absurdity in any signs of social opportunism or pretension. Socially, what his fame offered him was not the chance to take advantage of it as spectacularly as might be the case today, but a chance to run on the spot, as decorously as possible, saying no more than he could get away with, in more comfortable surroundings than an Ayrshire field. Hence the necessity with which Burns disguised in affable but devoted irony much of his real substance. '*Complaining* profits little,' Carlyle wrote; 'stating of the truth may profit. That a Europe, with its French Revolution breaking out, finds no need of a Burns except for gauging beer, – is a thing I, for one, cannot *rejoice* at!' But the social pressures on Burns were enormous, or he perceived them to be. Time and again his letters testify to his confusion. After listing Pope, Churchill, Shenstone, Gray, Thomson, Beattie, Littleton and Collins, he declared: 'I am not vain enough to hope for distinguished Poetic fame'.[14] A few weeks later, in February 1787, he writes to the Earl of Eglinton: 'Fate had cast my station in the veriest shades of Life, but never did a heart pant more ardently than mine to be distinguished . . .'.[15] Similar contrasts or contradictions could be multiplied many times. They indicate a genuine entrapment more than insincerity or pitching his confessions in the right tone to suit the propriety of his correspondents.

What Burns's poetry struggles with is to avoid becoming the captive of his circumstances in life. It is not exactly on the mark to believe that Burns 'accepts his limits' (as the late Professor Kinsley put it in his British Academy Warton Lecture of 1974) when he describes his intentions in 'The Vision'. After a hard day's work, the poet drowses by his fireside and imagines himself visited by Coila, his local Muse. It is when she speaks that Burns can be misinterpreted as opting for the minor or the wilfully lowbrow and populist, or regretting his remoteness from the styles of metropolitan high culture while claiming that it is beneficial:

> Thou canst not learn, nor can I show,
> To paint with *Thomson's* landscape-glow;
> Or wake the bosom-melting throe,
>> With *Shenstone's* art;
> Or pour, with *Gray*, the moving flow,
>> Warm on the heart.

> Yet all beneath th' unrivall'd Rose,
> The lowly Daisy sweetly blows;
> Tho' large the forest's Monarch throws
>> His army shade,
> Yet green the juicy Hawthorn grows,
>> Adown the glade.

> Then never murmur nor repine;
> Strive in thy *humble sphere* to shine;
> And trust me, not *Potosi's* mine,
>> Nor *King's regard*,
> Can give a bliss o'ermatching mine,
>> A *rustic Bard*.

Much of the first part of the poem – 'Duan First', in imitation of Macpherson's Ossianic poems – reads like ingratiating local historicism, riddled with the names of Ayrshire's great and good (especially when reinforced with additional stanzas from the Stair Manuscript). The dynamic of the verse could even be claimed to show Scots trumped by English within the same measure of Standard Habbie. It could be noted, too, that in the three stanzas quoted above, the rhymes are neatly monosyllabic, and that the conception of verse, even in this very Scottish form, is temporarily being obedient and well-mannered, or paying lip-service to a more 'literary' standard, an English one. The first eleven stanzas are, however, in Scots, although it is not so conspicuous in its diction as in Burns's less self-consciously 'literary' poems. But crowned in holly as he is, and not in bay, Burns is yet far from accepting a mediocre or provincial ambition. Instead, the poem expounds the dignity of who Burns is, and what he does, and it is an identity released in stately measure, opening up Burns's personality as a poet to a different kind of decorum, which is probably why it strikes the ear as oddly out of tune: certainly, in Burns's English, his handling of Standard Habbie is fluent and even majestic, but it contrasts oddly with the more engaging fullness of tone of 'Address to the Deil', 'Holy Willie's Prayer' or the epistles. 'The Vision' can be read as a poem of self-encouragement; Coila reassures the poet, drawing him away from doubts and despairs. She is native, local, rural and beautiful; her eye beams 'keen with *Honor*'. If anything, Burns seeks to dispel the limitations (if such they were; my view is that they are best understood as part of his poetic strength) imposed on him by place, poverty, nationality, humble birth and disadvantage in general. He *is* the great poet of the canon of the disadvantageous beginning, middle and end, and his metric, his resonance, his irony, the forms he used, are intimate and expressive aspects of his struggle with himself and his society. Although not in 'The Vision' itself (and which can therefore seem an incomplete, perhaps even a compromised poem), Burns was to transform these alleged disadvantages into the very stuff of his best art, aware, probably, that what society might see as his novelty (a poet who did not need to 'look down' for 'a rural theme') was, in the poetry itself, the material of a more original distinction.

In 'Sketch', Burns addresses the Muse (the 'interior paramour', as Wallace Stevens called her) in a more vigorous and vernacular style. It complicates and underlines the subject of 'The Vision', although the purpose here is to celebrate Allan Ramsay:

> Say, Lassie, why thy train amang,
> While loud the trumps heroic clang,
> And sock and buskin skelp alang
>   To death or marriage;
> Scarce ane has tried the Shepherd-sang
>   But wi' miscarriage?
>
> In Homer's craft Jock Milton thrives;
> Eschylus' pen Will Shakespeare drives;
> Wee Pope, the knurlin, 'till him rives
>   Horatian fame;
> In thy sweet sang, Barbauld, survives
>   E'en Sappho's flame.

But thee, Theocritus, wha matches?
They're no Herd's ballats, Maro's catches;
Squire Pope but busks his skinlin patches
        O' Heathen tatters:
I pass by hunders, nameless wretches,
        That ape their betters.

Demotic humour in these stanzas is the playfulness of a poet conscious of writing deliberately beyond a predictable idiom: 'Jock Milton', 'Wee Pope' – let alone the cocky familiarity of 'Say, Lassie', an amusing inversion of the more conventional 'Hail, Poesie!' with which the poem begins – are the touches of a proud prankster, their purpose serious and literary for all their easy light-heartedness and disavowals of ambition. When a poet like Burns says that 'For me, an *aim* I never fash;/ I rhyme for *fun*' ('To J. S****', lines 29–30), we can be sure that he means the opposite, and that smiling as he says it is a tactic in the exercise of a profoundly ironic habit of mind. His 'spavet *Pegasus*' ('Epistle to Davie', line 147) was anything but. The essential irony of Burns's poetry is that his apparent self-effacement (his forelock-tugging courtship of the Daisy and reverential acknowledgement of the Rose as 'unrivall'd') is a joke at the expense of those who fail to notice the irony: he expresses his allegedly humble, local verse and stunted artistry in vigorous, virtuosic measures. There is a bare-faced daring to his best poetry. Anyone who has attempted to write in Standard Habbie, the most characteristic of Burns's stanzas, will know the obstacles to be overcome before developing the fluency that delivers a dimeter phrase like 'Horatian fame' so neatly into its place while at the same time exposing a hazardous subject, the poet's intimate sociology: Burns was the representative of one culture (his own) and excluded from another (Milton, Shakespeare, Pope). His poetry is a struggle against the inferiorism implanted by the cultivated Scottish class of his time, and against self-engendered complexes of a man endowed by nature with extraordinary gifts of poetic erudition. What 'Sketch' shows, and very clearly, is that the pen is an accessory of a farmer – not the crook, smock and rosy cheeks, the accoutrements of a pastoral poet. When these dimensions of his artistry are compared with his largely unsuccessful attempts to write in English, then the contrast is between aboriginal smeddum and a version of 'refinement' remote from Burns's own.

Burns's approach to verse is reminiscent of an apocryphal story once current in low musical circles in Glasgow in the mid-1960s. A raggedy musician turns up in London to audition for a place in the trumpet section of a flash band. He arrives in a beaten raincoat and soft cap, bearing an ex-Salvation Army instrument much the worse for combat in the holy and charitable wars. Slowly, the instrument is unwrapped from its swaddling of brown paper and old copies of the *Evening Citizen*. As he does so, there is

much wincing mirth from suave chaps in tuxes, to which the Caliban retorts
mischievously in pellucid Glaswegian. There are two punchlines to the story.
One is that he plays like Gabriel, or, at least, like Harry James. Being alert to
this pose – in football it used to be known as that of 'the tanner-ball player'
– local jokesters in the West of Scotland sometimes (depending on the
company) traded on the other ending, which is that the man in the raincoat
and soft cap is absolutely rotten. Burns, of course, fits the first alternative. It
is not unknown in other cultures either. The obvious example is D'Artagnan
arriving from Gascony on *his* Pegasus, or Balzac's *Lost Illusions*, and his
obsession with provincial young hopefuls in Paris. Burns's great triumph
could depend on the fact that he knew better than to try it on in London.

The more Burns made these Scottish verse-forms his own, then the more
he became their servant (and to have done so strikes me as both astute and
inevitable, deliberate, self-aware and totally fated by literary history, the
coincidence of one poet's talent with time and place). They guided him, and
they refused to let him go. They controlled him as much as he controlled
them. Whatever their origins, those Scottish stanzas were, or were made to
be, and maybe they still are (but by now I think the matter is historical) as
aboriginal as native melodies. That Burns should have closed his relatively
short career as a lyricist was a natural development. He was led into submer-
gence in a national mode as he understood it, and it continued what he
began in his poems: it was announced as early as 1785 in his Commonplace
Book, while the rhotacistic euphony of such a line as 'Ye arena Mary
Morison' (Hugh MacDiarmid's favourite line in all of Burns's poetry and
song) is early proof of Burns's commitment and achievement in native
lyricism. More indigenous raw material for a poet can hardly be imagined.
Yeats's favoured lines, however, were quite different:

> The white moon is setting behind the white wave,
> And time is setting with me, O!

Yeats quoted, rewriting Burns's

> The wan moon sets behind the white wave,
> And time is setting with me, Oh: . . .

Either way, there is a quality of poetry in them which is uncharacteristic of
Burns, more imaginative and hazardous in its imagery; but it is so rare in
Burns as to have been accepted in Scotland as how a Scottish poet does not
proceed. This, I suppose, is what Lionel Trilling calls 'the disenchantment
of our culture with itself' – that is, what we have (Burns, say) fails to match
what we want, a poetry which might not be so infatuated with the demotic
and the plain-spoken, but more disinterested, more 'modern' in its

inclusiveness, and more open to recognitions which might not be 'national' in any meaningful way.

Between Burns's work as a poet and as a songwriter, the link is performance and the traditions which supported it. Indigenous Scottish poetry is abetted by the same or very similar traditions. Even in such a self-consciously written genre as the epistle, Burns's spokenness is unmistakable. Such stanzas as Standard Habbie, but especially the more ornate or complicated Montgomerie's Stanza, assist performance only if the writer is concerned to ground the poem in spokenness and direct address or feels obliged by tradition and expectation to do so, in which case the poet must feel at one with an imagined audience. Much of the pleasure of these verses arises from the flow of a speaking voice riding over the obstacles of rapidly-disclosed rhyme and line lengths, especially the awkwardness of the very short two-beat lines. Performance, that is, lies in the audible presence of a voice, the sustained inventiveness of rhyme, and an adroit, resourceful handling of a stanza, the shape of which is sculpted out of air so that it can be felt on the ear. (Stanzas, and poetic forms such as the sonnet, *sestina* and *terza rima*, were devised before the invention of printing: they might look like pleasing designs on the printed page, but clearly they were intended to be heard.) In Burns's poetry, or in Fergusson's, as in Sempill of Beltrees's elegy for the Piper of Kilbarchan, the artistic gist is one of demotic ceremonial, an aesthetic of common sense. While the sheer craftsmanship of their writing is important, it seems to have been equally indispensable that it be heard and seen to surpass mere proficiency. Rhyming 'for fun', along with Burns's other denials of seriousness, is therefore more than tongue-in-cheek. Behind the generous smile, the parade of good nature, there is an ironic grimace, an earnestness which Burns's characteristically high-spirited tone seems determined to disguise. In these lines, for example, it is possible that forecast disappointment or the fear of ultimate defeat can be heard leaking through the poet's ostensible modesty – his 'haughty modesty', as Carlyle described it – or ironically self-imposed local limitations, proclaimed in order to be surpassed by the poet's performance:

> For me, I'm on Parnassus brink,
> Rivan the words tae gar them clink;
> Whyles daez't wi' love, whyles daez't wi' drink,
>   Wi' jads or masons;
> An' whyles, but ay owre late, I think
>   Braw sober lessons.
>
> Of a' the thoughtless sons o' man,
> Commen' me to the Bardie clan;
> Except it be some idle plan

> O' rhymin' clink,
> The devil-haet, that I sud ban,
>   They never think.
>
> Nae thought, nae view, nae scheme o' livin',
> Nae cares tae gie us joy or grievin':
> But just the pouchie put the nieve in,
>   An' while ought's there,
> Then, hiltie, skiltie, we gae scrivin',
>   An' fash nae mair.
>
> Leeze me on rhyme! it's ay a treasure,
> My chief, amaist my only pleasure,
> At hame, a-field, at wark or leisure,
>   The Muse, poor hizzie!
> Tho' rough an' raploch be her measure,
>   She's seldom lazy.
>
> Haud tae the Muse, my dainty Davie:
> The warl' may play you [monie] a shavie;
> But for the Muse, she'll never leave ye,
>   Tho' e'er sae puir,
> Na', even tho' limpan wi' the spavie
>   Frae door tae door.
>
> ['Second Epistle to Davie',] lines 19–48

Poetry and poverty are associated, which is instructive in itself, and Standard Habbie, the Muse's 'measure', and the 'standard' verse of Scottish poetry, is included as 'rough and raploch' [*homely*]. Horizons are distinctly depressed in these stanzas, and if Burns's writing lacks its best technical bravura (the repeated *-ink* rhymes, for example) the expertise is obvious and strong enough to enforce an ironic contrast between the gestural acceptance of narrow aspirations and the actual *doing* of verse. What Burns *does* in the poem is not what he *says*, and the other way round, too. He describes his writing as a ploughman's pastime but performs this statement with considerable artistry. It is not, as it happens, at its highest pitch of ingenuity, but sufficient for the point to be made that what is being expressed is a restrained fury, the anger, the affront, of a poet who is also the representative of a culture, obliged to define himself as a hobbyist, even in the stanza, the primary artistic unit, of his country's literary culture. It is an essential meaning in Burns's poetry and is conveyed through the contrast of what he says with the dexterity of how he says it. Equally striking in these stanzas is the emphasis of a native acoustic in the bang or slide of his rhymes, either monosyllabic snaps (-ink, -an) or broad and open (treasure, pleasure, leisure, measure; Davie, shavie, leave ye, spavie), while the Scots diction (raploch, spavie) adds its own vocal contribution to the overall meaning of the passage in which the dynamic moves from the virtues of local poetry to a submission to the Muse of all poetry. Joseph Brodsky remarked, and very wisely: '"Sorrow controlled by meter" may do for you as a provisional definition of humility, if not of the entire art of poetry'.[16] Burns's sorrow is not a self-pitying regret that the choices imposed on him by his origins and circumstances determined his poetic career as one of local or national limitations, but that he should have been forced to contest the perceived prejudices of those who felt otherwise, and which he did through the sustained use of local and national prosody. Brodsky continued: 'As a rule, stoicism and obstinacy in poets are results not so much of their personal philosophies and preferences as of their experiences in prosody, which is the name of the cure'.[17] Stoicism and obstinacy are terms not normally associated with a high-spirited and often impatient poet like Burns, drawn to satire on the one hand and love lyrics on the other, as well as, significantly enough, addresses to representatives of the microcosm: he is a poet of lice, mice, wounded hares, dead mares, mountain daisies, peasant delicacies, and something nice to fill your glass with, as well as the passionate poet of 'A man's a man for a' that', and, above all, the poet of his own poetry (which is the poet Burns too long neglected), a defender of poetry and the place in it which he clears and defines for himself, and which he then inhabits.

No-one need philosophise too strenuously to see a connection between these vulnerable subjects and Burns's concern with poverty – his own and that of others in the society with which he was intimate. But his prosodic fortitude seems to me inescapable, radiant and meaningful. Instinctively, he relied on the security of national stanzas, rhythms, cadences, tones and melodies, to which a judiciously-distributed Scots diction added an acoustic that lifts the linguistic experience of his poetry and song above that of a mere accent. It matters not at all that it could have been less than deliberate on Burns's part, although I feel absolutely convinced that it was. To claim that he was not a self-aware artist is to diminish how his 'keenness of insight keeps pace with keenness of feeling', as Carlyle put it, with wonderful fineness, although Carlyle's insensitivity to verse blinded him to the extent, which is practically total, to which that 'keeping pace' is a matter of technical control, of the marvellous instinct which insists that an artist take such pains, the *versification* of insight and emotion, and not just their disclosure.[18]

'Love and Liberty – A Cantata', the poem once known as 'The Jolly Beggars', and never published in Burns's lifetime, is a perfect illustration of all that I have been trying to say about Burns's native metric. It contains Montgomerie's Stanza, Ballad Royal, Standard Habbie and the eighteenth-century derivative of the *Christ's Kirk on the Green* stanza, as well as, in the songs, trochaic metre (the rhythm, incidentally, of most of the songs in Shakespeare's plays: it could have been Shakespeare's way of asserting the voice of the people, of folk-poetry) and triple metre, in answer to Burns's composition into the cadences of a tune. Famously, 'Love and Liberty' is set in Poosie Nancie's in Mauchline, described by James Mackay in his recent biography as 'a disreputable dive' and a 'dosshouse for vagrants'.[19] Burns, Mackay says, 'would never have considered frequenting such a place', which does nothing to answer why he should have written about it with such an investment of vigour and passion and in all of his major, national poetic forms.[20] Whether Burns went there or not, he inhabited Poosie Nancie's low tavern in his imagination. As a brilliant dramatic stroke – the work, assuredly, is composed for performance – Burns draws down, reduces, the national circumstance, the matter of his contemporary Scotland, to its microcosm in a state of actively defiant misrule in which Burns is a participant, and that is what he boils in his alembic basin. Reductive impulses are common in Scottish literature, and in contemporary writing, too: they can be seen in novels by James Kelman and Irvine Welsh, and in Tom Leonard's poetry. It is a literary and political tactic in which a serious statement is made through the events and mouths of lives considered marginal or even outcast by the ruling ethos in culture and society. The Scots seem to love and crave the very edges of existence, although they are not concerned with spiritualising them, which seems to me the major flaw of the Scottish cultural psyche. The Scots language is riddled with reductive terms and diminutives. What other cultures find disgusting, Scots poetry revels in. Burns marginalises himself in such reductive phrases as 'Jock Milton' or 'Wee Pope', and through the broader implications of his irony; but the importance of the gesture lies in its covert disclosure that the 'margin' is not 'marginal' at all, or certainly not for Burns, and not for his countrymen. It is when a meaning of that kind is folded into the egalitarian blast of 'A man's a man', his racy satire and his love lyrics, that the complexity and force of his poetic (and political) identity become clearer; and what made that identity possible was an adroitness in verse superior to mere craft, but a prowess in the higher reaches of skill, from the details of alliteration and assonance to the architectural difficulties of stanzas.

'Love and Liberty' is more than a medley of Scottish stanzas, but, significantly, a heave from beneath, a splore, an outburst of indignant merriment, pride, sorrow, pathos and humour, voiced in the drunken substratum of society by individuals who momentarily transcend their miseries. The poem's characters are even lower down the social scale than the poet, and the poet could hardly have been 'lower' in terms of social origin and still have hoped to write and publish. These qualities are intrinsic to the identities and uses of the stanzas; it is what they are associated with: mischief, vernacular impertinence, speaking back, speaking when you have not been spoken to, letting your hair down, breaking an imposed code, sneering at and dismissing the holy cows of a society in which these voices are displaced. Scottish vernacular poetry is a phenomenon which comes in from the fields or off the streets. The poem's characters are a veteran with one arm and one leg, and his 'doxy', a former camp-follower of a regiment who doesn't know her own age ('And now I have lived – I know not how long') but loyal to her mutilated partner; the widow of John Highlandman (a hanged cateran or Jacobite); an itinerant, diminutive fiddler; a wandering tinker-thief; and a Bard. All of them share a grudge. The Poet (perhaps Burns himself, as witness to his own anger and affection, as a lord of misrule) politicises the entire scene. Lines like these are reminiscent of his inverting or reductive remarks elsewhere:

> I never drank the Muses' STANK,
> Castalia's burn an' a' that,
> But there it streams an' richly reams,
> My HELICON I ca' that.

'It' is usually taken to mean a glass of something very strong. I suggest that it could just as likely be a stream of piddle.

Burns's taste for misrule is at its best in the ballad with which 'Love and Liberty' ends:

> Life is all a VARIORUM,
> We regard not how it goes;
> Let them cant about DECORUM,
> Who have character to lose . . .

> Here's to BUDGETS, BAGS and WALLETS!
> Here's to all the wandering train!
> Here's our ragged BRATS and CALLETS!
> One and all cry out, AMEN!
> A fig for those by LAW protected,
> LIBERTY's a glorious feast!
> COURTS for Cowards were erected,
> CHURCHES built to please the Priest.

Even if Burns *is* imaginatively present in the poem, it remains a dramatic piece the revolutionary propulsion of which is determined as much by a tradition of writing and song set in low taverns and among beggars as by the French Revolution which was to begin about three years after the poem's composition.[21] In this context, though, it can look as if what Burns was doing was to associate his verse (and its typical stanzas, his metric, his resonance) with a more extreme, a more demotic, more vernacular occasion than any others in his work outside of *The Merry Muses of Caledonia*, even if there is present in the poem a characteristic sprinkling of eighteenth-century English diction. Lines like 'Full soon I grew sick of my sanctified *sot*,/ The Regiment AT LARGE for a HUSBAND I got', or

> But hurchin Cupid shot a shaft,
>   That play'd a DAME a shavie –
> The Fiddler RAK'D her, FORE AND AFT,
>   Behind the Chicken cavie ...

would have been what disposed Burns to withhold its appearance in print. However, the effect of 'Love and Liberty'[22] is not one in which its inhabitants feel either degraded or falsely esteemed. Instead, they are revealed as unsentimentally, animatedly *present*. Open the door on a place like Poosie Nancie's, and this is what you see:

> First, niest the fire, in auld, red rags,
> Ane sat; weel brac'd wi' mealy bags,
>   And knapsack a' in order;
> His doxy lay within his arm;
> Wi' USQUEBAE an' blankets warm,
>   She blinket on her Sodger:
> An' ay he gies the tozie drab
>   The tither skelpan kiss,
> While she held up her greedy gab,
>   Just like an aumous dish:
>   Ilk smack still, did crack still,
>   Just like a cadger's whip;
>   Then staggering, an' swaggering,
>   He roar'd this ditty up –

Burns's art transforms squalor – depicted initially with some distaste – into social portraiture in which neither disapproval nor applause is of any consequence, and in the expression of which the symmetry of Montgomerie's Stanza is very precisely drawn. The presence, too, of a Poet in the cast of the poem's characters unsettles the reader (or member of an audience) with the possibility that if the cantata makes no exact claims to autobiographical testimony in an immediate sense, then it does so emotionally and imaginatively. While 'Love and Liberty' is a poem in which seldom-heard voices are set free in their own melodies and life stories, in Scottish lyrics, and introduced in the stanzas of the Scottish tradition, the impression is one of powerful conviction, linking it to the rest of Burns's work as a kind of miscellaneous masterpiece, a demotic *summa*, a gob-stopping whoop of moral indiscipline. He was a poet who wrote his own finale early in his career, and who left it unpublished in his lifetime. That it should contain all these Scottish stanzas as well as songs is a curiously telling, unsettling truth: it is as if Burns saw the boundaries of his genius long before he ran up against them.

Burns's typical stanzas have been used since his death. Wordsworth, Longfellow and Swinburne, in their poems about Burns, demonstrate how enervated the stanza can seem without Scots diction. A host of minor Scottish figures in the late eighteenth and nineteenth centuries, for example, used Standard Habbie too. In some cases they wrote with considerable vigour and success, in some cases sufficient as to lead to the question of how minor they actually are.[23] In others it becomes clear how the directness of Scottish poetry leads into McGonagallese and that it calls for technical mastery to avoid it when statement occupies more poetic space than imagery in cases where all that a poet has to say is banal at best and slewed by incompetence at worst. R. L. Stevenson was fond of the stanza. Hugh MacDiarmid turned his back on these measures as obstacles to modernity (and he could have been right), although his high valuation of 'directness' led readily enough into passages of dire emptiness of imagery and yards of assertion and vehemence. It was left to Robert Garioch, through his attachment to Fergusson more than to Burns, to try to revive them significantly. It is difficult to see how these stanzas, or how Burns's metric and resonance, can inform contemporary and future Scottish poetry. In a sense that does not deny Burns and his forms their present usefulness, his poetry is a phenomenon of the past. There is something about Scotland which insists on living in the past, a species of national selfishness; it is the opposite of the spirit of Burns and his poetry: he was progressive and, in using the verse materials of tradition, experimental and courageous, given the tenor of his times. The stanza commonly named after him outwith Scotland could have been influential on W. H. Auden (the most interestingly stanzaic of all modern poets) in 'The Witnesses', for example.[24] More recently, Standard Habbie has been used by John Fuller[25] and by Seamus Heaney.[26] It is some time since a Scottish poet used it. Fuller and Heaney write nimbly in Standard Habbie, but break many of the rules implicit in Burns's eighteenth-century practice – stanzas run on into others, for example, with dodgier half- and near-rhymes than Burns's notion of 'clink' permitted, as well as other tendencies sanctioned by contemporary poetry.[27] In Heaney's case, the stanza is significant in that it had a long tradition of use in Northern Ireland.[28] At the same time, it is interesting and ironic that an Irish writer should have a poem published complaining at being called 'British' (which Seamus Heaney undoubtedly isn't) in a Scottish stanza.

Burns 'cults', Burns Suppers, and other phenomena of a like nature, are of very little consequence. What does it matter if those who otherwise do not read or care for poetry meet once a year to eat and drink in honour of Burns's memory? Is it even worth mentioning that Robert Burns's is the only poetry that they care to read or listen to? In this bicentenary year of Burns's death, the Scottish literati have once again raised their voices in complaint at the spectacle of celebrations deemed false or philistine, and the sound is as disagreeable as that of a dimwit trying to recite Burns after a dram too many (or one too few). To rescue Burns for poetry means paying attention to the significance of how he wrote as well as what he said. Burns's prosodic artistry, his fluency and confidence in metre and rhyme, his self-aware reliance on a range of native stanzas, and his expertise in their manip-ulation, which are crucial to the national spirit of his poetry, amount to a mighty artistic gesture, a big prosodic heave, a major artistic effort. To those for whom poetry and its understanding form a large part of their lives and devotions, it is the proof of the poet, and it is what has made his work last.

NOTES

1. T. S. Eliot, *Ezra Pound: His Metric and Poetry* (New York: Knopf, 1917).
2. For this kind of poem, its themes and its stanza, see Allan H. MacLaine, 'The *Christis Kirk* Tradition: Its Evolution in Scots Poetry to Burns', *Studies in Scottish Literature*, 2 (July 1964–April 1965), 3–18, 111–24, 163–82, 234–50.
3. W. E. Henley and T. F. Henderson (eds), *The Poetry of Robert Burns*, Centenary Edition, 4 vols (London: Caxton, 1896), I, pp. 336–42.
4. Allan H. MacLaine, 'New Light on the Genesis of the Burns Stanza', *Notes and Queries*, 198 (August 1953), 349–51.
5. Op. cit. in note 3 above, I, p. 337.
6. In Roderick Watson (ed.), *The Poetry of Scotland* (Edinburgh: Edinburgh University Press, 1995), p. 126.
7. In A. M. Kinghorn and A. Law (eds), *Poems by Allan Ramsay and Robert Fergusson* (Edinburgh: Scottish Academic Press, 1974), p. 134.
8. Ibid., p. 184.
9. Alexander Montgomerie, *The Cherrie and the Slae*, ed. H. Harvey Wood (London: Faber and Faber, 1937), p. 23.
10. Quoted by Henderson, op. cit. in note 3 above, I, p. 366.
11. George Saintsbury, *Historical Manual of English Prosody* (London: Macmillan, 1930), p. 270.
12. Unless someone else comes along with an active Scottish interest in these stanzas, their longevity – so called here – may have come to an end in the work of the late Robert Garioch or in the writings of Burnsian pasticheurs.
13. Edwin Muir, 'Burns and Popular Poetry', *Essays on Literature and Society* (London: Hogarth Press, 1949), p. 57.
14. G. Ross Roy (ed.), *The Letters of Robert Burns*, 2nd edn, 2 vols (Oxford: Clarendon Press, 1985), I, p. 88.
15. Ibid., I, p. 97.

16. Joseph Brodsky, 'On "September 1, 1939" by W. H. Auden', *Less than One: Selected Essays* (New York: Viking, 1986), p. 351.

17. Ibid.

18. Carlyle (in the 1828 *Edinburgh Review* essays on Burns from which I am quoting) defended Burns's poems as 'imperfect' and of 'small extent', and makes his proposition that 'his genius attained no mastery in its art' in a fulsome passage for which the excuse is Burns's early death at 37. All that can be said is that it is pathos, a moment of high intellectual sentimentality in an essay otherwise distinguished by remarkable and exhilarating fervour and insight. At the same time, Carlyle's opinions of Burns's artistry appear to be sadly replicated into our own time.

19. James Mackay, *A Biography of Robert Burns* (Edinburgh: Mainstream, 1992), p. 152.

20. Ibid., p. 153.

21. See Thomas Crawford, *Burns: A Study of the Poems and Songs*, 2nd edn (Edinburgh: Oliver & Boyd, 1965), pp. 130–46.

22. At times, I prefer the older title ('The Jolly Beggars') as one which leaves the uncanny elevation of Burns's treatment of anarchic 'low' life to the reader's experience of the poem. 'Love' and 'Liberty' raise the poem to high revolutionary prestige even before reading has begun.

23. Tom Leonard's anthology *Radical Renfrew* (Edinburgh: Polygon, 1990) shows a remarkable range of examples of poetry from John Robertson (1767–1810) and Alexander Wilson (1766–1813) to writers active throughout the nineteenth century who used Standard Habbie, the *Christ's Kirk* stanza and an eight-line ballad measure. Wilson is especially impressive as one of the major 'if only' cases in Scottish poetry.

24. W. H. Auden, 'The Witnesses', in Edward Mendelson (ed.), *The English Auden* (London: Faber and Faber, 1977), pp. 126–30.

25. John Fuller, *Epistles to Several Persons* (London: Secker and Warburg, 1973), is a collection of five poems in Burns's stanza.

26. Seamus Heaney, *An Open Letter* (Derry: Field Day Theatre Company, 1983) ('Field Day Pamphlet' No. 2).

27. And I do, too, in my poem 'Tannahill' in *St Kilda's Parliament* (London: Faber and Faber, 1981). I promise not to do it again.

28. See John Hewitt's anthology *Rhyming Weavers* (Belfast: Blackstaff Press, 1974), which contains much introductory and critical comment. Hewitt's examples include poems in Standard Habbie, the Christ's Kirk stanza and Montgomerie's Stanza.

BURNS AND POLITICS

Marilyn Butler

'Burns and Politics' is a topic that encompasses most of what Burns wrote, and much of the literary culture of his day. Burns's social position and his self-presentation, the deliberately simple and traditional language, verse-forms and metres, are all in the end political, but at a level hard to do justice to in a survey. In individual poems he may seem forthright and simple, yet considered as a whole the man and the phenomenal career seem complex and elusive. In addition, he withheld a larger proportion of his work than other poets, and this includes the best of what's overtly political. Those poems remain political in intention but not as action, and that distinction complicates the story.

Burns's first volume, which made him famous – *Poems, Chiefly in the Scottish Dialect* (Kilmarnock, July 1786) – contained only forty-four poems and songs, many of them short. The edition was reissued in Edinburgh (April 1787) with minor cuts and twenty-two additional poems; and again in Edinburgh in two volumes (1793), with nineteen additional poems. That formal core of Burns's oeuvre gets us to a total in the low eighties, not much compared with the traditional Scottish songs, set to Scottish airs, on which Burns spent much of his poetic energy from 1787. He communicated and often effectively rewrote about 200 of the songs in *The Scottish Musical Museum*, edited in six volumes by the Edinburgh engraver James Johnson between 1787 and 1803, and another seventy in *A Select Collection of Original Scottish Airs for the Voice*, edited by the Edinburgh clerk George Thomson from 1793 to 1818. Traditional song challenges the very notion of individual authorship by its essentially stereotypical themes, verse-forms, imagery and diction. Yet the songs can be as political as anything by Burns, and must play an important part in a survey of his engagement with politics. As for the latently political, that includes the erotica – for instance *The Merry Muses of Caledonia*, first prepared for publication around 1800, and at last in 1965 lawfully published in an edition by James Barke and Sydney Goodsir Smith (London: W. H. Allen).

I shall begin with what is openly political and leave what is latent until last. When people ask about Burns and politics, they will usually be thinking, at least if they live outside Scotland, of his interest in the major geopolitical feature of his day – revolution, especially the French. Burns does write directly political poems on current events and public personalities: at least twenty of the eighty-odd poems which he published are political in this state-political arena, which is a high percentage, especially from someone coming on the scene as a pastoralist. These divide into the following categories:

- poems which praise America as a land of freedom;
- poems on British-national, i.e. London-based, politics;
- poems on elections for Westminster in the Ayr/Dumfries region;
- poems alluding to the French Revolution and its Scottish reception;
- loyalist or equivocal poems, also post-revolutionary.

Because in Burns's case it would be misleadingly narrow to define politics that way, I shall also consider three other groups:

1. Those *Songs*, identified as Burns's work in the two *Collections*, which are Jacobite and/or nationalist, in the sense that they might rally opinion against England and government rather than against 'whigs' within Scotland.
2. Burns's poems (mostly written in 1785, most unpublished in Burns's lifetime) on the politics of Ayrshire Presbyterianism. Burns grew up in a locality where the Calvinists or 'Auld Lichts' contended vigorously with the Moderates or rationalists, and their disputes produced the significant ideological rifts in Burns's world. Burns's ten or so religious satires reveal more profoundly than any other issue what he stands for as a thinker, and place him socially in his community, as a man who challenged others and was in turn challenged by men in authority. In Ayrshire, the Kirk had far more significance than the political parties of faraway Westminster as a way of establishing a person's identity, as the chief forum of serious debate, and as a means of disciplining younger and poorer members of the community.
3. Implicitly, the Kilmarnock (and first Edinburgh) collection itself. In offering a diverse selection of popular poetry in the vernacular, Burns raises questions about hierarchy, class and cultural authority.

My formal political category yields a respectable number of examples, and a few important poems, but overall the aesthetic quality and intellectual interest is not great by Burns's high standards. The largest subgroup consists of seven satires on elections in the locality for seats at Westminster. Burns weighed in with three vigorous squibs in 1789–90, when the contest was for Dumfriesshire Burghs.[1] On his first visit to Edinburgh in 1786–7, Burns had mixed in Whiggish circles and worn the buff and blue clothes of the Whig faction, as his likely patrons did. Since the Whig candidate in the Dumfries election was the son of his own landlord, Burns would have been expected to support him. But Burns disliked what he knew of the Whig oligarch controlling this seat, the Marquess of Queensberry. He felt equally free to adopt an independent line on the twenty-year-old candidate, and in his letters described him as a youth of only modest abilities. Burns asserted himself when, as a self-styled local poet, he weighed into the national political fray, and further asserted himself by giving his services to the Tory.

Later, though, he did back a Whig, his friend Patrick Heron, who stood in 1795 and again in 1796 for the Stewardry of Kirkcudbright. Three of these four election poems (nos 492, 493 and 494) are, like the 1789 group, fairly tedious recitals of local personalities, usually opponents, none memorably portrayed as in the satires of Juvenal or Pope. In 'Wham will we send to London Town?' (490), however, Burns borrows freely from the ideas, metre and refrain of the most anti-aristocratic of his own songs, 'For a' that' (482). In this context, to call Heron an Honest Man and an independent commoner is in effect to align him with democrats. Boisterous and abusive – 'A lord may be a lousy loun' (l. 30) – Burns appears to be haranguing not so much the freeholders as the mob: 'We are na to the market come/ Like nowt and naigs and a' that' (ll. 39–40). If those who heard it had also heard its parent-poem and model, 'For a' that', with its fierce anticipation of revolution, they must have felt that Burns's contribution shifted the Heron campaign out of the polite confines of pre-reform party politics. The law agent for the other side, Young of Harburn, long afterwards reflected acidly that Heron's cause couldn't have been helped by Burns's 'libels and lampoons' on those who didn't serve Heron's interest – with which, Young said snobbishly, 'Burns [should have] had no more to do than he had with the affairs of the man in the moon'.[2]

The 'aristocratic' view that Burns should stay in his proper sphere, which would not have been confined to Tories, has always to be borne in mind when considering just what it was that he risked when he wrote on politics. It's easy to suppose that what he had to fear was solely arrest and imprisonment – and equally easy to patronise him retrospectively for having overrated this danger. By the summer of 1793, radicals were receiving savage treatment in the Scottish courts, and it was not obvious that satirists would be immune from prosecution. Burns, moreover, had something else to worry about, his foothold in a pursuit known at the time as 'polite letters'. A creative writer writes for the public and is dependent on fickle public taste, which for general social reasons often veers away from writers who present themselves as abrasive or contentious. Burns had to make very delicate judgements if he was to go on pleasing the educated public. In his first year of fame, in

Edinburgh in 1786, he already suspected that his independence would necessarily lose him the approval of middle-class readers of poetry. His shift of
interest towards Scottish song, with its potentially much wider, more open
popular market, looks like a shrewd move to diversify his market in order to
reduce his dependence on fashion.

Liberal causes which did command wide middle-class support in the
later eighteenth century were humanitarianism and the revolt of the American
colonies. The immediate approval which Burns won from first readers of his
first volume no doubt owes something to the presence there of just these
issues, originally handled. In particular, Burns writes brilliantly emblematic
poems on humanitarian themes, largely free of sentimental excess: 'To a
Mouse', gently attentive to a small defenceless creature, also lightly addresses
the human experience of homelessness. He uses the same tactic of doubling
up when, in the age of the profoundly threatening and increasingly unpop-
ular French Revolution, he continues to recall the American one. America
figures in the poems as an idealised region, offering Britons and particularly
Scots the goals of social equality and personal independence. Aged 16 when
the American War broke out, Burns remembers it without unnecessary
complication as a struggle for independence and liberty. 'When Guilford
Good', an early political poem, satirically itemises by name the intriguing
Westminster politicians headed by Lord North, the 'Guilford' of the first
line, and the unsuccessful generals, who among them lost the war. Lord
Glencairn, Burns's first patron, saw nothing wrong with a social inferior
lampooning favourite political targets like these, and on his advice Burns
included this poem in his Edinburgh edition of 1787.

But by 1794 a nearer and more threatening revolution had turned France
upside down and spread well beyond its borders. Burns wrote one savage
popular jingle (401), parodying a facetious comic song, which jeered at the
French General Dumourier for deserting the republic for the pay of France's
leading continental enemy, Austria. More ambitiously, he used the pretext of
an 'Ode' on Washington's birthday (451) to recall admiringly a revolution
moderate British opinion could still find acceptable:

> Where is Man's godlike Form?
> Where is that brow erect and bold,
> That eye that can, unmoved, behold
> The wildest rage, the loudest storm,
> That e'er created fury dared to raise!
>
> . . . come, ye sons of Liberty,
> Columbia's offspring, brave as free,
> In danger's hour still flaming in the van:
> Ye know, and dare maintain, The Royalty of Man.
>
> (ll. 13–28)

The three irregular stanzas, based on the classic Pindaric Ode, polarise three states and their politics: newly-liberated America, England, seen as despotic and disgraced, and Scotland, which Burns represents as led in history by Wallace, Washington's prototype as the challenger of English imperialism. It is the middle stanza on England that carries the political punch, for it seems to allude to the current European war of the 1790s rather than to the American revolt of the 1770s:

> Dare injured nations form the great design,
>   To make detested tyrants bleed?
> Thy England execrates the glorious deed!
>   Beneath her hostile banners waving,
>   Every pang of honor braving,
> England in thunders calls – 'The Tyrant's cause is mine!'
>   That hour accurst, how did the fiends rejoice,
> And hell thro' all her confines raise th' exulting voice,
>   That hour which saw the generous English name
>   Linkt with such damned deeds of everlasting shame!
>
>   (ll. 34–43)

With topical application apparent, the poem became too risky to publish. Burns merely sent it as a new work on 25 June 1794 to his regular correspondent Mrs Dunlop, who was no friend to the French Revolution, and may have noticed suspicious detail strengthening the poem's real animus against London. A 'birthday ode' was traditionally a poem flattering a monarch. George III's official birthday was in June, Washington's actually on 22 February. She may also have noticed the poet's brief personal appearance when at the opening to the last stanza he turns to Scotland:

> Thee, Caledonia, thy wild heaths among,
> Famed for the martial deed, the heaven-taught song,
>   To thee, I turn with swimming eyes.
>
>   (ll. 44–6)

In the most celebrated of the reviews which greeted Burns's Kilmarnock poems in 1786, the Scottish man of letters Henry Mackenzie greeted him as a 'Heaven-taught ploughman'. The adjective had a special significance at the time: it conveyed the rationalist and intrinsically democratic precept that right reason was universally available (without of course implying, as some modern commentators appear to think, that Burns was uneducated). Burns clearly accepted and valued Mackenzie's compliment: the tag would never be detachable, and was a master-stroke of public relations. In using the same word in this line to balance the adjective 'martial', Burns matches his own contribution of song to the actions of soldiers such as Wallace or Washington. It is one of the clearest cases – the 'Epistles' to friends supply others – where Burns claims for himself a national role.

He had used North America before as a promised land, and a focal point of anti-landlord, anti-aristocratic resentment, in what must surely be one of his finest political poems, 'Address of Beelzebub' (108). This magnificent diatribe, written in 1786, borrows the pulpit rhetoric of hellfire from the ecclesiastical satires which Burns was writing throughout the previous year. Here he reacts to newspaper reports that a group of Highland landowners had met in London to discuss the plan of 500 of their tenants to emigrate to Canada. It seems that the lairds hoped to avert this exodus by improving the cotters' conditions, particularly the condition of their land. Burns believed, or his persona Beelzebub professes to believe, that the lairds' attitude is one of near-diabolical rage and malice: 'up amang thae lakes an' seas/ They'll mak what rules an' laws they please' (ll. 11–12). In a far more intense and eloquent reprise of the American war than he had given in 'When Guilford Good', Burns-as-Beelzebub puts words in the lairds' mouths:

> Some daring Hancocke, or a Frankline,
> May set their HIGHLAN bluid a ranklin;
> Some Washington again may head them
> Or some MONTGOMERY, fearless, lead them;
> Till, God knows what may be effected,
> When by such HEADS an' HEARTS directed:
> Poor, dunghill sons of dirt an' mire,
> May to PATRICIAN RIGHTS ASPIRE;
> Nae sage North, now, nor sager Sackville,
> To watch an' premier owre the pack vile!
>
> (ll. 13–22)

This single verse-paragraph imagines the attempted revolution still to come, another American War, except that it will not happen because it will be arrested by the landlords' spite:

> THEY! an' be d–mn'd! what right hae they
> To Meat, or Sleep, or light o' day
> Far less to riches, pow'r, or freedom,
> But what your lordships PLEASE TO GIE THEM?
>
> (ll. 27–30)

At the halfway point in the poem, succinctly brought to an impasse in l. 30, Beelzebub turns aside to propose the regime needed at home to break the rebels' spirits. This is a matter, he supposes, of pushing their present regimen only a little further, since 'while they're only poined and herriet,/ They'll keep their stubborn Highlan spirit' (37–8). With the zeal of an aroused divine, Beelzebub calls down curses on the heads and backs of the cotter families:

But smash them! crush them a' to spails!	pieces
An' rot the DYVORS i' the JAILS! . . .	debtors
The HIZZIES, if they're oughtlins fausont,	women, decent
Let them in DRURY LANE be lesson'd!	
An' if the wives, an' dirty brats,	
Come thiggan at your doors an' yets,	begging, gates
Flaffan wi' duds, an' grey wi' beese,	flapping rags, vermin
Frightan awa your deucks an' geese;	
Get out a HORSE-WHIP, or a JOWLER,	
The langest thong, the fiercest growler,	
An' gar the tatter'd gipseys pack	
Wi' a' their bastarts on their back!	

(ll. 39–52)

When that's done, Beelzebub more suavely invites the lairds to reconvene; the poem ends imagining a party to match the friendly discussion at the Shakespeare, Covent Garden, where, according to Burns's headnote, the proposal to stop the emigration was first discussed. Next time the Earl of Breadalbane and Macdonald of Glengarry meet, it will be to sample the pleasures of Beelzebub's own fireside, and Breadalbane is promised the inglenook nearest the fire.

Invited in 1787 to advise which if any of Burns's political and ecclesiastical satires should be published in the forthcoming second edition, Hugh Blair nervously observed that Burns's politics always smelt of the smithy,[3] perhaps recollecting singed Breadalbane. 'The Address of Beelzebub' did not in fact achieve publication until 1818, maybe because its powerful assault on personalities would have been widely felt to go beyond the bounds of civility even if the motives of the landlords were not also being misrepresented. As it stands, Burns's published volume, even in its later amplified versions, evokes a sociable village world and an author who enjoys the camaraderie of men, women and even animals: an amiable rather than a harsh persona. The harshness of ll. 30–60 could have seemed risky at the outset, for being outside Burns's apparent range – the very reason why it impresses us now.

Comic poems in an established tradition of impertinence gave less offence and appeared even in the Kilmarnock edition. One of these is a cheerful mock-heroic 'Earnest Cry and Prayer' (no. 81) to the Scottish MPs at Westminster following the passing of the Wash Act (1784), which cracked down on illegal Scottish distilleries and taxed the legal ones more heavily than before. By the time the poem appeared in 1786, other protests from Scotland had secured a new Distilleries Act more to Scottish liking. A poem already essentially light-hearted and familiar has lost any appearance of threat that it might have had. All the same, Burns in his persona of the Ayrshire ploughman wagers his new plough-spade that if the measure isn't recalled he and his like, representing an irritated female 'auld Scotland', will take to violence:

> Her tartan petticoat she'll kilt,
> An' durk an' pistol at her belt,
>   She'll tak the streets,
> An' rin her whittle to the hilt,
>   I' the' first she meets!
>   (ll. 98–101)

More potentially transgressive is 'A Dream' (113), Burns's clever parody of an 'Ode' by the poet laureate Thomas Warton which had appeared in the newspapers for the traditional ceremonial purpose of celebrating the monarch's birthday (4 June). The main purpose is to invert the theme to one of disapproval, with George III, his sons the royal princes, and his ministers the main targets. The 'Birthday Ode' to Washington written eight years later is a straightforward substitution of another kind, since it praises a great republican who stands for 'the Majesty of Man'. But it's also worth noting the *literary* politics of the assignment which Burns sets himself when addressing George III. He is in effect parodying this routine courtly exercise by Warton, author of the stately, prestigious *History of English Literature, 1100–1603* (3 vols, 1774–81), which was under fire throughout the 1780s from historians and collectors of provincial literature for its court-centred, Tory and Anglican perspective on culture. The Kilmarnock volume has a real agenda, after all, one which is expressed pithily in Lallans in the verse Epistles which the volume includes to the other local vernacular poets and antiquarians, John Lapraik and William Simson. The second stanza of 'A Dream' throws down a challenge to hired flatterers such as Warton: 'The poets too, a venal gang,/ Wi' rhymes weel-turn'd an' ready' (ll. 14–15).

The 'dream sequence' is an original medieval device, regularly used to discourage prosecution for a political libel. The jingle which Burns uses as an epigraph adapts a well-known cynical rhyme from the long history of political controversy: 'Thoughts, words and deeds, the Statute blames with reason;/ But surely Dreams were ne'er indicted Treason'. For those with antiquarian interests, in England as well as Scotland, this historically sophisticated presentation, evocative of that other Ploughman created by

Langland, complicates Burns's status and further politicises him. In fact, if we were now to read 'A Dream' as a self-consciously provincial poem, joining a very old genre of cultural protest against the Court and the metropolis, we would be in tune with the semi-covert political agenda of the new medieval revival. Like Chatterton before him, Joseph Ritson in the 1780s, and Burns's friend of later years, Francis Grose, Burns here uses a virtually archaic form to dignify an essentially popular satire.

Treasonable the poem may not be, forthright it is; the polite Blair might fairly think that there wasn't much finesse in immediately informing the King that the Jacobite Pretender should have occupied his place:

> . . . nae reflection on YOUR GRACE,
>   Your Kingship to bespatter,
> There's monie *waur* been o' the Race,   worse
>   And Aiblins *ane* been better   maybe
>   Than You this day.
>
>   (ll. 23–7)

The blunt reference in line 26 to Charles Edward Stuart as George's superior rival is not developed, making its introduction seem awkward or irresolute. Instead, Burns fills successive stanzas with equally abrupt derogatory sketches of court personalities, in the manner of 'When Guilford Good'. If 'A Dream' is somewhat better than the American poem, it is because its literary self-consciousness seriously problematises the roughness attaching to the figure and voice of the ploughman. Burns seems uneasy, and he never loses his unease, when the genre requires him to place himself in a high-life setting.

Nevertheless, traditional, even medieval literary devices such as parody and the adoption of a clownish persona, served Burns in good stead in the 1790s, when to publish political poetry at all was even riskier in Scotland than in England. In the summer of 1792, the lawyer Thomas Muir set up a society, 'Friends of the People', which among other networking and campaigning activities circulated copies of Tom Paine's *Rights of Man*. Muir was arrested on a charge of sedition in January 1793, and, after provocatively visiting Paris while on bail, was tried for sedition on 30 August 1793, convicted on the following day and sentenced to transportation for the exceptionally severe term of fourteen years. Others came before the Scottish courts and were also transported in 1794. Apart from Muir himself, the reformer who attracted most sympathy was the respectable Unitarian clergyman Thomas Fyshe Palmer, who received seven years. Like Muir, Palmer endured many hardships during his life as a convict; both died on the homeward journey. Scotland's indicted 'revolutionaries' in 1793 were not men of violence but members of the learned professions. Their English opposites numbers Hardy, Holcroft and Horne Tooke, accused in 1794 of 'constructive treason' or 'imagining' the death of the King, were acquitted by the jury. By contrast, the harsh, overbearing conduct of the Scottish trials by Judge Braxfield was much criticised by quite moderate onlookers in England as well as Scotland. The image helped to create the climate for Burns's late political writings and frequent self-suppressions.

In private, Burns's sympathies lay with reform. As a young man he had read Locke, father of the English liberal tradition in the eighteenth century. In the summer of 1792 he read Thomas Paine, with approval, though otherwise he seems not to have followed the major texts associated with the French Revolution. Prior to that, legend says that he signified his approval of the French government in early 1792 by sending them guns from a ship arrested for smuggling. Though J. G. Lockhart sets out this story elaborately in his *Memoir of Burns* (1828), Burns's own friends (and enemies) seem unaware of it, a fair reason for suspecting that it did not happen. On the other hand, Burns did make his 'French' sentiments visible in late 1792 in ways that were immediately talked about and investigated. He wrote a letter on 13 November 1792 to Captain William Johnston, the proprietor of a new reformist newspaper, the *Edinburgh Gazetteer*, in which he enrolled as a subscriber and approved the paper's stance: 'Go on, Sir! Lay bare, with undaunted heart & steady hand, that horrid mass of corruption called Politics & State-Craft!'[4] Two weeks earlier, Burns had been present at an incident in Dumfries Theatre when one faction called for 'God Save the King', another for the revolutionary song 'Ça ira'. When in January these signs of radical sentiments were reported to his superiors in the Excise, Burns was forced to apologise and equivocate, but he could also argue that he had been misrepresented. Far from flaunting his views in the theatre, the more serious-looking of the charges, he claimed that he had sat out the near-riot, along with other respectable members of the audience, as a vulgar disturbance.

If Burns *was* associated with 'Ça ira', it could in fact be because he had teasingly used the slogan in the Epilogue which he wrote for the benefit night (4 December 1792) of a favourite actress, Louise Fontenelle – but in such a way that he robbed it of any connection with street violence, if not with more subtle forms of protest. The Epilogue (390) begins and ends daringly political:

> While Europe's eye is fixed on mighty things,
> The fate of Empires, and the fall of Kings;
> While quacks of State must each produce his plan,
> And even children lisp The Rights of Man;
> Amid this mighty fuss, just let me mention,
> The Rights of Woman merit some attention . . .

> But truce with kings, and truce with Constitutions,
> With bloody armaments, and Revolutions;
> Let MAJESTY your first attention summon,
> Ah, ça ira! THE MAJESTY OF WOMAN ! ! !
>
> (ll. 1–6, 35–8)

Everything that comes between is coy, decorous and polite; it would do very well read out in court by the counsel for the defence.

Though his superiors in the Excise accepted Burns's excuses, this episode marked only the beginning of tensions in Dumfries that followed Burns for the short remainder of his life. A group in the town calling themselves 'the Loyal Natives' formed themselves in January 1793, the month of Louis XVI's execution, presumably in opposition to the Disloyal Francophiles. Burns seems to have responded by himself joining the Dumfries Volunteers, the local militia formed nationwide to meet the possible threat of a French invasion. In his capacity as a Volunteer, he wrote appropriate verses (484) calling for solidarity against a foreign foe:

> Does haughty Gaul invasion threat,
>   Then let the louns bewaure, Sir
> There's WOODEN WALLS upon our seas,
>   And VOLUNTEERS on shore, Sir . . .
>
> O, let us not, like snarling tykes,
>   In wrangling be divided,
> Till, slap! come in an *unco loun*,
>   And wi' a rung decide it!
>
> (ll. 1–4, 9–12)

Composed in his last year, 1795–6, this appeared on 4 May 1795 in the *Edinburgh Courant*, a loyalist paper which evidently seemed the appropriate venue for it. Thus far, at least; but the remaining twelve lines turn back on themselves in a manner that leaves the writer's allegiance in doubt. 'For never but by British hands', the second stanza ends, 'Must British wrongs be righted'. The third and last stanza is perfectly equivocal, withholding support from either side:

> Who will not sing, GOD SAVE THE KING,
>   Shall hang as high's the steeple;
> But while we sing, GOD SAVE THE KING,
>   We'll ne'er forget THE PEOPLE!
>
> (ll. 29–32)

Behind this irresolute ending, it's easy to sense the rowdy Loyal Natives, who were happy to spar with Burns using his choice of weapons: 'Ye sons of sedition give ear to my song,/ Let Syme, Burns and Maxwell pervade every throng'. Syme was a friendly local landowner; Maxwell Burns's doctor, and notoriously a man who had been actually present at Louis XVI's execution. As is always the case in a community, a man's politics were most clearly spelt out by his choice of friends. Burns replied with a quatrain (450) expressing his contempt, and, with 475, returned to the fray on 10 June 1794:

> Pray, who are these *Natives* the Rabble so ven'rate?
> They're our true ancient *Natives*, and they breed
>   undegen'rate
> The ignorant savage that weather'd the storm,
> When the *man* and the Brute differed but in the form.

In Scotland as in England, loyalism appealed to the rabble, while outnumbered liberals felt and no doubt were intimidated. Given the context, it seems inappropriate to conclude of poems such as 'Does haughty Gaul' that they display uncertain loyalties, still less the ideological muddle that some of Burns's new acquaintances attributed to him on their first meeting in Edinburgh in 1787. On the contrary, in 1793, the year of the Scottish treason trials, and 1794, the year of the transportations, Burns knew that he was an unmistakable partisan of reform, and must accordingly have been in the state of tension so tellingly portrayed by Godwin in his novel *Things as they Are, or Caleb Williams* (1794). A direct allusion to the alarms of this period occurs in a poem 'Epistle from Esopus to Maria' (486), which Burns puts into the mouth of a friend imprisoned for vagrancy in the winter of 1794–5. The actor James Williamson (Esopus) had headed the group which formerly played the Dumfries Theatre:

> The shrinking Bard adown an alley skulks
> And dreads a meeting worse than Woolwich hulks –
> Tho there his heresies in Church and State
> Might well award him Muir and Palmer's fate.
>
> (ll. 39–42)

With his family to support, Burns was not looking for martydom. Yet he still sought devices that would permit forthright expression in forms that people understood. All his best work in the last post-revolutionary period comes in songs rather than in poems, verse epistles or formal satires. Because the property-rights in songs were indeterminate, they were unlikely to be looked at by the Home Office. They passed along the ground, under the nets of the censors. They had their own processes of transmission through performance, in public or private, including the rhyme and the air, which helped the memory to retain them. This was a cheaper, safer form of circulation than that of the sophisticated printed poem.

Many of Burns's songs came with their own airs; if not, Burns and other collectors suggested an air out of the Scottish folksong repertoire, perhaps one that already had powerful political connotations. This is the case with two of Burns's most successfully circulated songs of 1793. The first, 'Here's a health to them that's awa' (391), derives directly from a celebrated Jacobite song with the same first line, which in the form that Hogg prints it in his *Jacobite Relics* (1819) has the following refrain:

> It's good to be merry and wise,
> It's good to be honest and true,
> It's good to be aff wi' the auld king,
> Afore we be on wi' the new.

In Burns's hands in 1792, the chorus becomes:

> It's gude to be merry and wise,
> It's gude to be honest and true,
> It's gude to support Caledonia's cause,
> And bide by the Buff and the Blue.
>
> (ll. 5–8)

The Whig colours signify by this date not the dominant Parliamentary party but the pro-Reform, initially pro-French Opposition faction headed by Fox. So in each of the following verses, Burns in his old stereotyped satirical manner focuses in turn on a quick sketch of a different politician – the technique of the cartoonist. In stanza II, Burns impudently invites comparison with the Jacobite original: 'Here's a health to Charlie, the chief o' the clan,/ Altho' that his band be sma' (ll. 11–12); but a tune that familiarly belongs to Charles Edward Stuart smoothly attaches itself to Charles James Fox, and it will also accommodate his followers. In stanza III, 'Here's a health to Tammie, the Norland laddie,/ That lives at the lug o' the law!' (ll. 19–20) introduces the great Scottish lawyer, Thomas Erskine, who had defended another Thomas – Paine himself. The next verse names the two aristocrats who were picked out for attack in the royal proclamation against seditious writings of May 1792. James Maitland, eighth Earl of Lauderdale, had indeed been to France with Burns's friend and correspondent, the Edinburgh doctor and novelist John Moore. The Earl of Wycombe, later second Marquess of Lansdowne, was a son of the noted liberal Whig, the Earl of Shelburne, and hence another target of the proclamation: 'Here's to

Maitland and Wycombe! Let wha does na like 'em/ Be built in a hole in the wa'!' (ll. 27–8). Burns ends with Norman McLeod, MP for Inverness, not really a leading Foxite but a useful figure for a Burns interested in creating a large and respectable phalanx to which he could attach himself.

That song made its way into the radical *Edinburgh Gazetteer*, no less, though not necessarily at Burns's instigation; it could have been sent in by an approving friend. If the tune and words of an old song have much to do with the success of this adaptation, the same is even more true of 'Scots Wha Hae' (425, 1793). Again, the reader is expected to be aware of an old air 'Hey tutti taiti', traditionally held to be the tune to which Robert Bruce's army marched to Bannockburn in 1314; equally, readers of Scottish histories had read reconstructions of Bruce's address to his army before leading them to their heroic victory. What Burns did in 1793 was to give the emotive tune words which became instant history, the form in which that speech would always subsequently be remembered: 'Now's the day, and now's the hour;/ See the front o' battle lour;/ See approach proud EDWARD's power,/ Chains and Slaverie . . .' (ll. 5–8). The simple, apt promotional idea, of imposing a version of the supposedly real speech on the supposedly old tune, was opposed by the publisher George Thomson on the grounds that the tune was insufficiently dignified. In the same vein, he wanted to substitute 'Gallia' for 'Scotland' in stanza IV. Burns rightly held out, and made a powerful impact with what came across as a marching-song of great simplicity and naturalness. Less predictably, Burns found another powerful resource in the historical record to which he makes almost pedantic reference. As Macpherson in the previous generation noticed, a new poem claiming to be an authentically old one has quite different qualities from an invention, and for some purposes deeper qualities, whatever its literary merits. Perhaps because it seemed basically historical rather than political, 'Scots Wha Hae' found its way almost at once into different Scottish newspapers, before its first publication in book form in Thomson's *Select Collection* (1803).

Viewed one way, the poem is steeped in the specific historical record, nationalistic about and for the Scots. It is used for that purpose, and could be used only for that if it stopped at four verses. But Burns rarely continues levelly in one vein. He has a powerful sense of plot as well as of structure, influenced surely by drama and the dramatic element in ballad. Something happens, a dramatic turn, at the end of the best Burns poems. The fifth verse moves purposefully into the present tense:

> By Oppression's woes and pains!
> By your Sons in servile chains!
> We will drain our dearest veins,
> But they *shall* be free!
>
> (ll. 17–20)

Inviting his readers to die is a serious matter: he could be inciting the Scots people in the violent circumstances of the French revolutionary wars actually to fight. They would be on the side of Liberty, against Oppression, serfdom, Usurpation and Tyranny. If a Scottish reader were to apply these verses topically, he or she would have difficulty fitting serfdom and usurpation to the French republic, but might feel that the words fitted the government in London. Yet Burns could also reasonably say, and no doubt would have done if he had ever found himself in the dock, that the last two verses no longer address the people of Scotland. In the age of Revolutions nationalism drops away. The poem may be modernising and internationalising itself, as a universal call to anyone in chains to shake them off. Burns might have taken to addressing the world, like the Blake who at this very time wrote 'Continental' epics about and for America, Europe, Asia and Africa. The ambivalence here hardly belongs in the category of the prudent equivocation, though in a crunch it might have to serve as one. In a magnificent gesture, the last verse introduces every tyrant and usurper, making revolution a principle too capacious to limit itself to a particular government. The grandeur of the scale paradoxically absolves the poem from treason aimed at a particular state.

'Scots Wha Hae' may rate as Burns's best political song for its power to raise the blood, but 'For a' that' (482, written in 1795) has another kind of power: to bring in something of Burns's emotions and experience, and of who and what he stood for. Generically it's indeed a song, identified by the sprightly rhythm and the ingeniously varied use of the tag 'for a' that'. Compared with the run of songwriters, Burns aims to be forensic – he holds a topic up, quizzes it, argues towards a verdict. He alone seems to have detected in this non-committal, throwaway phrase (Heaven knows how it translates) a surprising range of nuance and diversity of functions. First encountered in the second line, it seems deliberately odd and out of place, because it is used to characterise the inarticulate mutter of a man ashamed of his poverty. Picked up by the vigorous speaker of the poem, whose tone is assertive and indignant, in the first stanza it still attaches to poverty, but not shamefully so – for the speaker refuses to be identified with or evaluated by his poverty. The first stanza, with its characteristic forceful turn in the last two lines, has the unexpected compacted power of the Shakespearean or Miltonic sonnet, an effect not often found in songs:

> Is there, for honest Poverty,
>   That hings his head, and a' that; . . .
> The rank is but the guinea's stamp,
>   The Man's the gowd for a' that.
>
>   (ll. 1–2, 7–8)

Where Burns's typical surveys of individual politicians tend to seem trivial, his sketch in the first four stanzas of 'the world' is tight and comprehensive: the world of the poor in the first two stanzas, of the rich in the third and fourth. It reminds us of similarly stylised works of literature, polarising the classes, many of them associated with popular culture: morality plays, Langland, *Timon of Athens*, Bunyan's *Pilgrim's Progress*, Wycherley's *Plain Dealer*, Gray's *Elegy*, Paine's *Rights of Man*:

> What though on hamely fare we dine,
>   Wear hoddin grey, and a' that.
> Gie fools their silks, and knaves their wine,
>   A Man's a Man for a' that . . .
> A prince can mak a belted knight,
>   A marquis, duke, and a' that; . . .
> The pith o' Sense, and pride o' Worth,
>   Are higher rank than a' that.
>
> (ll. 9–12, 25–6, 31–2)

Though the tinsel and ribband of the aristocrat always outshines the poor man' s hoddin grey, verse by verse the Man steps forward in the last two lines, and is more and more clearly identified with the poem's speaker. Though that speaker should be thought of as in some senses Everyman, he is also Burns as a self-fashioned ploughman poet. 'The pith o' Sense and pride o' Worth' recur regularly as admirable qualities in Burns's characters of lower status, even when they are talking sheep or dogs. 'The pith o' Sense' in particular evokes characteristics of language, and thus the work of a poet; above all, the phrase captures and epitomises the tough rationality of Burns's idiom when he appears to step forward in soliloquy.

After a poem with no slack, it was not an easy matter to make the last stanza yet more forceful. Burns manages it once more by moving from the plane of the human, social and familiar into a grand historical narrative. Each eighth line in each stanza is clinched by an 'a' that' which seems to signify resistance to progress, what must be pushed aside. As an adverbial phrase, it means 'despite seeming not to be so'. When the millennium arrives, this point of resistance is swept aside, and the auxiliary verbs 'may', 'will' and 'shall' seem to pour through the breach as though movement and energy, the laws of the physical world, will of themselves bear humanity ('Sense' and 'Worth') irresistibly forwards:

> Then let us pray that come it may,
>   As come it will for a' that,
> That Sense and Worth, o'er a' the earth
>   Shall bear the gree, and a' that,

> For a' that, and a' that,
>   It's comin' yet for a' that,
> That Man to Man the warld o'er,
>   Shall brothers be for a' that.
>
> (ll. 33–40)

As with 'Scots Wha Hae', the climactic verse opens out on to a visionary scene, as spacious as futurity itself. Given the date of writing (January 1795), the prophecy must be taken to mean that the French Revolution will achieve its main social goals, equality and fraternity. By projecting a voice consistent with his own, in real life and in his previous poems, Burns cannot this time evade his responsibility for the conclusion. It might of course be argued that the dénouement is impersonal, *come it will*, a process of history; he hasn't this time invited readers to achieve the millennium themselves by force of arms. But the ideologues of the French Revolution, like Marx and Engels after them, knew how empowered the disenfranchised might feel at the discovery that history was on their side. Burns's last verse here is probably the closest rendering in English of the letter and spirit of the notorious Jacobin 'Ça ira'. In the circumstances of 1795, it is surprising that it appeared that August in the *Glasgow Magazine*: further proof of the remarkable mobility of songs.

To sum up the story so far, Burns's twenty or so overtly political poems are indeed explicitly opinionated. Once the circumstances are borne in mind – the proper decorum required in a volume of polite verse, the atmosphere of the Scottish 'Terror', 1793–5 – they mostly sound notes that are firm, if some way short of foolhardy. Taken together as evidence of Burns's opinions, they outweigh his occasional letters to patrons, or to his employers the Excise, denying an interest in politics.[5] But the best of the poems so far discussed did not come out in his lifetime or even shortly after it in a volume of his work. Even when, in the early nineteenth century, they were acknowledged as his, the differences of form and spread of topic in (say) 'Address of Beelzebub', 'Ode on Washington's Birthday', 'Scots Wha Hae' and 'For a' that' dissipate their political impact.

What then might a contemporary have replied if asked about Burns's politics? The likely answers are (a) a 'patriot' in terms of Scotland at large, or of his region of western Scotland, (b) a moderate 'new light' Presbyterian, rather than a Calvinist, and (c) a writer, at times an antiquarian, concerned with the past and present of popular culture rather than or in addition to polite literature. All these dimensions of Burns then had more political significance, or a somewhat different political significance, than they do now.

It is not that Burns changes his mind, or that he may pretend to; as his readers, we are the problem. We have inherited, for example, influential but conflicting ideas about nationalism. Nineteenth-century 'big history' was locked on to national history; it was itself an expression of nationalism, and even Marxist history could fall into the pattern. Alternatively, Marxist historians, when they lingered on nationalism at all, might categorise its appearances say in colonial societies as a brand of libertarianism, as essentially progressive, and as a by-product of the French Revolution.

More recently, though, especially since the 1980s, the typical nationalist risings of the nineteenth century, and those of our own days in the former Soviet empire, have been identified as local, perhaps tribal, and in various ways conservative. Nationalists from Lithuania to Afghanistan react probably to a centralising, secular, commercially-driven government, which may also be a foreign colonial power. Regional nationalists of this kind may appear backward, intellectually simplistic, driven by emotion rather than reason, all the more because they tend to be bonded by a common religion, perhaps a local sect, and a language which also differs from that of their rulers. The first nationalist risings of the French revolutionary period were also in fact counter-revolutionary movements, localised, Catholic, peasant: they broke out against liberal reformist governments in the French Vendée (1793–4), Naples (1799) and Spain (1807). But Britain's apparently modern, centralising state also experienced internal resistance at the margins through the seventeenth and eighteenth centuries, most notably in Scotland, Ireland and North America.

This revisionist view of nationalism, developed spiritedly by scholars such as Ernest Gellner and Benedict Anderson,[6] throws light on Burns's career. It shows why an apparently local writer using a provincial idiolect at once found a receptive audience, and why the conditions were right for him to become a *national*, that is a Scottish, poet. True, Burns clearly expresses sympathy with the French Revolution; personally, he was of a type – educated but of humble origins, a man living on his talents – who typically became a middle-class liberal activist. Yet Burns's *nationalism*, equally plainly, has conservative rather than individualistic origins: at the very least, it has localised and rural roots; a family connection on his father's side to a great feudal family, that of the Jacobite Earl Marischal; a hard struggle to make a living from farming, which is under pressure from outside competition, commercial progress and social innovation; and cohesive factors locally, such as an influential, interventionist religion and a distinct language. Indeed, just as Ireland had the Catholic religion, an old native aristocracy, now largely dispossessed, and a Celtic language, so the Highlands of Scotland still had a defeated and largely unreconciled political culture in the earlier eighteenth century, which challenged the London government in armed uprisings in 1715 and 1745. Important work on Jacobitism by William Donaldson and Murray Pittock shows that it remains visible and even influential throughout the century in Scotland;[7] as sentiment, and as a form of group identity rather than as active political intrigue, it remains a significant trace element in Burns's Scotland. Most importantly, Jacobite sentiment quickly found effective cultural expression, and a revived or reconstructed culture became the basis of Scottish identity after the Act of Union (1707) between England and Scotland deprived Scotland of its political institutions. Scotland at the beginning of the century was hard to think of as one country, so deep were the divisions between the partly Gaelic-speaking and Episcopalian or Catholic Highlands and the English-speaking, Presbyterian and commercially active Lowlands. The religiously-polarised Scottish regions did not find a common cause in 1715 and 1745. But after the Jacobites' catastrophic defeat at Culloden, Lowlands as well as Highlands became preoccupied with their own songs and stories, increasingly told as one: after Culloden, Whiggish and Jacobite cultural streams intriguingly began to merge together.

A Scottish cultural revival can be observed throughout the eighteenth century following the Union with England in 1707. It puts the Scottish upper orders in touch with indigenous and folk traditions, with greater intimacy than was true of contemporary England. Allan Ramsay in the 1720s and Robert Fergusson in the 1770s are both educated poets, writing in the vernacular but enjoying the support of upper-class Jacobites. The same is essentially true of James Macpherson, the collector and translator of Gaelic songs, who has been rescued in our time from the slur of being merely a forger. Adam Ferguson and Hugh Blair, two key figures in maintaining Edinburgh's cultural rivalry with London, played important roles in briefing and promoting the Jacobite Highlander Macpherson in the early 1760s, and again in receiving the Ayrshire Presbyterian Burns a generation later. Burns did not then invent Scottish nationalism. But the key to understanding his career, and its political impact, is to grasp how he relates to post-Jacobite nationalism and substantially influences its course.

Burns made the impact which he did with the Kilmarnock volume because it was essentially sophisticated, the work of an evidently receptive reader of good late eighteenth-century writing. Burns has rifled the conventions of sensibility to arrive at a formulation all his own which is nevertheless reminiscent of the refinement of Mackenzie, the humour of Sterne and the physicality of Smollett. Beneath the pervasive echoes of these writers, readers can discern a contemporary theory of sociability, which Burns would have found in Adam Smith, especially in *The Theory of Moral Sentiments*. As a poet of rural life, Burns chose to be simple but in the best manner, as in the elegant French fables of La Fontaine, which are knowledgeably simple. The witty effect of this style is seen at its best in 'The Twa Dogs', the great satirical dialogue that opens the Kilmarnock volume, or in 'To a Louse', where the didactic lesson is tactfully kept in abeyance, or in the cluster of poems concerning Mailie, a pet sheep endowed with the idiolect and attitudes of a sensible wife and mother. Burns places the volume in this sophisticated tradition, both literary and natural, in a preface which describes the poems as pastorals, written 'with an eye to Theocrates [sic] and Virgil' yet also as accurate reports from homely real life – the sentiments and manners of himself and his 'native compeers', expressed 'in his and their native language'.

Indeed, the Kilmarnock volume *is* extraordinarily well populated, by vociferous animals as well as people; and by Burns himself, writing 'letters', that is, verse epistles, to friends or to men whom he wants to recruit as friends. In his 'Epistle to William Simson', a local antiquarian (59), Burns sets out his ambitions to write the missing poetry of the Ayrshire region, with friends and new contacts such as Simson making a circle of activists in the cause. When addressing John Lapraik (57), another stranger who is currently in prison for debt, Burns declares himself keen to write in Lallans, the native Scots dialect of English, in the tradition of Ramsay and Fergusson. (A later contribution to these poems of friendship and confederacy, 'Epistle to J[ames] S[mith]' (79), affectionately establishes Smith, a drinking companion at the Whitefoord Arms, Mauchline, as a 'russet coat' comrade from ordinary village life, one of 'The hairum-scairum, ram-stam boys/ The rattling squad'.) Taken together, the 'Epistles' are a significant, expressive feature of Burns's writing – just as similar poems make an eloquent part of the oeuvres of Ben Jonson, Dryden, Swift, Pope and Samuel Johnson. They place the poet in a small republic of friends, partly defined by its enemies in society at large.

Just as Thomas Muir in 1792 set up 'the Friends of the People' to disseminate reformist books and ideas, so Burns from 1785 set up as a networker in Scotland's cultural politics, initially within one Lowland region. The circle that met at the Whitefoord Arms called itself jocularly 'The Court of Equity', shorthand no doubt for 'Equality', but also parodic of the Mauchline Kirk Session, the disciplinary panel of elders presided over by the Minister. The Freemasons were another of Burns's clubs, societies or 'cells', and they could even more cogently appear to be set up to balance or negate the authority of the Kirk. Burns wrote 'The Farewell. To the Brethren of St. James's lodge, Tarbolton' (115) to his own Masonic Lodge, after planning in 1785 to emigrate to the West Indies. Again, he depicts a small group – 'dear brothers of the mystic tye' – as a model for an ideal sociability, one which is founded on communitarian principles but also seeks to disseminate these principles, by corresponding with lodges elsewhere. Fears were already being voiced that these secret networkers might have subversive aims. In France, recent historians have speculated, Masonic lodges *were* a breeding-ground of revolution because they symbolically substituted for traditional religion, and also because their cell-like structure trained their members to organise in safety.

The largest single group which Burns targeted as appropriate recipients for a verse epistle were local critics of the hardline faction in the Ayrshire

Kirk. Among the five 'Epistles' to appear in the Kilmarnock volume, two ('to W. S.' and 'Dedication to Gavin Hamilton', 103) are essentially or partly concerned with Kirk politics; two more, 'Epistle to J. Goldie, Kilmarnock' (63) and 'Epistle to the Rev. John M'Math' (68)', were written in 1785 but published later. The detail and personnel of the Kirk disputes need not concern us. In 1785 a new Minister was ordained, an event which polarised the 'Auld Lichts' or orthodox Calvinists on the one side, and a more moderate secular group, the 'New Lichts', on the other. Burns would no doubt have found much to admire in the vigour, independence and 'moral worth' of Knox, and indeed in the egalitarian, radical part which the Calvinist tradition played in sixteenth- and seventeenth-century Scottish history. But, in the 1780s, secular, educated young men were likely to come into conflict with the Kirk's dogmatism, that is, its intellectual as well as its moral discipline. Under the instruction of John Murdoch, the tutor appointed by his father, Burns moved in the direction of Deism, a religion of God and Nature which accepted the body and sexuality as natural rather than condemning it as an innately sinful part of our human make-up.[8] As the father of illegitimate children by two local women, Bess Paton and Jean Armour, Burns fell foul of Kirk discipline in 1785 and 1786, and was obliged to sit on the stool of repentance at the Sunday service. His dispute went wider than this, and in private letters especially he quarrelled with authoritarianism as a principle: 'Your children of Sanctity move among their fellow creatures with a nostril snuffing putrescence – and . . . that conceited dignity which your Scots lordlings of seven centuries' standing display when they accidentally mix among the many-aproned sons of mechanic life'.[9]

Personal anger and no doubt humiliation were involved, all the more because the Kirk pursued Burns relentlessly for the Armour affair, though he and Jean sought to marry. Burns's anger is a poetic asset, and the group of poems representing the language and world-view of the Kirk enhances Burns's volume and makes it more serious. Paradoxically yet powerfully, the Kirk's hellfire rhetoric resounds in 'To the Deil' and parts of 'Holy Fair' – while, in the more secular stanzas of 'Holy Fair', it offsets the animal instincts and desires of ordinary men and women, and their simple pleasure in one another's company. These poems show how closely religion can coexist for the mass of the population with 'superstition' or practices of pagan or unknown origin. But where 'To the Deil' is the monologue of a credulous villager, 'Hallowe'en' (73) resembles a report by an antiquarian on the religious practices of an unfamiliar community, complete with headnotes and footnotes. Burns emerges here as a pioneer of the common Romantic practice (adopted by Darwin, Southey, Scott, Byron and Coleridge) of accompanying a poem about 'simple' beliefs with a learned paratext, as though expecting readers to proceed to serious study. As a reasoning opponent of Calvinist orthodoxy, then, Burns distances himself from religion, and views it comparatively, that is neutrally. The poems themselves, by speaking in different voices, indicate a tolerant or even agnostic author. The Kilmarnock volume is rare among eighteenth-century poetic productions in avoiding didacticism: but the democratic cast list and eclectic topics are politically suggestive, because they evoke a charmed world resembling the 'land of Cockayne', the medieval Utopia which already jibbed at Church discipline. Burns's characters are small-town people who do not recognise any single human source of authority, but live interdependently within their natural habitat.

Burns cannot have been read as a naive poet in rational, secular Edinburgh. The sophisticates who became his hosts – Dugald Stewart, Adam Ferguson, Lord Monboddo, John Moore – and the tough, worldly, foul-mouthed, self-educated men who joined his group of lifelong correspondents – William Nicol, William Creech – saw well enough where he was coming from. Contrary to the representation of Edinburgh literati by some of Burns's admirers, these new acquaintances did not as a whole urge him to change his style to suit polite or English taste. Burns evidently concluded that he should not live independently by the pen, and perhaps could live independently only in his own region; and no-one in Edinburgh seems seriously to have given different advice. Though he looked for patrons in Edinburgh, he wanted funds to support him in Ayrshire, and these eventually he found.

Equally importantly, in Edinburgh he mapped out his central creative task for this time, the collecting and reshaping of traditional songs and ballads from both the Lowlands and the Highlands. It's interesting to see how open Burns was to advice, from very different quarters. He may not wholly have relished the interference in 1786 of the eleventh Earl of Buchan, whose idiosyncratic radicalism laid him open to his contemporaries' ridicule, but in 1787 Burns did follow Buchan's crucial and nationalist recommendation to travel in the Borders in order to get to know his country – first exploring the Borders with Robert Ainslie, a young lawyer and Mason as a companion, then tackling the Highlands with the ultra-democratic Edinburgh schoolmaster William Nicol. And in devoting 1787 to these tours, Burns mapped out his writing future with a purposefulness that is generally underrated. In the second and more rewarding of these trips, Burns and Nicol travelled through beautiful scenery and past historical sites – Stirling, Crieff, Aberfeldy, Dunkeld, Killiecrankie and Blair Atholl – to Ruthven, Macpherson's home town, where the Jacobite army briefly regrouped for the last time after Culloden. Afterwards they turned east to flatter country, the university city of Aberdeen and Kincardineshire, where Burns met his cousins on his father's side (who spelt their name Burness) at Stonehaven, Laurencekirk and Montrose. Apart from these cousins, he had letters of introduction to several noble households, including those of the Dukes of Atholl and Gordon and the Earl of Aberdeen. Interestingly, both the cousins and the peers provided him with Highland songs, no doubt often Jacobite songs, evidence of the enthusiasm for the popular tradition among different classes. In spite of Nicol's entrenched dislike of aristocratic company, Burns reported in one letter that the journey had been 'perfectly inspiring'; in another, to John Skinner, the veteran author of over sixty Scottish songs, he declared his nationalist ambition 'to form a kind of common acquaintance among the genuine sons of Caledonian song'.[10] This was in fact the definitive move into the cultural networking that he envisaged in so many of his poems to Ayrshire friends.

Burns's letter to Skinner claims enthusiastically that Scottish songs have 'a wild happiness of thought and expression which peculiarly mark them, not only from English songs, but also from the modern efforts of song-wrights, in our native manner and language'. He hints moreover that those who band together to collect and preserve 'these spells of the imagination' both share a secret enjoyment in the style of conspirators, and create a stronghold from which to fight back:

> The world, busy in low prosaic pursuits, may overlook most of us; – but 'reverence thyself'. The world is not our *peers*, – so we challenge the jury. We can lash that world, – and find ourselves a very great source of amusement and happiness independent of that world.

The difference this time is that Burns has a wider, more genuinely collaborative activity in view than writing – collecting. Significantly, he seems to have felt that it meant independence, a gentlemanly or amateur pursuit, compared with earning one's living by the pen, which might be thought of as trade. All the same, it might be used to make criticisms – another connotation of the word 'independent'. Above all, it might be a radical gesture, to turn from a volume of poems enjoying drawing-room success (Burns often sounds uneasy and shamefaced about his drawing-room success) to collecting old anonymous ballads which were the shared property of the people.

In the decade before Burns emerged in 1786, this very field of the popular ballad had been politicised by an English antiquarian. The Northumbrian ballad-collector Joseph Ritson, most truculent of contemporary popular antiquaries and editors, had attacked both Thomas Percy, editor of the pioneering *Reliques of English Poetry* (1765), and Thomas Warton, historian of medieval literature, for gentrifying the texts which they handled, and for falsifying the nature of popular culture as a derivative of written culture rather than (as Ritson believed) a largely autonomous tradition, which transmitted itself orally. Ritson published first a pamphlet (1782) about Warton's *History of English Literature 1100–1603,* then a more thoroughgoing 'Historical Essay on National Song', introducing his major *Historical Collection of English Song* (1783). It is in the latter that Ritson brushed aside attacks on

Macpherson and Chatterton, whom Ritson thought of as 'experimenters on the public taste' and significant local patriots. He proceeded to turn the tables on Percy and other gentlemanly scholars as themselves practitioners of 'forgery and imposition'.[11] It would be very odd if Burns, as Macpherson's compatriot and himself a cultural localist, did not recognise the relevance to his own position of Ritson's contemporary polemics, with their shrewd analysis of the restrictive social implications of much scholarship, and the radical power of the notion that the masses too had a culture.

Burns is not adversarial in Ritson's style as a collector of historical Scottish song. But he achieves a cumulative nationalistic consciousness by specialising in heroic moments and heroic figures, and by gathering in a large percentage of explicitly Jacobite songs. Indeed, he is responsible for more Jacobite songs than for political poems on all other topics put together. Burns's interventions in the songs which he collected may often be minimal; even then, he is a craftsman whose habit is to tighten a poem and simplify its structure, thus giving more power to the message delivered at the end. A fine example of this power recurs in the impressive 'Ye Jacobites by name, give an ear . . .' (371). Verse by verse, this stern song calls someone to task – apparently the Jacobites – for unleashing the horrors of war. Then, in the fourth and last verse, the speaker identifies his true allegiance, or perhaps a second, weaker voice replies:

> What makes heroic strife, fam'd afar, fam'd afar?
> What makes heroic strife, fam'd afar?
> What makes heroic strife?
> To whet th' Assassin's knife,
> Or hunt a Parent's life
> Wi' bludie war. –
>
> Then let your schemes alone, in the State, in the State,
> Then let your schemes alone in the State,
> Then let your schemes alone,
> Adore the rising sun,
> And leave a man undone
> To his fate. –
>
> (ll. 13–24)

Elsewhere, Burns forcefully and succinctly preserves songs as the popular records of recent historical landmarks – the Union of 1707 with England and the battles of the Jacobite wars ('A Parcel of Rogues in a Nation' (375)), Sheriffmuir or Falkirk ('Johnnie Cope' (297)) and, in many examples, Culloden. Sometimes headnotes draw out a historical reference, as when, apropos of 'The Campbells are Coming', he observes that their destination was supposed to be Mary Queen of Scots's island prison, Loch Leven. At other times, Burns utilises in a variety of forms the trope which Macpherson uses and comments on, when he observes that a mourning woman in the Old Testament often stands for a defeated nation: 'It was a' for our rightfu' king' (589) and 'The Highland Widow's Lament' (590) are two contrasted examples. Sometimes, as in 'Highland Laddie' (578), a stylised dialogue between the Laddie and his Lowland Lassie moves away from historical fact towards a sentimental resolution of the old hatreds. One by one these poems may have an agenda, together what they actually stand for is a diverse field of Scottish experience apparently randomly rooted in the popular consciousness. By implication, the people may remember and feel for an identity that their betters have forgotten or never knew. The basic posture of modern nationalism as a *grassroots* movement, conveyed by irregular cultural means, is thus plainly visible in Burns's Jacobite songs. Much less apparent are the recognisable signs or slogans of Jacobitism. Indeed, compared with Burns's poetry, these songs lack a sense of physical reality; they contain fewer proper names, dates and physical objects; sentiments, often nostalgia or bitterness, have taken over. The Jacobite songs do not compete aesthetically with Burns's more realistic poems and songs of Ayrshire; intellectually they complement them, by supplying a historical and political dimension, and filling in what would otherwise be blank spaces on the map of Scotland.

A second famous English antiquarian of the day, Francis Grose, paid Burns a visit in the summer of 1789. Grose, like Ritson, had an adversarial reputation: he described himself as 'a staunch Opposition-man and Grumble-man', and in 1791 published a collection of essays called *The Grumbler*. In addition to his interests in general antiquities – he was collecting materials for a two-volume study of Scottish monuments – Grose was expert in two topics which must have strongly appealed to Burns: English dialect and vulgar slang. His most recent books were two notable works of popular lexicography, the bawdy *Classical Dictionary of the Vulgar Tongue* (1785) and the more decorous *Glossary of the Provincial Tongue* (1787). The latter, which included a substantial section of local folklore and superstition, again coincided with Burns's tastes, and they were soon discussing the superstitions of the locality. Burns related to Grose some of the stories told of the ruined church at Kirk Alloway. Grose promised to include an illustration of the church, if Burns would write one of these legends down. Burns obliged with two, in prose, and afterwards, in 1790, forwarded a complete tale in verse – 'Tam o' Shanter', which was first published in the unlikely location of an Appendix to Grose's *Antiquities of Scotland* (1791), vol. II. In what proved to be the last year of his life, Grose provided an oddly prestigious location for perhaps the finest of Burns's poems, which is also the harbinger of other quintessential poems of the 1790s – 'Lenore', 'The Ancient Mariner' and 'The Idiot Boy'.

Grose's visit is fondly memorialised in one of the most convivial of Burns's fraternal songs, 'On the late Capt. Grose's Peregrination thro' Scotland, Collecting the Antiquities of that Kingdom' (275):

> Hear, Land o' Cakes, and brither Scots,
> Frae Maidenkirk to Johny Groats! –
> If there's a hole in a' your coats
>   I rede you tent it:
> A chield's amang you, taking notes,
>   And, faith, he'll prent it.
>
> (ll. 1–6)

The interests which these two shared spread across language and story: their politics was expressed, in the last resort, by an energetic and diverse immersion in popular culture. Where Ritson among English antiquarians resembles Burns as a commanding figure in getting traditional songs into print, only Grose matches the breadth and eclecticism of Burns's sympathy with every aspect of popular expression, including the foulest – the reductive physicalities and four-letter words of common-life oral communication.

Early Romanticism is very rich in popular if not always vulgar materials – in England represented with more propriety by the ballad and romance revival and Blake's *Songs of Innocence and Experience*, in Germany by the theorising of Herder and Goethe's popularity-derived *Faust* Part I. Herder's equivalents in England were in effect the provincial antiquarians who challenged narrowly-based and London-centred 'polite letters', and thus had a major input into much of the best poetry of the 1780s and 1790s. Surviving members of Grose's circle, Ritson and Francis Douce, indeed remained in contact with some of the first Romantic generation of poets, most particularly Southey and Scott, but also Wordsworth and Coleridge. If Burns had lived, he would have had access to a network, and students of the period's literature would have had no difficulty in thinking of him as a Romantic. Most of the poets whom we commonly call Romantic did, after all, recognise Burns posthumously as a brother.

If Burns does belong to a decentred, localised British Romanticism, it is genuinely popular in its verse-forms, social origins and ideal audience; and it has a short but brilliant Prolegomenon, encompassing the songs as well as the poems of Burns, the Songs, 1793 Notebooks and *Marriage of Heaven and Hell* of Blake, the best of the broadsheet and Gothic ballads of Southey. Burns's simplicity and naturalness go on speaking to Wordsworth's; his strength to Byron's. Burns is the first of our cultural nationalists, through his brilliantly-imagined construction of modern Scotland. In drawing together a nation, he both anticipates Scott and outdoes him: for, though the same elements are present in both, the emphases are different. Scott the laird goes on to make more of the historically picturesque – Bannockburn, and the Border and Jacobite songs. Burns, more active and contemporary, gives us the parish Scotland of the creepy-stool and the Excise, the 'Court of Equity', the mutual benefit society and the cornrigs.

NOTES

1. Robert Burns, *The Poems and Songs*, ed. James Kinsley, 3 vols (Oxford: Clarendon Press, 1968), poems number 269 (The Five Carlins'), 270 ('The Laddies by the Banks o' Nith'), 318 ('Epistle to Robt. Graham Esq: of Fintry on the Election for the Dumfries string of Boroughs, Anno 1790'). Poem numbers and references in this essay refer to Kinsley's three-volume edition, though the same system of poem numbering is also used in Kinsley's one-volume edition (Oxford University Press, 1969).
2. Robert Fitzhugh, *Robert Burns, his Associates and Contemporaries* (Chapel Hill: University of North Carolina Press, 1943), p. 65.
3. Quoted in Ian McIntyre, *Dirt and Deity: A Life of Robert Burns* (London: HarperCollins, 1995), p. 123.
4. Robert Burns to Captain William Johnston, 13 November 1792, in *Complete Letters of Robert Burns* (Ayr: Alloway Publishing, 1987), p. 681. This is the edition of Burns's letters used in the present essay.
5. Robert Burns to Henry Erskine [December 1786], *Complete Letters*, ed. cit., pp. 435–6.
6. Ernest Gellner, *Nations and Nationalism* (Oxford: Blackwell, 1983); Benedict Anderson, *Imagined Communities* (London: Verso, 1983).
7. See, for example, William Donaldson, *The Jacobite Song: Political Myth and National Identity* (Aberdeen: Aberdeen University Press, 1988); Murray G. H. Pittock, *The Invention of Scotland: The Stuart Myth and the Scottish Identity, 1683 to the Present* (London: Routledge, 1991); Robert Crawford, *Devolving English Literature* (Oxford: Clarendon Press, 1992).
8. Murdoch argues that 'the rational part should be set above the animal . . . not to the utter destruction of the animal part, but to the real and true enjoyment of it': John Murdoch, *Manual of Religious Belief in the Form of a Dialogue between Father and Son* (Kilmarnock: McKie and Drennan, 1875).
9. Robert Burns to Alexander Cunningham, 10 September 1792, *Complete Letters*, ed. cit., p. 466.
10. Robert Burns to John Skinner, 25 October 1787, *Complete Letters*, ed. cit., p. 363.
11. Joseph Ritson, 'An Historical Essay on National Song', in *Select Collection of English Song*, 3 vols (London, 1783), I, p. xii.

BURNS AND GOD

Susan Manning

Poetic imagination is determined finally by the state of negotiation – in a person or in a people – between man and his idea of the Creator. This is natural enough, and everything else is naturally enough subordinate to it. How things are between man and his idea of the Divinity determines everything in his life, the quality and connectedness of every feeling and thought, and the meaning of every action.[1]

Of all Nonsense, Religious Nonsense is the most nonsensical . . .[2]

What can we ever tell of the 'state of negotiation' between any poet and his 'idea of the Creator'? Ted Hughes suggests that we should try, not merely if we wish to understand 'everything in [the poet's] life', but as a route to the 'poetic imagination' itself. That is to say, if it is not the most nonsensical nonsense, 'Burns and God' may be a very important subject indeed. Which is just as well, given that it is not only a daunting and difficult, but also not a very enticing one. More than once in writing this essay, I have wished that 'Burns and Satan' rather than 'Burns and God' had been the brief. Burns and Satan seems immediately a more welcoming topic, more fun, perhaps in an essential sense more Burnsian. Relationship with Satan was after all a key element in Burns's self-dramatisation, and it is easy to see it at work in the forge of his imagination: well before it became a kind of proto-Revolutionary orthodoxy among Romantic poets to declare that Satan was the real hero of Milton's epic attempt to 'justify the ways of God to Man', Burns wrote rhetorically to his friend William Nicol:[3]

I have bought a pocket Milton which I carry perpetually about with me, in order to study the sentiments – the dauntless magnanimity; the intrepid, unyielding independance; the desperate daring, and noble defiance of hardship, in the great Personage, Satan. – 'Tis true, I have

113

just now a little cash; but I am afraid the damn'd star that hitherto has shed its malignant, purpose-blasting rays full in my zenith; that noxious Planet so baneful in its influences to the rhyming tribe, I much dread it is not yet beneath my horizon. Misfortune dodges [*sic*] the path of human life; the poetic mind finds itself miserably deranged in, and unfit for the walks of business; add to all, that, thoughtless follies and harebrained whims, like so many Ignes fatui, eternally diverging from the right line of sober direction, sparkle with step-bewitching blaze in the idly-gazing eyes of the poor heedless Bard, till, pop, 'he falls like Lucifer, never to hope again' – God grant this may be an unreal picture with respect to me! (*Letters*, I, 123)

Proclaimed affinity with Satan energises the language of this letter and propels it into a meditation on the relationship between the poet's nature and the nature of poetic imagination. The figure of Satan, that is, becomes at once the occasion for and the stimulus to verbal elaboration and imaginative self-creation.

Or again, here is Burns gleefully leaping off the tightrope of decorum into the liberating arms of Satanic extravagance in a letter written in the year of the storming of the Bastille, to Provost Maxwell of Lochmaben: 'Shall I write you on Politics, or Religion, two master-subjects for your Sayers of nothing?' No indeed:

I shall betake myself to a subject ever fertile of themes, a Subject, the turtle-feast of the Sons of Satan, and the delicious, secret Sugar-plumb of the Babes of Grace; a Subject, sparkling with all the jewels that Wit can find in the mind of Genius, and pregnant with all the stores of Learning, from Moses and Confucius to Franklin and Priestly – in short, may it please your Lordship, I intend to write BAUDY! (*Letters*, I, 462)

So vivid was Burns's delight in playing the 'son of Satan' that his religious detractors swallowed the self-dramatisation whole and disgorged it as accusation. James Maxwell, 'poet in Paisley', writing in 1788:

Of all British poets that yet have appear'd,
None e'er at things sacred so daringly sneer'd,
As he in the west, who but lately has sprung
From behind the plough-tails, and from raking of dung.
A champion of Satan, none like him before,
And his equal, pray God, we may never see more:
For none have like him, been by Satan inspir'd,
Which makes his rank nonsense by fools so admir'd . . .

His jargon gives rakes and vile harlots delight,
But all sober people abhor the vile sight.
He makes of the scriptures a ribaldry joke;
By him are the laws both of God and man broke.[4]

With such enemies to hand, being a son of Satan must have been nearly irresistible.

But Burns's satanism was much more than a calculated offence to cultural authority in all its forms. More importantly in terms of the genesis of poetic imagination, it was a self-conception which seemed to stimulate his language into liberating virtuosity. Linking this defiant grasping of expressive freedom to the Scottish Calvinist tradition, Alan Bold declares that Burns's 'rebellious outlook on life put him firmly in the radical Scottish tradition of Knox, if not the Knoxists'.[5] In this sense, we can say that Burns was a better Calvinist than the Kirk whose once-revolutionary spiritualism had ossified into a new theological orthodoxy, and against whose constrictions he fought to articulate personal and poetic independence. Burns learned more, though, from Auld Licht harangues than his hatred of intolerance. He learned to speak and write with its very accents, to project Calvinism's eloquent preoccupation with human depravity into the very person of Satan himself. It was the Reverend Rowland Hill, a contemporary of Burns, who is reputed to have said that 'he did not see any reason why the devil should have all the good tunes'.[6] Burns's poetry might have supplied him with a few:

THEY! an' be d–mn'd! what right hae they
To Meat, or Sleep, or light o' day,
Far less to riches, pow'r, or freedom,
But what your lordships PLEASE TO GIE THEM? . . .
But smash them! crush them a' to spails!
An' rot the DYVORS i' the JAILS!
The young dogs, swinge them to the labour,
Let WARK an' HUNGER mak them sober!
The HIZZIES, if they're oughtlins fausont,
Let them in DRURY LANE be lesson'd!
An' if the wives, an' dirty brats,
Come thiggan at your doors an' yets,
Flaffan wi' duds, an' grey wi' beese,
Frightan awa your deucks an' geese;
Get out a HORSE-WHIP, or a JOWLER,
The langest thong, the fiercest growler,
An' gar the tatter'd gipseys pack
Wi' a' their bastarts on their back![7]

This, from one of his most viciously satirical poems on the gentry's oppression of the poor, shows just what extraordinary rhetorical brilliance the Devil's persona could call forth from Burns. It is the flyting voice of earlier Scots poetry re-released against the established powers of late eighteenth-century Britain. Adopting the very voice of Evil itself, as he does in this 'Address of Beelzebub', Burns pits an older Scottish cultural authority against the new order: Satan in person (or im-personated) embodies a vigour and vindictive skill which invokes the enormous historical presence assumed by the Devil in Scotland's living out of the Augustinian, Manichaean dimension of Calvinist theology.

So where does this leave God? Or – since I haven't a hope of answering that one – where does it leave Burns and God?

> Dear –, I'll gie ye some advice,
>   You'll tak it no uncivil:
> You shouldna paint at angels, man,
>   But try and paint the Devil.
>
> To paint an angel's kittle wark,
>   Wi' Nick there's little danger;
> You'll easy draw a lang-kent face,
>   But no sae weel a stranger.
>
> (*Poems*, I, 323–4)

Burns wrote this on the back of a sketch in an artist's studio, after examining the work of a well-known painter engaged on a study of Jacob's dream.[8] As Jacob found to his cost, wrestling with an angel can be a curiously insubstantial business, the kind of struggle a mere mortal is bound to lose. Within its sly wit at the expense of the hapless, hopeless painter's artistic talent, Burns's little poem points to a real problem for his own poetic imagination. The angel of God with whom Jacob wrestles refuses to be named. In the Calvinist tradition, the Devil can be characterised, where God can only be conceptualised. God is that threatening, all-seeing, all-knowing, unknown omniscience beyond, imaged in the self largely through the Conscience, the unwelcome super-ego or 'vice-regent of God' within us, as Adam Smith put it in the year of Burns's birth, in a work later read and admired by the poet.[9] Popular Victorian sentimentality would subsequently confect a comforting but altogether implausible Divine image out of paternal benignity, long white robes and cottonwool clouds; eighteenth-century sentimentalists, however, were saddled with a coldly abstract conception of 'the Deity', or the 'divine Watchmaker', whose mechanistic fiats could be approached only with a diffuse pattern of benevolent 'sensations'.

In Christian theology, the figure of Jesus Christ is the incarnation of the idea of the 'Good', an approachable figure who provides a humanised pattern, an example, to bring the believer closer to God. But Christ makes a shadowy figure in Calvinism, and He is notably absent from both Burns's poetry and correspondence. The Devil, however, is our right-hand man, our familiar in both senses of the word. It is not too much to say that Burns – like many, doubtless – came to God through intimate acquaintance with Satan. The easy 'Address to the Deil' is no personification of an abstract quality:

> O Thou, whatever title suit thee!
> Auld Hornie, Satan, Nick, or Clootie,
> Wha in yon cavern grim an' sooty
>   Clos'd under hatches,
> Spairges about the brunstane cootie,
>   To scaud poor wretches!
>
> Hear me, *auld Hangie*, for a wee,
> An' let poor, *damned bodies* bee;
> I'm sure sma' pleasure it can gie,
>   Ev'n to a *deil*,
> To skelp an' scaud poor dogs like me,
>   An' hear us squeel!

(Poems, I, 168)

The Deil is incontrovertibly, almost physically, conjured by the language here; God, on the other hand, is nowhere in this poem. In fact, as soon as one begins to look for 'God' anywhere in the poems and letters, it becomes apparent what an elusive subject 'Burns and God' is, once we separate it from historical accounts of 'Burns and the Kirk', 'Burns and Calvinism', or even 'Burns and Religion'. The foremost cultural authority in Burns's lifetime – and, one might say also, his life – was the Scottish Presbyterian Church. Burns's confrontational, turbulent relationship with the Kirk has formed a necessary chapter in almost every full-length study of the poet, as well as being the theme of several books. But 'Burns and the Kirk' is not my subject.

It may also, in some senses, not have been all that important to Burns himself. Concocting a 'moral' for an imagined reader at the end of his first Commonplace Book, Burns instruct this 'Pupil', 'as he tenders his own peace, [to] keep up a regular, warm intercourse with the Deity'.[10] This, we are to infer, the poet himself failed to do. In his autobiographical letter to Dr John Moore written in August 1787, Burns described his youthful initiation into religious controversy in revealing terms:

Polemical divinity about this time was putting the country half-mad; and I, ambitious of shining in conversation parties on Sundays between sermons, funerals, &c. used in a few years more to puzzle Calvinism with so much heat and indiscretion that I raised a hue and cry of heresy against me which has not ceased to this hour. – (*Letters*, I, 136)

It's Burns's ambition to have his voice noticed, rather than his beliefs, which he remembers to have dominated and directed these early polemical efforts. This could well be equally true of the impulse which produced his subsequent 'religious satires'; it should certainly make us wary of deriving Burns's 'true' religious or doctrinal opinions too directly from them. Apart from one or two phrases of conventional rationalistic piety – 'the providential care of a good God placed me under the patronage of one of his noblest creatures . . .' – this long letter contains notably little information about Burns's religious beliefs. It leaves 'Burns and God', for my purposes, much where they were, or weren't, to start with.

That is, they are in the vexed and essentially unknowable biographical area of Burns's beliefs. Scholars have trawled the evidence of his letters for direct statements of faith which might land the poet in one or another doctrinal category. The problem here is that the more he sought to emulate Pope's highly self-conscious dictum that letters should present 'thoughts just warm from the brain without any polishing or dress, the very déshabille of the understanding', the more Burns's epistolary style treated language, as Walter Scott put it, 'rather so as to gratify his correspondent, than communicate his own feelings'.[11] It is easy to see how, in such circumstances, Burns *could not* write about God without Him becoming 'God', a construct at least as much of Burns's idea of his reader's faith as of his own.

To derive a view of the poet's relationship to his Maker directly from statements in the writing is therefore a hopeless case – which is not to say that it hasn't been tried. I have my own anthology of confident assertions: Burns was 'the enem[y] of God'; 'fun [wa]s more to him than God Almighty'; 'he [was] a Jacobite, an Arminian, and a Socinian'; 'he believed in God, but God was not the controlling power in his life'; 'Burns was more of a Calvinist than most of his critics admit'; 'he believed in a benevolent and paternal God'; 'Burns himself was quite clearly a Socinian or Unitarian'; he 'combine[d] Calvinist predestination with his own notion of "Nature's plan" '; 'Burns developed as a Deist'.[12] Such positivism is no longer possible in our postlapsarian state of critical self-consciousness, not least because for every statement in Burns's writing which might be taken to support any of these views, one can very easily find another which appears to contradict it directly. In each case, the 'Burns' so described probably reflects nothing so much as the beliefs of the describer.

David Daiches, taking a more literary line, has usefully enumerated the ways in which poets place themselves in relation to God: direct address or supplication; visionary experience and its explication; describing Him as present in His works ('Natural Religion'); explaining or justifying His ways (Milton's purpose in *Paradise Lost*, or Pope's in *An Essay on Man*); agonising about His existence, or (more latterly) doubting or denying it.[13] It's a fairly comprehensive range of possibilities. It also suggests (though Daiches himself does not) something rather startling about Burns. All these forms of poetic relationship *are* vividly evoked by him – but characteristically in relation to Satan rather than to God.

There's a yet more arresting, and more troubling, fact: the most fervent address to God in all of Burns's writing is spoken by his most hypocritical, perhaps his most despicable persona:

> O thou that in the heavens does dwell!
> Wha, as it pleases best thysel,
> Sends ane to heaven and ten to h–ll,
>   A' for thy glory!
> And no for ony gude or ill
>   They've done before thee. –
>
> I bless and praise thy matchless might,
> When thousands thou hast left in night,
> That I am here before thy sight,
>   For gifts and grace,
> A burning and a shining light
>   To a' this place. –
>
> What was I, or my generation,
> That I should get such exaltation?
> I, wha deserv'd most just damnation,
>   For broken laws
> Sax thousand years ere my creation,
>   Thro' Adam's cause!
>
> When from my mother's womb I fell,
> Thou might hae plunged me deep in hell,
> To gnash my gooms, and weep, and wail,
>   In burning lakes,
> Where damned devils roar and yell
>   Chain'd to their stakes, –
>
> Yet I am here, a chosen sample,
> To show thy grace is great and ample:

> I'm here, a pillar o' thy temple
> Strong as a rock,
> A guide, a ruler and example
> To a' thy flock. –

('Holy Willie's Prayer', *Poems*, I, 74–5)

David Craig writes that in 'Holy Willie', Burns 'has created a style commensurate to the whole life, personal, social, cultural, of his subject'.[14] There is no doubting the solidity of Willie's *presence* before his God and before the reader: twice in these opening stanzas he asserts '*I am here*'; and he brings his whole Calvinist culture with him. God is also very much there. Holy Willie knows his God intimately – indeed, they're gossips, in the old sense of the word:

> L–d mind Gaun Hamilton's deserts!
> He drinks, and swears, and plays at cartes,
> Yet has sae mony taking arts
>   Wi' Great an' Sma',
> Frae G–d's ain priest the people's hearts
> He steals awa'. –

(*Poems*, I, 77)

The relationship is one of sublime, and sublimely self-betraying, confidence. It is indeed a masterpiece of impersonation, perhaps the classically self-revealing address to God – but it is not Burns's own self-revelation.

Much has been written about Burns's savagely accurate satire of Scottish Calvinism; I want here to concentrate rather on Burns's poetic relationship to Holy Willie's voice as it addresses God. The 'Argument' prefaced by Burns to the poem introduces the character of his speaker and sets out the occasion for his prayer. It ends: 'On losing his Process [i.e. Suit against Gavin Hamilton in the Kirk Session], the Muse overheard him at his devotions as follows–' (*Poems*, I, 74). The idiom of the eavesdropping Muse is Popean, of course, but what Burns is drawing attention to in this precisely-placed introduction is the operation of his own poetic imagination across the poem's impersonation. How things are between Holy Willie and his idea of God determines everything in *his* life: the quality and connectedness of every feeling and thought, and the meaning of his every action. It also defines what we might call the satiric angle of the poem. Satanic verbal exuberance – 'To gnash my gooms, and weep, and wail' – here transfers itself to the object of Burns's derision. One of poetry's most famous invocations of the deity comes through the deeply ironic voice of Holy Willie. What can the imaginative evocation tell us about the 'state of negotiation' between *Burns* and God?

One possible answer is simple antithesis: Burns's God is everything that Willie's is not, and nothing of what He is. Graham Hough, referring to the energy and attractiveness of its portrayal of Satan, has described Milton's *Paradise Lost* as 'a poem that lives by meanings that its author must have repudiated'.[15] Perhaps the same is true, and for some of the same reasons, of 'Holy Willie's Prayer'. But there's a problem here: the beliefs exploded by the very perfection of their expression in 'Holy Willie's' sanctimonious self-justification are indistinguishable – as doctrine – from those apparently expressed 'straight' in Burns's earlier 'Prayer in Prospect of Death':

> Maybe thou lets this fleshly thorn
> Buffet thy servant e'en and morn,
> Lest he o'er proud and high should turn,
>   That he's sae gifted;
> If sae, thy hand maun e'en be borne
>   Until thou lift it. –
>
> (Poems, I, 76)

> If I have wander'd in those paths
>   Of life I ought to shun –
> As something, loudly, in my breast,
>   Remonstrates I have done –
>
> Thou know'st that Thou hast formed me
>   With passions wild and strong;
> And list'ning to their witching voice
>   Has often led me wrong.
>
> (Poems, I, 20-1)

Voice is all that distinguishes the sentiments – and no-one would quibble, I think, as to which is the more commanding voice of the two, nor with which the poetic imagination is the more fully engaged. Burns Jamieson concludes that the disconcerting overlap of sentiments between hypocritical Holy Willie and 'sincere Robert Burns' must be put down to 'contradictoriness': 'the habit among Scots of turning into ridicule their own sincerest feelings and profoundest experiences'.[16] It was a discrepancy, or perhaps more properly a doubleness, noted early on. J. G. Lockhart mused in 1828: 'that the same man should have produced *The Cottar's Saturday Night* and *The Holy Fair* about the same time – will ever continue to move wonder and regret'.[17] Something more is at issue here than imaginative inconsistency or even 'contradictoriness', however; to find it, we have to look to the circumstances of the poem's composition.

In 1785, the year of 'Holy Willie's' composition, Burns's first illegitimate child, by Elizabeth Paton, was born, and he became embroiled with Jean Armour and her family – circumstances which landed him, as he later wrote to Moore, in the hands of the Kirk Session on his own account. An extended image in this letter connects the verbal energies which project Holy Willie's voice to the impulses which led Burns (as he put it himself) 'astray':

> Holy Willie's Prayer . . . alarmed the kirk-Session so much that they held three several meetings to look over their holy artillery, if any of it was pointed against profane Rhymers. – Unluckily for me, my idle wandering led me, on another side, point blank within the reach of their heaviest metal. (*Letters*, I, 144).

Something of the same energy, that is, which propelled Burns's 'passion wild and strong' into illicit amours and subsequent conflict with the kirk authorities, invigorates the idiom of Holy Willie and makes his utterance a commensurate threat to the established order. The physical and the verbal exuberance, the love and the detestation, both belong to the *animus*, in an almost Jungian sense: that resisting spirit which asserts its right to expression against the 'holy artillery' of cultural authority in all its forms:

> Welcome! My bonie, sweet, wee Dochter!
> Tho' ye come here a wee unsought for;
> And tho' your coming I hae fought for,
>   Baith Kirk and Queir;
> Yet by my faith ye're no unwrought for,
>   That I shall swear!
>
> ('A Poet's Welcome to his love-begotten Daughter',
> *Poems*, I, 99)

Opposition engages Burns's imagination and launches his language into verse.

In contrast, the uncertain tone of the 'Epistle to a Young Friend' shows Burns's weakness when he does not reserve his own religious position by inhabiting an opposing voice:

> The great Creator to revere
>   Must sure become the *Creature*;
> But still the preaching cant forbear,
>   And ev'n the rigid feature:
> Yet ne'er with Wits profane to range,
>   Be complaisance attended;
> An *atheist-laugh*'s a poor exchange
>   For *Deity offended*!

When ranting round in Pleasure's ring,
    Religion may be blinded;
Or if she gie a *random-fling*,
    It may be little minded;
But when on Life we're tempest-driv'n –
    A Conscience but a canker –
A correspondence fix'd wi' Heav'n,
    Is sure a noble *anchor*!

(Poems, I, 250)

The metrical mastery of that last stanza, as it docks itself in the triumphantly stressed rhyme, is more evident than any sincerity of feeling on Burns's part; this is a *tour de force* of 'approved' diction. Jog-trot metre renders the sentiments almost as doggerel; poetically this seems at best an exercise, an apprenticeship in Enlightenment. The distanced and abstracted rhetoric of 'Deity offended' belongs rather to the theory of Deism than the experience of God. The normative stance of the poet distances the voice from experience, neutralises the emotional engagement. What it lacks is the energy, the sheer pace and momentum of the 'Address of Beelzebub', 'Holy Willie' or 'A Poet's Welcome'. Perhaps, under the conditions of Scottish Presbyterianism of the late eighteenth century, religious directness was simply no longer a possible position for a poet such as Burns. Candid address to God had become a contaminated area, appropriated by the Elect for their own self-justification; only by 'becoming' one of them, impersonating that voice, as Holy Willie, could Burns adopt it and, in becoming, oppose it.

The quotation from Ted Hughes which I've used as an epigraph is taken from his discussion of 'the groundplan of Shakespeare's imagination', which, he argues, 'very closely fits the groundplan of the religious struggle which . . . embroiled every fibre of Elizabethan life'.[18] I have been suggesting that something similar informs and indeed defines the characteristic idiom of Burns's poetic imagination in relation to Calvinism, and that in his case one of its manifestations is the difficulty of finding a stable idiom of 'positive' religious expression. In contrast to the rhetorical command and enjoyment when he writes about or as Satan, or Death, something happens to unsteady the register of Burns's prose when he writes directly about God. It's as though the language can't hold its tone when it loses touch with a ground of opposition. In the Lockean terms familiar to Burns, it's as though 'God' is an abstract idea, a slippery 'absence' formed in the mind alone, while Satan is imprinted on it, the impression of a concrete experience:

In this light I have often admired Religion. – In proportion as we are wrung with grief, or distracted with anxiety, the ideas of a compassionate Deity, an Almighty Protector, are doubly dear. –

' 'Tis this, my friend, that streaks our morning bright;
        'Tis this that gilds the horrors of our night' –
I have been this morning taking a peep thro', as Young finely says, 'the
dark postern of time long elaps'd'; and you will easily guess, 'twas a
rueful prospect. – . . . I kneeled down before the Father of mercies, and
said, 'Father, I have sinned against Heaven and in thy sight, and am no
more worthy to be called thy son!['] (*Letters*, II, 210)

Not trusting his own words to speak of God, he resorts to posturing or to
quotation. The expressive authority is not found within, but appropriated
from elsewhere. Such appropriation makes questions of sincerity unaskable:
we cannot get behind the posture to 'Burns's' belief. This is not an unfamiliar state of affairs: in one of the classic accounts of Scottish literature, Kurt
Wittig describes how 'it is often the feelings of others that are expressed, from
inside their minds'.[19] Critics and scholars have investigated this negative
rhetoric from various angles; I'm interested here in looking at its provenance,
and its effects on Burns's writing about God.

    John Knox had described Ayrshire as 'a receptacle of God's Saints',[20] but
by the mid-eighteenth century, religious discourse in south-west Scotland
was complicated both by the incursions of Enlightenment science and by
controversies between the 'Auld Licht' popular Calvinist and 'New Licht'
ministers trained in the Glasgow compromise of Moderatism.[21] Three religious
idioms were therefore available to Burns. There were the fundamentalist
opposites of orthodox Calvinism, and Atheism or religious Scepticism (with
its barely respectable theological expression, Deism). And, between these
extremes, there was the third voice of Moderatism, which attempted to
articulate a livable (perhaps a touch too livable) creed of a more optimistic,
enlightened and humanist kind. Burns, of course, knew all three positions
intimately – not only what they meant, but (more importantly for a poet)
what they sounded like. For anyone temperamentally unable to accept a
fundamentalist stance, as Burns himself clearly was, a certain degree of
scepticism was unavoidable. He wrote to Cunningham:

If there be any truth in the Orthodox faith of these Churches, I am
damned past redemption, and what is worse, damned to all eternity. – I
am deeply read in Boston's fourfold State, Marshal on Sanctification,
Guthrie's trial of a Saving Interest &c. &c. but 'There is no balm in
Gilead, there is no physician there,' for me; so I shall e'en turn
Ariminian [*sic*], and trust to 'Sincere though imperfect obedience. –'

After a strategic break, the letter continues:

Luckily for me I was prevented from the discussion of the knotty point
at which I had just made a full stop. – All my fears and cares are of this

world: if there is Another, an honest man has nothing to fear from it. –
I hate a Man who wishes to be a Deist, but I fear, every fair, unprejudiced
Enquirer must in some degree be a Sceptic. (*Letters*, II, 16)

Quite a deal of theology is crammed into this *tour de force* of 'controversial
divinity'. But its calculatedly 'lucky' rhetorical hiatus alerts us to yet another
pose; once again, the letter really reveals very little about 'Burns and God'.

Between alternative dogmatic certainties – atheistic or fideistic – lies a
much more nebulous, calculatedly ill-defined middle ground, the area of
the provisional and the uncertain which has notoriously been particularly
hard both to sustain and to articulate in countries such as Scotland where
the oppositional forms of Calvinism were so highly developed and fully
articulated. The central tenet of predestination presented stark alternatives;
salvation, or damnation. Thomas Boston's *Human Nature in Its Fourfold
State*, in which Burns claimed to be 'deeply read', spells out the implications
of the doctrine graphically and mercilessly:

There shall be a separation made between the righteous and the
wicked; the fair company of the elect sheep being set on Christ's right
hand, and the reprobate goats on His left. . . . The elect, being 'caught
up together in the clouds, meet the Lord in the air' (1 Thess. 4.17), and
so are set on His right hand; and the reprobate left on the earth, are
placed upon the Judge's left hand. Here is now a total separation of two
parties, who were always opposite to each other in their principles,
aims, and manner of life.[22]

The very terms of the absolutism meant that it was a slippery slope towards
atheism, once you set off from the high predestinarian ground.[23] Intellectual
rigour and emotional momentum both point – once the positions have been
defined in the ways that they irretrievably had been by the mid-eighteenth
century in Scotland – either to strict Calvinism or to radical scepticism
(implying either downright atheism or a mystically-achieved faith-without-
reason).

Into the space between these equally unpalatable alternatives the
Moderates attempted to step, tempering intellectual absolutes with feeling
and sentiment. Burns's poetic imagination easily inhabited the language, the
diction and the point of view of those whose religious views he most despised:
we hear their characteristic voices canting, praying, preaching, and always
full of vigour. Rejecting and ridiculing the extremes of Determinism and
Enthusiasm which it mimicked, the poetry is nevertheless at its weakest
when it adopts the tones of sentiment without edge; its idiom slackens in the
equivocating logic of the middle ground. Emotional and poetic power lie at

the extremes, the outer edges of hellfire terror or enthusiastic raptures; it's hard to be a passionate Moderate. Little wonder, then, that the 'cauld harangues,/ On *practice* and on *morals*' in 'The Holy Fair' lead the godly to desert the tent in throngs, 'to gie the jars an' barrels/ A lift that day' (*Poems*, I, 133).

When it comes to the sermons in 'Holy Fair', Burns's exact impersonation of the outraged Auld Lichter holds us far more than the opinions of the Moderate preacher whose *position* he might be said to support:

> What signifies his barren shine,
>   Of *moral pow'rs* and *reason*;
> His English style, and gesture fine,
>   Are a' clean out o' season.
> Like SOCRATES or ANTONINE,
>   Or some auld pagan heathen,
> The *moral man* he does define,
>   But ne'er a word o' *faith* in
>   That's right that day.
>   (*Poems*, I, 133)

The Moderate voice was one which could never be unequivocally Burns's own, involving as it did too many conflicts of class and ideology. The interests of its proponents were, by and large, those of the educated middle class: genteel, anti-democratic, pro-patronage; and they were, in everything but their doctrinal liberalism, far removed from Burns's natural sympathies. More important still, they had no imaginative language. The devil, it seemed, really did have all the good tunes.

'Orthodoxy' (in Burns's case represented by the Auld Licht Calvinists) embraced one extreme of religious emotion (fear) *and* its opposite (enthusiasm or rapture) within an abhorrent but logically tight conceptual framework. Availing itself of all the dark recesses of human experience, its expression carried always the animating frisson of passion-with-guilt. It is an intractable problem for the poet: the fires of Hell or the Holy Spirit's tongues of flame may be doctrinally dangerous and morally repugnant, but at least they're ardent and vital enough to warm the imagination. The 'fine excess' which Keats would declare to be intrinsic to poetic language seemed given over in Burns's Ayrshire to the prior claims of doctrine.[24]

So we come to a different kind of paradox: that Burns's greatest religious poetry was fabricated from the theological positions which he most despised, and that he had no *imaginative* language in which to write directly of his beliefs. Neither the devotional nor the doctrinal register of poetic intercourse with God is available to his writing, except negatively, as it

were, through comic and satiric impersonation of positions which he
abhorred emotionally and intellectually. Burns's relationship to the religious
expression of his day was, then, essentially destructive. An alternative, 'positive' religious vernacular was not readily available, and his poetry does not
create one. The religious expression of the Moderates was essentially an
Anglicised one, borrowing its pieties from the attenuated idioms of natural
theology, Deism and Sentiment. The contradictions referred to above here
become literally that: contrary dictions – and they led Burns's poetry into
false positions and fatally compromised its integrity when he was tempted to
adopt it without edge.

God makes a shadowy figure even in Burns's invocations of humane
principles and fraternity; these are expressed fervently but hardly with piety.

> Who made the heart, 'tis *He* alone
>   Decidedly can try us,
> He knows each chord its various tone,
>   Each spring its various bias:
> Then at the balance let's be mute,
>   We never can adjust it;
> What's *done* we partly may compute,
>   But know not what's *resisted*.
> ('Address to the Unco' Guid', *Poems*, I, 53–4)

What's most striking is just how distant God – that '*He*' – is from any kind
of human approach, understanding, or even relevance. In this sense, Burns
can scarcely be called a religious poet at all – certainly not as George Herbert,
Donne or Gerard Manley Hopkins was. Where is 'God's presence' in
Burns's writing? It is nowhere felt directly as in, for example, 'Batter my
Heart, three-person'd God', or 'Thou art indeed just, Lord, if I contend
with thee', or 'Kill me not ev'ry day, Thou Lord of life'.[25] His poetry belongs
instead perhaps with that other poet of the dying embers of a Puritan idiom,
Emily Dickinson.

> Those – dying then,
> Knew where they went –
> They went to God's Right Hand –
> That Hand is amputated now
> And God cannot be found –[26]

Like hers, Burns's poetic voice is dominated by the still-powerful rhetoric of
a decaying belief-system; like hers too, his own religious impulses seem to
struggle in vain for other than a negative expression in its shadow:

It's easy to invent a Life –
God does it – every Day –
Creation but the Gambol
Of His Authority –

It's easy to efface it –
The thrifty Deity
Could scarce afford Eternity
To Spontaneity –

The Perished Patterns murmur –
But His Perturbless Plan
Proceed – inserting Here – a Sun –
There – leaving out a Man –[27]

We might compare this with the self-imposed post-mortem effects elaborated in Burns's 'A Bard's Epitaph', written ten years before he died. It ends with the kind of repentance demanded by its occasion, but the idiom is as disengaged from poetic emotion as Dickinson's apparently cool acquiescence in the 'Perturbless Plan' of the Calvinist deity:

Reader, attend – whether thy soul
Soars fancy's flights beyond the pole,
Or darkling grubs this earthly hole,
    In low pursuit,
Know, prudent, cautious *self-controul*
Is wisdom's root.

                (*Poems*, I, 247)

One feels this should end, not with a full stop, but – like her characteristically unconcluded lyrics – with a dash, so full of unspoken 'buts' and incompletions is it. Partly, though, in Burns's writing, this is simply the weakness of the poems' endings when the projected voices die away; with all his ventriloquistic virtuosity, he doesn't always seem to know what to do with a voice once he has mastered it for the occasion. This inconclusiveness must surely also bear on the want of 'an AIM' which he laments in his letters, the essentially negative relation in which his writing stood to the religious culture of this time and place (*Letters*, I, 139). Was Burns, then, no more than an inspired ventriloquist, an eighteenth-century Felix Krull or a latter-day Rameau's Nephew, impersonating his way through life and literature in a series of poses adopted and discarded as they offered hope of immediate rhetorical advantage? It would be a melancholy conclusion to reach about Scotland's favourite, perhaps her greatest, poet.

And yet, and yet. Burns remained a churchgoer throughout his life, and for all the poetic ridicule, there is plenty of evidence for the respect in which he held many individual ministers of his acquaintance. Making due allowance for the postures and pieties which inform the studied epistolary displays, it is hard not to hear sincerity in his assertions to Mrs Dunlop that 'we can no more live without Religion, than we can live without air' and, more particularly, 'a Mathematician without Religion, is a probable character; an irreligious Poet, is a monster' (*Letters*, II, 57; I, 230). If Burns's poetic imagination, that is, *is* invested with an idea of God which is more than purely negative, where do we see it active in what Ted Hughes calls the 'quality and connectedness of every feeling and every thought' in his writing?

I have argued that the cultural authority of the Scottish Kirk was such that it left no rhetorical space for an independent poetic voice in relation to God – as direct address, praise, explanation or even doubt. All the positions were already pre-occupied by doctrines with whose forms of expression Burns was only too familiar. I want to suggest now that this forced his poetry in two directions: first, towards exposing and undermining these positions from within (reappropriating their voices in satire or parody); and second, away from direct religious engagement altogether, towards exulting in life evoked in entirely this-worldly terms. This is the impulse behind his great song-collections. By 1787, the 'state of negotiation' between Burns and religion had reached an uneasy impasse; though it would be a few more years until he wrote to Cunningham that 'of all Nonsense, Religious Nonsense is the most nonsensical; so enough, & more than enough of it', after this year, he wrote little which engaged directly with religion. From the beginning, Burns had written songs; but, quite suddenly, song became the centre of his life. Perhaps paradoxically, but not nonsensically, these songs whose voices free themselves completely from doctrinal issues were his truest and final revenge on the Kirk idiom which oppressed and preoccupied his early poetic expression. Again, only an inflection separates Holy Willie's

> O thou that in the heavens does dwell!
> Wha, as it pleases best thysel,
> Sends ane to heaven and ten to h–ll,
>   A' for thy glory!
> And no for ony gude or ill
>   They've done before thee. –

from

> The Kirk an' State may join, an tell
>   To do sic things I maunna:
> The Kirk an' State may gae to Hell,
>   And I'll gae to my Anna.

– but what a difference. Between a voice that is devouring itself from within, consumed by its own hypocrisy, and one which has abandoned hope of preferment for the preferment of hope. The illicit energies which impel the *animus* against Calvinist intolerance and propel his satiric personae to utterance are here directly engaged. Reckless assertion of the natural self against order and discipline informs this and *The Jolly Beggars*, whose songs enter the voices and emotions of their speakers without the ironic meta-consciousness which in the religious poetry works to qualify or to undermine the interiority of expression. Their speakers, or rather singers, articulate a relationship to reality which escapes from both satirical demolition and crippling self-consciousness; they re-find the energy of satanic self-expression in a secular idiom which goes behind the 'pre-occupied' ground of religion to direct celebration.

> What is TITLE, what is TREASURE,
>   What is REPUTATION'S care?
> If we lead a life of pleasure,
>   'Tis no matter HOW or WHERE.
>
> A Fig for those by law protected!
>   LIBERTY'S a glorious feast!
> Courts for Cowards were erected,
>   Churches built to please the PRIEST. . . .
>
> Life is all a VARIORUM,
>   We regard not how it goes;
> Let them cant about DECORUM,
>   Who have character to lose.
>
>   (*Poems*, I, 208)

What kind of relationship with the world, then, do these songs inhabit? How can we say that they represent the expression of 'Burns and God' when their poetic stance so resolutely eschews any idiom of transcendence? Natural theology, with its logical progression towards Romanticism, was not intuitively available to Burns; unlike Wordsworth, he didn't readily see evidence of God in nature; his contact with it was not as a sportive child or a promenading poet, but primarily as a labourer on harsh, unyielding land. Relationships – friendship and love – occupy the hub of emotional existence in the songs:

> I hae been blythe wi' Comrades dear;
>   I hae been merry drinking;
> I hae been joyfu' gatherin' gear;

I hae been happy thinking:
But a' the pleasures e'er I saw,
    Tho' three times doubl'd fairly,
That happy night was worth them a',
    Amang the rigs o' barley.

(Poems, I, 14)

Repeatedly refusing the transcendent in favour of a heightened, intensified immanent, these songs are a distillation of emotion:

Had we never lov'd sae kindly,
Had we never lov'd sae blindly!
Never met – or never parted,
We had ne'er been broken-hearted. –

(Poems, II, 592)

Scott said of this 'exquisitely affecting stanza' that it 'contains the essence of a thousand love tales'.[28] Its language, to return for a moment to Keats, has 'fine excess' of a much less rhetorically lurid kind, which surprises the reader not by its singularity, but 'almost [as] a Resemblance'.[29] The words and the air together hold in tension the completed and the freedom of the unfinished; their idiom refuses the irrevocable closure of Calvinist determinism. What might have been is not overwhelmed by what can never be.

From about 1790, the son-of-Satan posturing, references to the 'want of an AIM' and the aping of Sterne's whimsical style all disappear from Burns's letters. It may be that in these great song-collections Burns saw himself gathering together the scattered fragments of the Scottish past into a new emotional coherence. Whatever the exact meaning of the enterprise to him, it seems clear that amid illness, financial insecurity and harassment of all kinds, his final years retained an undeviating conviction, at last, of the importance of something larger than the assertion of individuality in rebellion. A faith, in other words. Burns described his project of song-collection in religious terms; he wrote to George Thomson in January 1793 of himself as an 'enthusiast' making a 'pilgrimage' to pa[y his] devotions at the particular shrine of every Scots Muse' (*Letters*, II, 181). Immersing himself in the impersonality of the traditional airs, Burns finally by indirections found directions out. The genesis of his lyrics is revealing:

Untill I am compleat master of a tune, in my own singing, (such as it is) I never can compose for it. – My way is: I consider the poetic Sentiment, correspondent to my idea of the musical expression; then chuse my theme; begin one Stanza; when that is composed . . . I walk out, sit down now & then, look out for objects in Nature around me that are in unison or harmony with the cogitations of my fancy & workings of my bosom; humming every now & then the air with the verses I have framed: when I feel my Muse beginning to jade, I retire to the solitary fireside of my study, & there commit my effusions to paper. – (*Letters*, II, 242)

Here is a different 'negative capability', shifted now from energetic possession-in-opposition of the voices and thoughts of his satiric victims, to a kind of wise passiveness which found within the imagination a harmonising response to the energy of the airs which absorbed him. In his first Commonplace Book, Burns wrote, 'Rhyme and Song were, in a manner, the spontaneous language of my heart'.[30] It suggests prayer, something which bypasses the normal organising processes of the understanding of the drives of the will, an answering internal energy. In *The Marriage of Heaven and Hell* (completed as Burns wrote 'Tam o' Shanter'), Blake declares:

Energy is the only life and is from the Body and Reason is the bound or outward circumference of Energy.
    Energy is Eternal Delight.[31]

It is an energy at once intensely of the self and completely self-forgetful:

There's nought but care on ev'ry han',
    In ev'ry hour that passes, O:
What signifies the life o' man,
    An' 'twere na for the lasses, O.

The warly race may riches chase,
    An' riches still may fly them, O;
An' tho' at last they catch them fast,
    Their hearts can ne'er enjoy them, O.

But gie me a canny hour at e'en,
    My arms about my Dearie, O;
An' warly cares, an' warly men,
    May a' gae tapsalteerie, O!

For you sae douse, ye sneer at this,
    Ye're nought but senseless asses, O:
The wisest Man the warl' saw,
    He dearly lov'd the lasses, O.

(*Poems*, I, 59–60)

A final word. Jacob never did get the angel's name, though the angel had his, sure enough. Naming is control, power, authority. Burns's songs show just how much of life escaped the power of the Kirk which claimed to have a monopoly on how to speak to God. In a dedicatory poem, Ben Jonson lamented how the corrupt currency of flattery had made it impossible to praise a benefactor and patron without hypocrisy and disingenuousness:

> 'Tis grown almost a danger to speak true
>   Of any good mind now, there are so few.
> The bad, by number, are so fortified,
>   As, what they've lost t'expect, they dare deride.
> So both the praised and praisers suffer: yet,
>   For others' ill, ought none their good forget.[32]

In songs, Burns found a way of evading the debased religious discourse which surrounded him, and learned to 'speak true' to another:

> Oh wert thou in the cauld blast,
>   On yonder lea, on yonder lea;
> My plaidie to the angry airt,
>   I'd shelter thee, I'd shelter thee:
> Or did misfortune's bitter storms
>   Around thee blaw, around thee blaw,
> Thy bield should be my bosom,
>   To share it a', to share it a'.
>
> Or were I in the wildest waste,
>   Sae black and bare, sae black and bare,
> The desert were a paradise,
>   If thou wert there, if thou wert there.
> Or were I monarch o' the globe,
>   Wi' thee to reign, wi' thee to reign;
> The brightest jewel in my crown,
>   Wad be my queen, wad be my queen.

> (*Poems*, II, 813)

NOTES

1. Ted Hughes, 'Note' to *A Choice of Shakespeare's Verse* (London: Faber & Faber, 1971), pp. 184–5.
2. *The Letters of Robert Burns*, ed. J. De Lancey Ferguson, 2nd edn ed. G. Ross Roy, 2 vols. (Oxford: Clarendon Press, 1985), II, p. 146. Subsequent references to the *Letters* appear in the text.
3. *Paradise Lost*, Book I, 1. 26, in *The Poetical Works of John Milton*, ed. Douglas Bush (Oxford: Oxford University Press, 1966), p. 213. Dryden was perhaps the first

British poet to 'discover' Satan as the true hero of Milton's epic; Burns's contemporary William Blake wrote in *The Marriage of Heaven and Hell* (1789–90) that 'The reason Milton wrote in fetters when he wrote of Angels & God, and at liberty when of Devils & Hell, is because he was a true Poet and of the Devils party without knowing it' (Plate 6); facsimile, intro. Geoffrey Keynes (Oxford: Oxford University Press, 1975). Subsequently, Percy Bysshe Shelley would develop the praise of Satan's revolutionary heroism to bolster his own atheistic anarchism in his Preface to *Prometheus Unbound* (1820), and, more fully, in the 'Essay on the Devil and Devils' (written 1819–20).

4. *Animadversions on some poets and poetasters of the Present Age* . . . (Paisley, 1788), p. 4.
5. *A Burns Companion* (London: Macmillan, 1991), p. 94.
6. As cited by Vernon J. Charlesworth in *Rowland Hill: His Life, Anecdotes, and Pulpit Sayings*, intro. C. H. Spurgeon (London: Hodder & Stoughton, 1876), p. 156.
7. 'Address of Beelzebub', *The Poems and Songs of Robert Burns*, ed. James Kinsley, 3 vols (Oxford: Clarendon Press, 1968), I, p. 255. Subsequent references to the poems appear in the text.
8. Genesis 32, 24–30.
9. *The Theory of Moral Sentiments*, ed. D. D. Raphael and A. L. McFie, *The Glasgow Edition of the Works and Correspondence of Adam Smith*, 6 vols (Oxford: Clarendon Press, 1976), I, p. 166. See Burns's 'First Commonplace Book' (1783–5; publ. 1872), ed. and intro. Raymond Lamont Brown (Wakefield, Yorkshire: S. R. Publishers, 1969), p. 7.
10. Ibid., p. 54.
11. Pope, letter to Caryll, 5 December 1712, *The Correspondence of Alexander Pope*, ed. George Sherburn, 5 vols (Oxford: Clarendon Press, 1956), I, pp. 160–1. The letter to Moore gives Burns's own account of the importance of the studied forms of the 'Wits of Queen Ann' in forming his own epistolary style. Walter Scott, unsigned review of Cromek's *Reliques of Robert Burns*, in *The Quarterly Review* (February 1809); reprinted in Donald A. Low (ed.), *Robert Burns: The Critical Heritage* (London: Routledge & Kegan Paul, 1974), p. 199.
12. The quotations come, in order, from (Anon.) [Rev. William Peebles], *Burnomania: The Celebrity of Robert Burns Considered in a Discourse addressed to all Real Christians of Every Denomination* . . . (Edinburgh: J. Ogle, 1811), p. 5; ibid., p. 19; John Ramsay of Ochtertyre, *Scotland and Scotsmen in the Eighteenth Century*, 2 vols (Edinburgh: William Blackwood & Sons, 1888), I, p. 554; Rev. Dr W. C. Bitting, Pastor, Second Baptist Church, St Louis, 'Burns and Religious Matters', in Walter B. Stevens (ed.), *St Louis Nights Wi' Burns* (St Louis MO: The Burns Club of Missouri, 1913), p. 27; A. Burns Jamieson, *Burns and Religion* (Cambridge: W. Heffer & Sons, 1931), p. xiv; David Daiches, *Robert Burns* (1950; rev, edn London: Andre Deutsch, 1966), p. 82; David Cairns, 'Robert Burns and the Religious Movements in the Scotland of His Day', Carlyle Society, Thomas Green Occasional Lectures, no. 3 (Edinburgh, 1962), p. 13; Carol McGuirk, *Robert Burns and the Sentimental Era* (Athens GA: University of Georgia Press, 1985), p. 29; Alan Bold, *A Burns Companion* (London: Macmillan, 1991), p. 97.
13. *God and the Poets* (Oxford: Clarendon Press, 1984), pp. 69f.

14. *Scottish Literature and the Scottish People, 1680–1830* (London: Chatto & Windus, 1961), p. 110.
15. *Selected Essays* (Cambridge: Cambridge University Press, 1978; 1980), p. 40
16. *Burns and Religion*, p. 48.
17. *Life of Robert Burns* (1828; London: J. M. Dent & Sons, 1912), p. 53.
18. *A Choice of Shakespeare's Verse*, p. 185.
19. *The Scottish Tradition in Literature* (Edinburgh and London: Oliver & Boyd, 1958), p. 215.
20. Cited by Andrew O'Hagan, 'Thin Ayrshire', *The London Review of Books* (25 May 1995), p. 19.
21. H. N. Fairchild, *Religious Trends in English Poetry*, 6 vols (New York: Columbia University Press, 1939–68), III, pp. 23, 35.
22. *Human Nature in Its Fourfold State of Primitive Integrity, Entire Depravity, Begun Recovery and Consummate Happiness or Misery* (1720; Edinburgh: Banner of Truth Trust, 1964; 1989), pp. 407–8. Burns referred to this book as 'stupid', however, it was among the 'damned trash' which, several months later, he ordered from the Edinburgh bookseller Peter Hill for the Monkland Friendly Society (*Letters*, II, pp. 36, 66); cf. John S. Robotham, 'The Reading of Robert Burns', *The Bulletin of the New York Public Library*, vol. 74 (1970), p. 563.
23. As a contemporary of Burns, the Rev. Samuel Hopkins, put it in his biography of a great American eighteenth-century theologian, 'if these [Calvinist doctrines], in the whole length and breadth of them were relinquished, he did not see, where a man could set his foot down with consistency and safety, short of Deism, or even Atheism itself; or rather universal Skepticism' (*The Life and Character of Mr Jonathan Edwards* (1765), in *Jonathan Edwards: A Profile*, ed. David Levin [New York, 1969], p. 52).
24. *The Letters of John Keats*, ed. Maurice Forman, 4th edn (Oxford: Oxford University Press, 1952), p. 107.
25. 'Holy Sonnets', 10, *The Divine Poems of John Donne*, ed. and intro. Helen Gardner (Oxford: Clarendon Press, 1952, 1978), p. 11; 'Justus quidem tu es, Domine', *The Poems of G. M. Hopkins*, ed. Catherine Phillips (Oxford: Oxford University Press, 1986), p. 183; 'Affliction II', *The English Poems of George Herbert*, ed. C. A. Patrides (London: J. M. Dent & Sons, 1974), p. 80.
26. *The Complete Poems of Emily Dickinson*, ed. Thomas H. Johnson (Boston and London: Faber & Faber, 1970; repr. 1975), Poem 1,551.
27. Ibid., Poem 724.
28. *Critical Heritage*, p. 208.
29. *Letters of Keats*, loc. cit.
30. Burns, 'Commonplace Book', p. 3.
31. Blake, Plate 4, op. cit.
32. Epistle, To Katherine, Lady Aubigny, *The Poems of Ben Jonson*, ed. Ian Donaldson (London: Oxford University Press, 1975), p. 111.

HAUNTED BY AUTHORITY:
NINETEENTH-CENTURY AMERICAN CONSTRUCTIONS OF ROBERT BURNS AND SCOTLAND

Carol McGuirk

'The world seems always waiting for its poet.'
(Ralph Waldo Emerson)

Abraham Lincoln, invited in January 1865 to address a gathering of the Burns Club in Washington DC, declined by memorandum: 'I can not frame a toast to Burns. I can say nothing worthy of his generous heart and transcending genius. Thinking of what he has said, I can not say anything which seems worth saying.'[1] Fortunately for this essay, Lincoln's reticence was shared by few of his fellow citizens. At one splendid Centenary dinner held at the Parker House hotel in Boston on 25 January 1859, the keynote speech by Ralph Waldo Emerson was followed by new poems on Burns written for the occasion and recited by James Russell Lowell, Oliver Wendell Holmes and John Greenleaf Whittier. That last-named poet was a Quaker temperance activist known in those days as 'the American Burns', which may give some preliminary idea of the wilfulness of nineteenth-century American constructions of Burns.

Even hostile commentaries show the power of Burns's nineteenth-century reputation in the USA. In 1859, a hard-bitten editor at *The New York Times* – we can almost hear the stream of tobacco juice hitting the side of his spittoon – puts Burns in his place as *only* 'fourth or fifth' among what he laconically terms 'the dead poets of Britain':

There is a sure method for testing the popularity of a poet, and that is by the popular demand for his works, and, tried by this standard, Burns ranks only fourth or fifth among the dead poets of Britain. One of the most extensive books dealers in this country states that where one copy of BURNS' poems is sold there are five of BYRON's. The poets rank, according to the trade scale, as follows: first SHAKESPEARE, then BYRON, MOORE comes third, and after him WORDSWORTH and BURNS.[2]

I will begin with analysis of America's official Burns, repeatedly debated – whether to be finally certified or rejected – as a Major Dead Briton by such poets and theorists of US literary nationalism as Emerson, Whittier, Holmes, Lowell, Nathaniel Hawthorne, Henry Wadsworth Longfellow and Walt Whitman. I will briefly touch in concluding on an unofficial Burns who also travelled to the USA in the early nineteenth century. Unlike the poems of the once adulated, now neglected poet, Burns's unsigned Scottish songs, because of their early entry into American popular mythology, became permanently assimilated as part of US cultural heritage.

> 'His Presence Haunts This Room Tonight.'
>
> (Longfellow)

The first oddity to strike me as I began research on this essay was the frequency with which nineteenth-century Americans imagine, wish, or even roundly assert that Robert Burns is not dead. As with Elvis Presley sightings in our time, this is most likely a sign that mere celebrity has been transcended and cult status achieved. The cult of Burns included prominent Scottish-Americans such as Andrew Carnegie but also such marginal persons as Mina S. Seymour, a psychic who in 1900 published a book said to be 'transmitted' or channelled directly from the mind of Burns. An introductory 'poem' in Seymour's deranged little volume lists some of the distinguished company which Burns keeps in the spirit world, to which Thomas Edison (d. 1931) is evidently making an informal early visit:

> Wallace, Bruce, Dante, men of history
> Washington, LaFayette, Paine,
> Lincoln, Gladstone, the warlock Edison, aye!
> Passive instruments of unseen powers,
> Frien's, ye'll understand it bye an' bye.[3]

Seymour's profession was communicating with ghosts, but even a person so well grounded in the natural world as John Muir (1838–1914), the Scottish-born naturalist who was, with Theodore Roosevelt, chief architect of the US National Parks system, describes a powerful sense of communion with Burns's spirit:

On my lonely walks, I have often thought how fine it would be to have the company of Burns. And indeed he was always with me, for I had him by heart . . . So real was his companionship, he oftentimes seemed to be with me in the flesh, however wild and strange the places where I wandered.[4]

Seymour and Muir both lived in the USA at the end of the nineteenth century; both expressed their strong conviction that Burns was somehow 'with' them.

An earlier and more specifically literary example of a face-to-face encounter between Burns and a nineteenth-century admirer may be seen in the poem read by Oliver Wendell Holmes (1809–94) at the Centenary dinner in Boston:

> The century shrivels like a scroll, –
> The past becomes the present, –
> And face to face and soul to soul,
> We greet the monarch-peasant.[5]

And in a tribute to Burns by Henry Wadsworth Longfellow (1807–82) that nineteenth-century illustrators found irresistible, Burns is described as actually materialising in Longfellow's study in Cambridge, Massachusetts:

> His presence haunts this room to-night,
> A form of mingled mist and light
>   From that far coast.
> Welcome beneath this roof of mine!
> Welcome! This vacant chair is thine,
>   Dear guest and ghost![6]

In 1845, Nathaniel Hawthorne offered a kind of prescient deconstruction of these face-to-face encounters. In 'P's Correspondence', the protagonist (known only as 'P') is an American, a confined mental patient who is convinced he is visiting London – a madman's alternative London in which Lord Byron, grown conservative and enormously fat by 1846, is engaged mainly in expurgation of his own best early poems. Robert Burns, spry as a cricket but senile at 87, is visiting London for a reading (that does not go well) at the British Museum. John Keats is a ghostlike wraith, still afflicted with tuberculosis; and ten years after a stroke, Sir Walter Scott lingers on at Abbotsford, paralysed and semi-conscious. Two promising young English writers, on the other hand – William Wordsworth and Charles Dickens – have, in 'P's' deranged account, died prematurely – Dickens after completing only the first numbers of *The Pickwick Papers*.

'P's' insanity, we are told, has been caused by his failure as a poet, a failure which 'P' projects onto popular American poets of the 1840s, whom 'P' imagines as dead before their time:

> Most of our writers have come to untimely ends . . . Bryant has gone to his last sleep, with the Thanatopsis gleaming over him, like a sculptured marble sepulchre by moonlight . . . Somewhat later there was Whittier, a fiery Quaker youth, to whom the muse had perversely assigned a battle-trumpet, and who got himself lynched, ten years agone, in South Carolina. I remember, too, a lad just from college, Longfellow by name, who scattered some delicate verses to the winds, and went to Germany, and perished, I think, of intense application, at the University of Göttingen.[7]

Hawthorne, with his search-and-destroy instinct for the USA's nascent myths, poses two questions: what if Bryant, Whittier and Longfellow had been fated to die young, before their essential mediocrity could be detected by the reading public? (Incidentally, though Hawthorne could not have known this in 1845, the American poets did live out 'P's' contrast to the full, his Bowdoin College classmate Longfellow surviving well into his seventies and Whittier and Bryant into their eighties.) And what if the canonised figures of British Romanticism had long outlived their talent, instead of being translated into Major Dead British status while still at the height of their powers? The British authors named in 'P's Correspondence' were the very writers who most impressed and intimidated literary Americans, including the young Hawthorne. Indeed, the three poets in his college novel *Fanshawe* (1828) – Fanshawe, Walcott and Crombie – likewise constitute, as Patricia Crain has recently argued, a meditation on the literary careers of Keats, Wordsworth and Burns respectively.[8]

'P's' ambiguous tale of transcultural and transatlantic 'correspondence' is darkly comic, dramatising the extent to which, in Hawthorne's view, American literary culture during the 1840s remained colonised by Great Britain. As Walt Whitman wrote rather mournfully in 'Poetry Today in America' (1881), 'Long, long are the processes of the development of a nationality'.[9] 'P' could stand equally well for 'Poet' or for 'Patient': his narrative asks readers to consider whether American 'P' will ever emerge from its sickroom or from its paralysing dream of grey British literary eminence. Amused but also alarmed at the dis/ease in contemporary US writing, Hawthorne mocks his compatriots' sick longing for a British literary culture no longer native or natural. That the mature Hawthorne is not prone to reverencing British forebears may be seen in his *English Notebooks* (1857), where a visit to Dumfries stimulates a mixed evaluation of Burns:

Seeing [Burns's] poor, mean dwelling and surroundings . . . one does not so much wonder that people of his day should have failed to recognise what was immortal in a disreputable, drunken, shabbily clothed and shabbily housed man, consorting with associates of ill reputation, and, as his only ostensible occupation, gauging liquor casks . . . I only wonder that his honor came so soon; there must have been something very great in his immediate presence to have caused him to seem like a demi-god so soon.[10]

If a cool customer like Hawthorne ultimately acknowledges the magnetism of Burns's 'immediate presence', it is not surprising that so many other American poets imagine Burns as a kind of ghost: for like the other British Romantics, Burns surely did haunt even the least susceptible literary Americans.

Wholesale exorcism of the Dead Poets of Britain did not come about in the USA during Hawthorne's lifetime, though Dickinson and Whitman broke free. Burns's stylistic influence was greatest early in the century, and (as with Hawthorne) early in literary careers. In 1837, James Russell Lowell (1819–91) published his first poem, 'Imitation of Burns'. One of Hawthorne's victims above, John Greenleaf Whittier (1807–92), was a Massachusetts farmboy who dated his consciousness of literary vocation from the summer afternoon during the 1820s when he sat down under a tree with a borrowed volume of Burns's poems:

> How oft that day, with fond delay,
>   I sought the maple's shadow,
> And sang with BURNS the hours away,
>   Forgetful of the meadow! . . .
>
> New light on home-seen nature beamed,
>   New glory over Woman;
> And daily life and duty seemed
>   No longer poor and common. . . .
>
> Why dream of lands of gold and pearl,
>   Of loving knight and lady,
> When farmer boy and barefoot girl
>   Were wandering there already?[11]

Longfellow was the nineteenth-century American most engrossed in probably misguided efforts to synthesise a new American style using traditional metres borrowed from Britain and Europe. His poem 'Robert Burns',

quoted briefly above, is of special interest because Longfellow adapts
Burns's Standard Habbie measure:

> I see amid the fields of Ayr
> A ploughman who, in foul and fair,
>   Sings at his task
> So clear, we know not if it is
> The laverock's song we hear, or his,
>   Nor care to ask. . . .
>
> At moments, wrestling with his fate,
> His voice is harsh, but not with hate;
>   The brushwood, hung,
> Above the tavern door, lets fall
> Its bitter leaf, its drops of gall
>   Upon his tongue. . . .
>
> For now he haunts his native land
> As an immortal youth; his hand
>   Guides every plough;
> He sits beside each ingle-nook,
> His voice is in each rushing brook,
>   Each rustling bough . . .[12]

By contrast with Burns's poetic practice, Longfellow uses dimeter in lines
three and six (the short lines are lines four and six in Burns). Longfellow has
used enjambement (e.g. between lines four and five of the first two stanzas
quoted), usually employed in English blank verse and not well adapted to
Standard Habbie, as it results in a diminishing of the effect of rhyme in a
stanza-form designed to emphasise rhyme. Repetition of sounds is also
de-emphasised in Longfellow by the introduction of a third rhyme in every
stanza – 'Ayr' (a), 'fair' (a), 'ask' (b), 'is' (c), 'his' (c) and 'task' (b) in
Longfellow's opening stanza. (Burns uses two rhymes in Standard Habbie,
repeating the (a) rhyme three times and the (b) rhyme once.) Longfellow's
worst mistake, however, may be his choice of one-syllable, masculine
rhymes: Burns's success with heavily-rhymed Scottish measures results
from his revelling in repetition and emphasis – he uses predominantly multisyllabic or feminine rhyme, even in octosyllabics:

> I've aften wondered, honest Luath,
> What sort o' life poor dogs like you have;[13]

or

> That ev'ry naig was ca'd a shoe on,
> The smith and thee gat roaring fou on.[14]

In Standard Habbie, frequent feminine rhyme (with masculine rhyme mainly introduced for variety, especially in the short dimeter lines) was traditional for Scots poets, a major factor in creating the illusion of casual speech despite the stylising effect of short lines and frequent rhyming. And, though often comic or satiric in effect, the emphatic rhyme and metre can also convey intensity and urgency of expression:

> I saw thy pulse's maddening play,
> Wild-send thee Pleasure's devious way,
> Misled by Fancy's *meteor-ray*,
>   By Passion driven,
> But yet the *light* that led astray,
>   Was *light* from Heaven.[15]

In this stanza from 'The Vision', only the first two lines have single-syllable rhymes; all the other rhymes are multisyllabic or feminine.

Wordsworth achieves a more consistently stately – occasionally pompous – simplicity of expression using monosyllables and slant-rhyme to achieve an apparent naturalness of diction much more often emulated by nineteenth-century poets in the USA; hence, probably, Longfellow's choice of masculine rhyme even in a poem written in imitation of Burns.[16] The strong influence of Wordsworth may have made Burns's emphatic rhyming sound too stylised or too informal for direct and full imitation by nineteenth-century American poets: Walt Whitman is both amazed and rather put off by what he calls the 'careless nudity' and 'idiomatic ear-cuffing' of Burns's versification.[17]

In his Standard Habbie tribute, Longfellow may be refusing outright imitation of Burns's colloquial, racy language because (like other American readers) he has been taught by the false report of Burns's early biographies to associate a free-spirited poetic diction with a corresponding (and deplorable) freedom in morals. Indeed, it is surprising to find no less a figure than Walt Whitman in essential agreement not only with Longfellow but with the conduct book *The Young Woman's Guide to Excellence* (1845) on the matter of Burns's deficient idealism: '[Burns] has . . . little or no spirituality. This last is his mortal flaw and defect';[18] 'Burns . . . sought some power that would bestow on us the gift "to see ourselves as others see us". Poor Burns! this was as high as he could be expected to go. But how much more to be desired is it, that we could see ourselves as *God* sees us?'[19] In tone, then, Longfellow's tribute to Burns strikes a rather typical American note of affectionate remembrance, tinged with regret for Burns's presumed transgressions. Burns is a ghost – one of those awe-inspiring Dead Britons who haunt the reveries of ambitious nineteenth-century American poets. But Longfellow makes it clear that Burns is, among those figures and in part because of his perceived failings, the least intimidating, the dearest 'ghost'.[20]

For Walt Whitman, writing in 1882, 'dear Rob' is counted among the 'tenderest, manliest and (even if contradictory) dearest flesh-and-blood figures in all the streams and clusters of by-gone poets' ('Burns', 415). Whitman's ghost-Burns is specifically androgynous: manly, but also tender. In Whittier's poem, Burns's presumed carnality and his endeared presence become explicitly feminised in the image of Mary Magdalen:

> Lament who will the ribald line
>   Which tells his lapse from duty,
> How kissed the maddening lips of wine
>   Or wanton ones of beauty;
> But think, while falls that shade between
>   The erring one and Heaven,
> That he who loved like Magdalen,
>   Like her may be forgiven.[21]

Such constructions of the ghost-Burns as 'erring one' result from the reading of Burns by Americans as middle-class like themselves, therefore presumably pledged to a respectability and high-mindedness as ostentatious as their own. Figured as female, the poet's transgressiveness becomes disarming – 'dear' instead of dangerous. This feminised construction is a ghost-Burns in that it is easy enough, at least at this historical distance, to see through. All that is needed is what readers in the USA during the nineteenth century never had – a full knowledge of all Burns's writings (which would have precluded the misguided cult of Saint Robin) and a full and fair biography (which would have precluded the equally delusionary myth of Demon Rab).

For Burns was not appropriately judged by American middle-class standards. He was a peasant, born into a cycle of hereditary poverty and landlessness that never ceased to enrage him, even after he had abandoned his last farm at Ellisland in late 1791 and had become a full-time officer in the Excise. In *Democracy in America*, De Toqueville mused in 1835 that

> Americans never use the word *peasant*, because they have no idea of the class which that term denotes; the ignorance of more remote ages, the simplicity of rural life, and the rusticity of the villager have not been preserved among them; and they are alike unacquainted with the virtues, the vices, the coarse habits, and the simple graces of an early stage of civilization.[22]

Americans writing on Burns during the nineteenth century may approach
the topic of Burns's social class from an oblique angle (as in William Alcott's
observation that the moral in 'To a Louse' goes 'as high as [Burns] could be
expected to go'). But they 'never use the word *peasant*' unless it is accompanied by some qualifier to neutralise it, as in Oliver Wendell Holmes's
oxymoronic phrase 'monarch-peasant' in his Centenary poem.

Americans commiserate with their ghostly Burns, yet often see his miseries as largely self-inflicted. James Currie's first biography and edition of
Burns (Liverpool, 1800) initiated the falsehoods about Burns's conduct that
were so widely believed during the nineteenth century. In a generous effort
to create sympathy for Burns's wife and surviving children (to whose benefit
the sales of his edition were dedicated), Dr Currie was nonetheless moved
to tug at his readers' heartstrings by inventing tragic motifs. James Currie,
the first full-scale biographer, repeatedly asserts that Burns wilfully caused
his own death; venereal disease is hinted at as well as alcoholism. Currie,
whose edition was the most popular in the USA, is often echoed by nineteenth-century Americans, as in the 'Sketch of the Life of Robert Burns' that
appeared in *The Ladies' Pearl* for December 1840. That essay is prefaced by
a melodramatic couplet from an elegy for Burns printed in Currie's edition:
'An ideot laugh the welkin rings,/As genius thus degraded lies'. (William
Roscoe, author of the elegy, was to become an abolitionist Member of
Parliament for Liverpool, and was Currie's close friend.) *The Ladies' Pearl*
biographer also draws from Currie in sketching her portrait of turpitude:
'That a mind, sensitive, powerful and vigorous as his – . . . that such a mind
should be the duped victim of the grosser faculties, the slave of the senses,
is a melancholy and deplorable thought: yet such was the fact in Robert
Burns'.[23] In fact, the poet's death at 37 is now agreed to have been caused
by a chronic bacterial infection that followed rheumatic fever during Burns's
teens: rather than a weak victim of self-destructive passions, Burns was so
determined to live that he survived for twenty years despite increasingly
defective heart valves. James Currie's moralising edition, whether imported
or pirated, was the only one available in the USA until around 1815, and it
remained the most popular until the later 1840s, when Allan Cunningham's
(just as unreliable) surpassed it. Dr Currie's Burns was the edition which
young Hawthorne checked out of the Salem library.

Even Americans who think that they are rejecting the easy moralising of
the Burns biographers may still be influenced by them, as in Whitman's
case: 'from his own rank appetites . . . [Burns] never extricated himself'
('Burns', 413). Furthermore, even sympathetic American readers are
inclined to define Burns's chief problem as poverty, which is only a small
part of the truth. As Burns's poetry shows, the haughtiness of the privileged
classes in lording it over the poor galled Burns far more than poverty itself:

But, then, to see how ye're negleket,
How huff'd, an' cuff'd, and disrespeked!
L–d man, our gentry care as little,
For *delvers*, *ditchers*, an sic cattle;
They gang as saucy by poor folk,
As I wad by a stinkan brock.
    I've notic'd, on our Laird's *court-day*,
An' mony a time my heart's been wae,
Poor *tenant-bodies*, scant o' cash,
How they maun thole a *factor*'s snash;
He'll stamp an' threaten, curse an' swear,
He'll *apprehend* them, *poind* their gear,
While they maun stan', wi' aspect humble,
An' hear it a', an' fear an' tremble![24]

The tools, equipment and livestock of Burns's own father were impounded by a factor for non-payment of rent in exactly the manner described in these lines: like other Scottish tenant farmers oppressed by eighteenth-century rack-renting, Burns was denied even the hope of the slow, generation-by-generation upward mobility possible for equally poor nineteenth-century Americans – at least those living in freedom, those who were not slaves. He wrote in 1787 of his despair during early manhood as he watched his dying father fighting bankruptcy proceedings, knowing his own responsibilities as eldest son: 'I saw my father's situation entailed on me perpetual labor'.[25] Unlike any middle-class American, Burns was expected to shoulder his burden *submissively*, 'wi' aspect humble'. Submissiveness was the sticking point, breeding in Burns a reflex rebelliousness, an outright hatred of privilege that Burns's American admirers simply fail to fathom.

Burns's nineteenth-century audience in the USA, however poor, has an expectation of future prosperity that would be incomprehensible to most of Burns's speakers, who typically imagine release from sorrow and hardship only in death ('Man Was Made to Mourn') or a better world beyond ('The Cotter's Saturday Night'). Thus, Burns's anger is unreadable to Americans: they may even interpret it as neurotic or self-destructive. In the USA, homesteading made eventual landownership at least a common hope and theoretical possibility, so that vagrancy and homelessness, recurring topics in Burns's poems, suggested to Americans not so much a failure of luck as a lack of enterprise – even (as with Huck Finn's father) a hankering after disreputable leisure. And the idea (something of an obsession with Burns in his vernacular epistles) that a bright, hard-working, active person might find him- or herself involuntarily and permanently clothed in rags is unthinkable. Burns's most enthusiastic American admirers were themselves descendants of British or European peasants, risen to a degree of prosperity: perhaps they are resisting any slippage backwards in time and status when they express their frequent wish that Burns were 'higher'. Or perhaps they are judging Burns according to standards that would have been appropriate if indeed he did still live among them, the beneficiary, like them, of several generations of gradual upward mobility. Robert Burns becomes during the nineteenth century the fading ghost or muffled echo of his American readers' own discarded class-origins.

The mismatch between Burns's expressed class sympathies and those of his middle-class American readers helps to account for one of the more mysterious aspects of nineteenth-century America's cult of Burns: the enshrinement of his sentimental songs to 'Highland Mary' as his finest works. The Highland Mary songs are written in Burns's most self-conscious and exalted English. Furthermore, as urgent addresses to a dead girl, they achieve the focus on morbidity and mortality that nineteenth-century Americans found so perversely attractive:

> O pale, pale now, those rosy lips
>   I aft hae kiss'd sae fondly!
> And clos'd for ay, the sparkling glance,
>   That dwalt on me sae kindly!
> And moldering now in silent dust,
>   The heart that lo'ed me dearly!
> But still within my bosom's core
>   Shall live my Highland Mary.[26]

In 1818, the popularity of William Cullen Bryant was established by 'Thanatopsis', a precocious meditation on death written in 1811 (when he was 16) by a poet so hale that he lived to be 85: 'approach thy grave,/ Like one who wraps the drapery of his couch/ About him, and lies down to pleasant dreams'.[27] Three generations later, James Whitcomb Riley (1849–1916) mines an adjacent vein – infant death – in a poem that recalls the pre-interment photographs of dead children so common in the Midwest during the late nineteenth century:

> This is the way the baby slept:
>   A mist of tresses backward thrown
> By quavering sighs where kisses crept,
>   With yearnings she had never known:
> The little hands were closely kept
>   About a lily newly blown –
> And God was with her. And we wept –
>   And this is the way the baby slept.[28]

Mark Twain parodies this taste in the adolescent republic as itself adolescent. Emmeline Grangerford in *Huckleberry Finn* produces the lugubrious 'Ode to Stephen Dowling Bots, Dec'd,' and a 'slim, melancholy girl' on 'Examination Day' in *Tom Sawyer* perceives her exile from Alabama as a metaphoric death:

> Welcome and home were mine within this State,
> Whose vales I leave – whose spires fade fast from me;
> And cold must be mine eyes, and heart, and tête,
> When, dear Alabama, they turn cold on thee![29]

Burns's Highland Mary songs suited the taste of this Prairie graveyard-school: no off-putting sympathy for the devil or for ragged people in these songs. Though today we would think them an odd choice to stand as exemplary of Burns's genius, Andrew Carnegie's praise – he thought 'To Mary in Heaven' Burns's finest song – was not uncommon. In the schoolbook *A First View of English and American Literature* (Scribners, 1909), the Burns canon is anthologised as follows: 'The Cotter's Saturday Night', 'The Twa Dogs', 'To a Mouse', 'Address to the Unco Guid', 'A Red, Red Rose', 'Bonnie Doon', 'Of a' the Airts', 'Scots Wha Hae' and 'To Mary in Heaven'.[30]

In 'Robert Burns as Poet and Person' (1882), the complex and ambivalent essay already quoted from, Walt Whitman ignores the sentimental or Highland Mary component in the American Burns myth, preferring such racier texts as 'Love and Liberty' and 'Epistle to John Rankine'. Nonetheless, Whitman emphasises the misleading terms 'average' and 'middle class'. 'Manly, witty, fond, friendly' 'Rob' is hailed as a happy worker and well-adjusted proto-American:

> [T]here are many things in Burns's poems and character that specially endear him to Americans. He was essentially a Republican – would have been at home in the Western United States, and probably become eminent there. He was an average sample of the good-natured, warm-blooded, proud-spirited, amative, alimentive, convivial, young and early-mid-aged man of the decent-born middle-classes everywhere and any how. Without the race of which he is a distinct specimen, (and perhaps his poems) America and her powerful Democracy could not exist today. ('Burns', 409)

This projected image of Burns as a flourishing cowpoke somewhere in Wyoming or Montana has its appeal, but it is also typical of American appreciations of Burns in its refusal to grant Burns either his Scottishness or his 'peasantness'. While praising Burns as a person, the passage also implies the reservations about Burns as a poet that will surface later in Whitman's essay – for what poet is simply average? We usually think of the poet as defining human experience, not as tranquilly exemplifying it. In Emerson's words, 'the Poet . . . stands among partial men for the complete man'; '[People] behold in the hero or poet their own green and crude being – ripened'.[31]

Whitman rejects what he calls Burns's 'feudalism': 'He prided himself in his songs on being a reactionist and Jacobite – on persistent sentimental adherency to the cause of the Stuarts – the weakest, thinnest, most faithless, brainless dynasty that ever held a throne' (413). In an outburst included in the earliest published version of his essay (*The Critic* 1882) but deleted in later printings, Whitman explicitly dissociates himself from the Scottish nationalism which he perceives as marking Burns's cult as well as Burns's poems: '[I will not consider Burns] from the zealous points of view of his clannish and foreign race (for to Americans, he and all of them, are they not foreigners and clannish enough?)'.[32] In truth, Burns's and Whitman's nationalism and patriotism are expressed in conflicting ways, though both see national identity and destiny as crucial concerns of poetry, which is to say that both define themselves as bards.

Whitman cannot praise Burns's Scotland-centred bardic consciousness because he sees it as tied to a decadent political system and to superseded values: 'As to the old feeling of pride in the rustic because he was rustic – Burns, Millet, Whittier, I do not share that pride myself: whatever it may be it is not modern'.[33] Whitman's view is insistently progressive: the bard is a far-seer, looking ahead to national destiny. Burns's view, like that of most Scots poets, is, at least on a superficial reading, more often retrospective: the bard recuperates (as opposed to new-forging) national identity. Burns can 'imagine' Scotland only by various means of dimming his consciousness of England's cultural and political dominance – by his distinctive emphasis on Scottish dialect, for instance, and by his displacements of time. Most of Burns's songs suggest a time-frame either vaguely or specifically in the pre-Union past. In 'My Bonie Mary', a single reference to the 'glittering spears' of the departing soldiers establishes the setting as medieval, for instance; and even Burns's first song, written at the age of 15 to charm his 14-year old harvest-partner, begins 'O *once* I lov'd'. Burns's temporally displaced and even archaic frames of reference ('Auld Lang Syne') are assisted by the fragments of old songs and ballads that he collected throughout his life. From 'John Barleycorn' (written before 1782) to 'Charlie is My Darling' (1796), Burns reused old Scots music and words, interweaving what he called 'the old scraps' with his own new stanzas. And that songs recreating Scottish battles of 1314, 1688, 1715 or 1746 might be read as calls to battle in the revolutionary 1790s was clear at least to Burns himself, for he almost never signed these songs, despite keeping a private record of which words in a given song were his and which were drawn from the old fragments.

For Whitman, true poets embrace (*create*) a new world, an emphasis which he may derive from Emerson's theorising of America:

> Why should not we [Americans] have a poetry and philosophy of insight and not of tradition . . . The sun shines today . . . There is more wool and flax in the fields. There are new lands, new men, new thoughts. Let us demand our own works and laws and worship.[34]

In 'Works and Days', Emerson rejects all retrospective gazing: 'whatever is old corrupts, and the past turns to snakes. The reverence for the deeds of our ancestors is a treacherous sentiment'.[35] Yet Burns would have read such passages in Emerson very differently from Whitman, for making a 'new' land with 'new' men was the very argument that had led to the Union of Parliaments (1707) and the rule of the Hanoverian kings (1714). 'New-fangled' was a Jacobite term of insult.

Whitman, like many nineteenth-century Americans, cannot see that Burns's vision of Scotland, far from representing a sad case of ancestor-worship, is essentially (if implicitly) addressed to the future: a reborn sovereign Scotland, and a Scottish posterity that – the poet even italicises the future tense – one day '*shall* be' free:

> By Oppression's woes and pains!
> By your Sons in servile chains!
> We will drain our dearest veins!
> But they *shall* be free![36]

Whitman's thesis on Burns's essential 'normalcy' finally cannot be reconciled with the integration of Real and Ideal which he sees as essential to poetry: 'Burns is not at all great for New World study . . . is not to be mentioned with Shakespeare – hardly even with Tennyson or our Emerson . . . – [T]hose universal strivers . . . show . . . man's crowning, last victorious infusion in himself of Real and Ideal' (413–14). The intimate scale, stylised metre and insistent rhyme of Burns may be too unlike Whitman's own looser-limbed and larger-scaled poetic practice. For, liking the tart flavour of the 'Scotch patois' itself, and loving the personality of the man, or at least his fantasy of the man, Whitman sees Burns's achievement as fatally restricted by too 'contracted and low' a 'notion' of poetry (411): 'He has, moreover, little or no spirituality. This last is his mortal flaw and defect, tried by the highest standards' (413).

Though Emerson's emphasis on America's transcendental destiny may well be behind Whitman's dismissal of Burns's relevance to 'New World study' (limited because of Burns's immersion in tradition), Emerson himself evades the trap of class-prejudice, partly by acknowledging (rather than, like Whitman, denying) Burns's class differences, and also partly by looking beyond subject matter to language itself. Emerson's Centenary oration, to my mind the warmest and most perspicuous of nineteenth-century American appreciations, insists that through his language Burns does achieve the necessary poetic integration of Real and Ideal:

> And as he thus was the poet of the poor . . . so had he the language of low life . . . He had that secret of genius to draw from the bottom of society the strength of its speech, and astonish the ears of the polite with these artless words, better than art, and filtered of all offence through his beauty.[37]

To Emerson, Burns does not transcribe, but 'filters', meeting the formal demands of art through his self-consciously constructed vernacular language, which nonetheless evokes the speech-acts of the artless. Emerson concludes that Burns provides 'the only example in history of a language made classic through the genius of a single man' (442).

Burns, says Emerson, reconstitutes within an artistic context the intensity of language-usage characteristic of people uninhibited by literary codes and practices. In a journal entry, Emerson notes that

> The language of the street is always strong . . . I confess to some plea-sure from the stinging rhetoric of a rattling oath in the mouth of truckmen & teamsters. How laconic and brisk it is by the side of a page of the *North American Review*. Cut these words & they would bleed; they are vascular & alive; they walk & run. Moreover they who speak them have this elegancy, that they do not trip in their speech. It is a shower of bullets, whilst Cambridge men and Yale men correct them-selves & begin again at every half sentence.[38]

The forthright language employed by Burns's peasant speakers is often 'vas-cular' in Emerson's sense. Burns learned how to construct his distinctive poetic language by listening to his contemporaries, but also by listening to the Scottish past through his collection and revision of old folk fragments. Burns's poetry renovates the Scottish language, putting the demotic speech of Scotland's past and present to lyric uses, and using the vernacular to dramatise rural speakers unheard in British poetry (outside the genres of pastoral and burlesque) until Burns himself showed Wordsworth that it could be done.

'[Burns] displays, and as it were embalms, the peculiar manners of his
country.'

(James Currie)

Burns's commitment to a bardic role (he worked almost exclusively on song-
writing and revision during the last ten years of his life) was accompanied by
an increasingly secretive attitude towards authorship. He signed songs of
personal compliment, but otherwise commonly represented himself as the
editor or collector rather than the writer of his songs. Even his characteristic
displacements to the past ('O *Once* I Lov'd', 'There *Was* a Lad') assisted in
oral and anonymous transmission by depersonalising texts. It is not surprising, then, that so many of Burns's songs travelled to the USA without being
associated with his name, or with any source except Scottish culture itself.
In his Centenary lecture of 1859, Emerson noted that 'the people who care
nothing about literature and poetry care for Burns' (441). It is more paradoxical still that people who knew nothing of Burns were nonetheless learning
his songs and echoing his language, and in so doing disseminating Burns's
strong idealisation of Scotland throughout the USA.

The dividing line between the official Burns (a canonised literary figure,
though somewhat controversially so) and the unofficial Burns (an anonymous bard and cultural influence) thus falls between his poems, which he
signed and for which he was celebrated, and his songs, whose authorship he
often suppressed and which – even when signed – often travelled to the USA
anonymously. In a study conducted between 1938 and 1942, the Writer's
Project of Roosevelt's Works Progress Administration collected texts of
songs for deposit in the archives of the University of Virginia: among these
songs, folk-collected as 'Virginian', are 'Banks o' Doon', 'Banks of Allan
Water', 'Bonnie Jean', etc.[39]

Burns's anonymous influence through his songs began early. Describing
his visit to Sir Walter Scott in 1817, Washington Irving (1783–1859) writes
in 'Abbotsford' of his intense pleasure in seeing Scotland for the first time,
tracing this pleasure to his recognition of the landscape through his childhood memories of Scottish songs:

> every turn [in the landscape] brought to mind some household air–some
> almost forgotten song of the nursery, by which I had been lulled to
> sleep in my childhood; and with them, the looks and voices of those
> who had sung them, and were now no more. It is these melodies,
> chanted in our ears in the days of infancy, and connected with the
> memory of those we have loved, and who have passed away, that clothe
> the Scottish landscape with such tender associations.[40]

These half-remembered Scottish lullabies of American childhood are almost always songs by Robert Burns. Indeed, as infant schools in the USA during the nineteenth century often taught the alphabet to the tune of 'Auld Lang Syne', the earliest experiences of literacy itself were for many nineteenth-century Americans intertwined with Burns's song-revision project.[41] It is not surprising, then, that even Americans (like Irving) without family ties to Scotland itself nonetheless experience Scottish songs as speaking from a deeply compelling place in their own past – and speaking, at that, in the 'voices of those . . . who were now no more'. In this light, the ghost of Burns bears the face not of a Major Dead Romantic Poet but of a beloved, long-lost parent or family friend.

This American association of Burns's songs with childhood's home and hearth may also explain the frequency with which the songs are quoted in popular children's fiction; in the novels of Louisa May Alcott (1832–88), for instance. In *An Old Fashioned Girl* (1870), Alcott describes an American child's embarrassment while attending a French play (probably an early vaudeville) incorporating African-American songs and dance:

> Never mind what its name was, it was very gorgeous, very vulgar, and very fashionable . . . At first, Polly thought she had got into fairyland, and saw only the sparkling creatures who danced and sung in a world of light and beauty; but, presently, she began to listen to the songs and conversation, and then the illusion vanished; for the lovely phantoms sang negro melodies, talked slang, and were a disgrace . . .[42]

The invariable hostility of this influential children's author to French and African-American culture is matched by her invariable praise for the 'purity' of Scottish literature and song. In *Eight Cousins* and *Rose in Bloom*, a two-novel exploration of a Scottish-American family, the Irish poorhouse orphan and kitchen-maid Phebe Moore has a gift for singing and so is taught all 'the dear old songs'–by which is meant Scottish, not Irish, folksongs. Every song-text specifically named in *Eight Cousins* (1874) and its sequel *Rose in Bloom* (1875) is either a hymn or a song by Robert Burns:

> 'I'll give you some of the dear old songs you used to like so much. This was a favorite, I think'; and sitting down she sang the first familiar air that came, and sang it well in a pleasant, but by no means finished, manner. It chanced to be 'The Birks of Aberfeldie.'[43]

That Burns's vernacular ('Bonie lassie will ye go/ To the birks of Aberfeldie') does not sound like 'slang' to Alcott suggests the transparency of Burns's song-language for nineteenth-century Americans, perhaps because of associations with early childhood and elementary schooling. Burns is never named by Alcott, but in *Eight Cousins* and *Rose in Bloom* she is evidently aware of his authorship of the Scots songs which she uses, drawing a picture of his failings (as rendered by James Currie) in the character of Charles Campbell, the brightest yet the weakest of the seven Campbell boys who together form a composite meditation on male Scottish character. The Scottish women in the two novels – Aunt Peace, Aunt Plenty and Aunt Jessie – are, by contrast, rocks of feminine integrity, a matter in which Alcott agrees with the educator Emma Willard, who in fact adds as Burns's sole strong point his appreciation of strong-minded Scotswomen: 'The general female character in Scotland I hold in high estimation . . . Burns, though not much to be praised when morality is in the question, shows yet an honest regard to women'.[44]

In portraying the most attractive of the cousins – Charles Campbell is nicknamed 'Prince' and 'Bonnie Prince Charlie' – Alcott draws most obviously on Prince Charles Edward Stuart, leader of the doomed 1745 Jacobite rebellion; but also on the tragic Burns of early biographers. Just before Rose Campbell, the heroine, extracts a promise from Charlie (a gifted artist but a problem drinker) that he will take the pledge, both historical Scotsmen are introduced:

> a quick step sounded in the hall, and a voice drew near tunefully humming:
> 'As he was walking' doun the street
>   The city for to view,
> Oh, there he spied a bonny lass,
>   The window lookin' through.
>
> 'Sae licht he jumped up the stair,
>   And tirled at the pin;
> Oh, wha sae ready as hersel'
>   To let the laddie in?'
> sung Rose as the voice paused and a tap came at the door. (*Rose*, 72)

Charlie sings of his royal namesake using the words of the Burns song 'Charlie is My Darling' (1796), and he courts Rose with the song which Burns wrote during his last illness to his nurse, Jessie Lewars:

> turning to the little cabinet piano behind him, he sung in his best style the sweet old song, – 'Oh, were thou in the cauld blast,' dwelling with great effect not only upon the tender assurance that 'My plaid should shelter thee,' but also that, even if a king, 'The brightest jewel in my crown/ Wad be my queen, wad be my queen.' It was very evident that Prince Charming had not gone troubadouring in vain; for Orpheus himself could not have restored harmony so successfully. (85)

Alcott's Charlie Campbell is most closely linked to Dr Currie's tragic-alcoholic Burns when, breaking his pledge and injuring himself fatally in a fall from his horse (the same poetic justice from which Burns rescues Tam o' Shanter), he faces a premature death with courage. (Another possible connection between Burns and this doomed, gifted character in Alcott is that in the USA during the nineteenth century Burns was thought to be related to the Campbell clan; a story to that effect was printed in *The New York Times* during the 1850s and is repeated in numerous biographies.)

Alcott is not unusual among Americans in seeing Burns's life as an example of self-destructive genius. She is unusual in attempting to integrate Burns's reputed life and temperament into the prevailing nineteenth-century American cult of what Henry James referred to in an essay for *The Nation* as Scottish 'physiognomy' and 'style'.[45] Not herself of Scottish descent, Alcott nonetheless treats Scotland in *Eight Cousins* and *Rose in Bloom* rather as she treats Germany in *Little Women* and its sequels – as an exemplary (as opposed to alien) European culture, and – more so than German culture, personified by the kindly but mild-mannered Professor Bhaer – a culture apt to nurture turbulent genius as well as solid domestic virtue.

Americans during the nineteenth century often see Burns as a fallen spirit, to be stigmatised as a mere sensualist (as in Hawthorne's *Fanshawe*), generously forgiven his presumed trespasses (as in the assessments of Whittier, Longfellow and even good, grey Walt), or primly shown the error of his ways (as in Alcott's *Rose in Bloom*).[46] Burns's peasant class-loyalties were often taken as proof that he was a low, 'mean' fellow – spirited, no doubt, but far from spiritual. Yet during the same years that this patronising consensus on Burns as a person was being reached, Burns's unsigned songs were becoming synonymous with cultural sweetness and light – with a wholesome simplicity in Scottish culture itself.[47] It is a secret triumph, this final transfiguration of Burns's unsigned songs in an idealised American vision of Scotland. And any conclusion to be drawn from study of Burns's nineteenth-century American reception must be drawn with respect to this hidden triumph of his songs as well as his hotly and publicly debated – but finally less influential – signed poems.

Nineteenth-century Americans typically see their 'official' Burns as a ghostly echo of the past, whether endeared or rejected. Publicly celebrated as a peasant-poet, Burns is for Americans a haunting, at times chafing reminder of their own superseded class-origins. As a poet generally perceived – though not without some controversy – as a major figure in the Romantic canon, the official Burns is for many literary Americans during the nineteenth century a disquieting reminder of Great Britain's continuing colonisation of US literary culture: though hailed by Emerson as a progressive spirit, Burns is ultimately rejected by Whitman as a 'feudal' representative of the 'obsequious and flunkey tasselage' of a patronage system best exorcised from a democratic literary culture.[48]

Only in the reception of his unofficial writings – those Scottish songs which he never signed, or which lost their identification with him over the years – did the figure of Burns become liberated from American preconceptions about genius, social class and high seriousness. Ironically enough, given the vagaries of Burns's personal reputation, his Scots songs came to symbolise, over the course of the nineteenth century, the power and purity of Scotland itself – which was exactly what Burns intended for his song-revision project. For, far from lacking an ideal purpose in his writing, Burns sought nothing less than to be the bard who defined and disseminated, to all places and for all time, a vision of Scotland transfigured and perfected: Scottish language, Scottish history and Scottish character. The total assimilation of the songs of Burns into American cultural identity – for, as has been shown, this 'Scotland' of Robert Burns somehow becomes conflated with the imaginary realms of US childhood – has its own ironies.[49] For Burns – of all Dead British Poets – is thus enlisted as a phantom-soldier in the bitter culture wars of the nineteenth century, that long and acrimonious debate about which cultures in the US melting pot were, to use Alcott's terms, 'dearest', 'sweetest' and best. And that same hand wrote the poems perceived in the USA as the 'lowest' and most problematic of Romantic canonical poems, and the song-lyrics perceived as the sweetest and most innocent of childhood's dream-songs, simply gives one more reason for the ghost of Burns – if it does still walk – to assume a particularly knowing and sardonic smile.

NOTES

1. Abraham Lincoln, *The Collected Works*, ed. Roy P. Basler et al., 8 vols (New Brunswick NJ: Rutgers University Press, 1953), VIII, p. 90.

2. 'The Popularity of Burns', Editorial, *The New York Times* (28 January 1859), section 4, p. 6.

3. Mina S. Seymour (ed.), *Pen Pictures Transmitted Clairaudiently or Telepathically by Robert Burns. Received and Edited by Mina Seymour* (Lily Dale NY: privately printed, 1900), p. 11.

4. John Muir, Journal entry for 25 January 1906, repr. in Linnie Marsh Wolfe (ed.), *John of the Mountains: The Unpublished Journals of John Muir* (Boston MA: Houghton Mifflin, 1938), pp. 434–5.

5. Oliver Wendell Holmes, repr. in John Ross (ed.), *Round Burns's Grave; The Paeans and Dirges of Many Bards; New and Enlarged Edition* (Paisley: Alexander Gardner, 1892), p. 34. Subsequent references to this volume are abbreviated as Ross, *Round Burns's Grave*.

6. Henry Wadsworth Longfellow, repr. in Ross, *Round Burns's Grave*, p. 26.

7. Nathaniel Hawthorne, *Mosses from an Old Manse* (Columbus: Ohio State

University Press, 1974), Centenary Edition X, pp. 378–9.

8. Nathaniel Hawthorne, *Fanshawe*, in *The Blythedale Romance and Fanshawe* (Columbus: Ohio State University Press, 1964), Centenary Edition III. Hawthorne's preoccupation in *Fanshawe* with Burns, Keats and Wordsworth is noted by Patricia Crain in 'Nathaniel Hawthorne', in Eric Haralson and John Hollander (eds), *The Garland Companion to Nineteenth Century American Poetry* (New York: Garland, forthcoming [1996]).

9. Walt Whitman, 'Poetry Today in America', *Complete Poetry and Prose of Walt Whitman*, 2 vols (New York: Pellegrini and Cudahy, 1948), II, p. 305.

10. Nathaniel Hawthorne, *The English Notebooks*, ed. Randall Stewart (New York: Russell and Russell, 1941), p. 500.

11. John Greenleaf Whittier, 'Burns: On Receiving a Sprig of Heather in Blossom' (1854), *Poetical Works*, 4 vols (Boston: Houghton Mifflin, 1892), IV, pp. 93–4. Subsequent citations abbreviated as Whittier.

12. Henry Wadsworth Longfellow, repr. in Ross, *Round Burns's Grave*, pp. 25–6.

13. 'The Twa Dogs', *The Poems and Songs of Robert Burns*, ed. James Kinsley, 3 vols (Oxford: Clarendon Press, 1968), I, p. 139. Subsequent quotations are taken from this edition, abbreviated as *Poems and Songs*.

14. 'Tam o' Shanter', *Poems and Songs*, II, p. 558.

15. 'The Vision', *Poems and Songs*, I, p. 112.

16. The influence of Wordsworth may also be seen in Whittier's ballad stanza in 'On Receiving a Sprig of Heather', with its Wordsworthian a-b-a-b rhyme scheme (rather than a-b-c-b, as in popular ballad stanza). Whittier differs from Longfellow and Wordsworth in at least attempting Burns's feminine rhyme and ono-matopoeia, though he lacks Burns's bravura skill:

> Bees hummed, birds twittered, overhead
> I heard the squirrels leaping,
> The good dog listened while I read,
> And wagged his tail in keeping.
> (Whittier, IV, p. 93)

17. Walt Whitman, 'Robert Burns as Poet and Person', in *November Boughs, Complete Poetry and Prose of Walt Whitman*, 2 vols (New York: Pellegrini and Cudahy, 1948), II, pp. 414, 415. Subsequent references to this essay, keyed to this edition, are abbreviated as Whitman, 'Burns'.

18. Ibid., p. 413.

19. William Alcott, *Young Woman's Guide to Excellence* (Boston MA: George Light, 1840), p. 162.

20. For Burns, the word 'dear' is a favourite rhyme, occurring with 'tear', 'drear', 'bear' (barley), 'frere' (brother), 'fear', 'gear' (wealth): it is possible that American writers are remembering and echoing Burns's own habitual usage.

21. Whittier, IV, p. 96.

22. Alexis de Tocqueville, *Democracy in America*, 2 vols (New York: Knopf, 1945), I, p. 316.

23. *The Ladies' Pearl: A Monthly Magazine, Devoted to Moral, Entertaining, and Instructive Literature* (Lowell MA: P. D. and T. S. Edmands, 1843), III, p. 1. Cf. also James Currie (ed.), *The Works of Robert Burns: With an Account of his Life, and a Criticism On his Writings*, Second Edition, 4 vols (London: Cadell and Davies, 1801).

24. 'The Twa Dogs', *Poems and Songs*, I, p. 140.
25. J. De Lancey Ferguson and G. Ross Roy (eds), *The Letters of Robert Burns* (Oxford: Clarendon Press, 1985), I, p. 139.
26. 'Highland Mary', *Poems and Songs*, II, p. 660.
27. Edmund Clarence Stedman, *An American Anthology, 1787–1900* (1900; repr. New York: Greenwood, 1968), p. 54.
28. Ibid., pp. 560–1.
29. Mark Twain, *Tom Sawyer* (New York: Holt, Rinehart and Winston, 1961), p. 107.
30. *A First View of English and American Literature* (New York: Scribners, 1909); cf. also Andrew Carnegie, 'Genius Illustrated from Burns', *Speeches and Essays* (Washington DC: Jean Armour Burns Club, 1908).
31. Ralph Waldo Emerson, 'The Poet', *Essays: Second Series* in *Works* (1904; repr. New York: AMS, 1968), III, p. 5; Emerson, 'The American Scholar', *Nature: Addresses and Lectures* in *Works* (1903); repr. New York: AMS, 1968), I, pp. 106–7.
32. Walt Whitman, *Collected Writings* (New York: New York University Press, 1963), VI, pp. 560–1n.
33. Quoted by F. O. Matthiessen, *American Renaissance: Art and Expression in the Age of Emerson and Whitman* (London: Oxford, 1941), p. 613.
34. Emerson, 'Nature', *Nature: Addresses and Lectures*, *Works* (1904; repr. New York: AMS, 1968), I. p. 3.
35. Emerson, 'Works and Days', *Society and Solitude*, *Works* (1904; repr. New York: AMS, 1968), VII, p. 177.
36. 'Scots Wha Hae', *Poems and Songs*, II, p. 708.
37. Emerson, 'Robert Burns', *Miscellanies*, *Works* (1904; repr. New York: AMS, 1968), XI, p. 442.
38. Emerson, *The Journals and Miscellaneous Notebooks*, ed. A. W. Plumstead and Harrison Hayford (Cambridge MA: Belknap Press, 1969), VII, p. 374.
39. Bruce A. Rosenberg, *The Folksongs of Virginia: A Checklist* (Charlottesville: University of Virginia Press, 1969), pp. 5, 11, 14.
40. Washington Irving, 'Abbotsford', *Works* (1848–51; repr. New York: Co-Op Press, 1948), III, p. 531.
41. 'The children may sometimes march together, all saying the letters aloud – sometimes sing an easy tune, perhaps "Auld Lang Syne," arranged to "a, b, c, d, e, f, g, h,"' in Samuel Read Hall, *Lectures to Female Teachers on School Keeping* (Boston MA: Richardson, Lord & Holbrook, 1832), p. 146. Cf. also Ephraim Bacon, *Infants School Teacher's Guide to Which is Added, A Source of Instruction Suited to Infants' Sunday Schools* (Philadelphia PA, 1829).
42. Louisa May Alcott, *An Old Fashioned Girl* (Boston MA: Roberts, 1886), p. 15.
43. Louisa May Alcott, *Rose in Bloom* (New York: Burt, 1917), p. 20.
44. Emma Willard, *Advancement of Female Education: or a Series of Addresses, in Favor of Establishing at Athens, in Greece, a Female Seminary, Especially Designed to Instruct Female Teachers* (Troy NY: Norman Tuttle, 1833), p. 26.
45. Henry James, describing his first journey to Scotland, remarks on Scotland's modishness: 'Something . . . has occurred to me more than once since I have been in Scotland – the idea, namely, that if that fine quality of Scotch conceit which, if I mistake not, all the world recognizes, is, as I take it to be, the most robust thing of its kind in the world, the wonder after all is not great . . . [I]f I were a Scotchman, I too should be conceited . . . I should be proud of Scott and Burns, of Wallace and Bruce, of Mary Stuart and John Knox . . . Above all, I should take

comfort in a country in which natural beauty and historical association are blended only less perfectly than they are in Italy and Greece; whose physiognomy is so intensely individual and homogenous, and, as the artists say, has so much style' (in *The Nation*, 3–10 October 1878, p. 225).

46. Alcott's *Rose in Bloom* – in this matter, oddly like Hawthorne's *Fanshawe* – offers in the character of Mac Campbell a Keats-like alternative poet-figure to Burns. Cousin Mac writes a volume of sonnets and succeeds in winning Rose Campbell after Charlie's death.

47. For a discussion of Matthew Arnold's 'sweetness and light' as it relates to his denial to Burns of 'high seriousness' in 'The Study of Poetry' (*Essays in Criticism: Second Series*), see Carol McGuirk, *Robert Burns and the Sentimental Era* (Athens GA: University of Georgia Press, 1985), pp. xiv–xv.

48. Walt Whitman, *Notebooks and Unpublished Manuscripts*, ed. Edward Grier, 6 vols (New York: NYU Press, 1984), III, p. 1,141.

49. Burns's songs also form an important component in the education and acculturation of the pioneer children in Laura Ingall Wilder's 'Little House' books. The heroine Laura's favorite song – never identified as a Burns song – is 'Bonnie Doon'; her elder sister's is 'Highland Mary'. The series was published beginning in the 1930s, so is not nineteenth-century material, though it is based on idealised memories of Ingall's childhood during the 1870s and 1880s, spend on unsuccessful homesteads in Wisconsin, Kansas, Minnesota and South Dakota.

AUTHENTICATING ROBERT BURNS

Nicholas Roe

> Nothing so difficult as a beginning
> In poesy, unless perhaps the end . . .
> (Lord Byron, *Don Juan*, IV, 1–2)[1]

> Try and reconstruct Burns as he was.
> (*The Glasgow Herald*, 22 July 1896)

DEATH AND THE 'NAMELESS BARD'

On 26 January 1859, *The Daily Scotsman* marked the centenary of Burns's birth:

> From every corner of the land, from every class of the people, there has arisen in speech and song, an utterance so fervid, so heartfelt, so spontaneous, so truly and intensely personal, that Scotland may now, in pride if also somewhat in penitence, stand up before the world and say that she has rendered to her Poet, if not justice, such an homage as no other nation has paid to any similar man.[2]

In tempering celebration with a reminder that such wholehearted homage paid 'now' was belated, the *Scotsman* identified Burns's posthumous reputation as a focus of cultural anxiety. One does not need to look far to discover why. Two days previously, in a column headed 'Pulpit Trash', the *Scotsman* had declared its 'disgust' at a lecture in which Burns was denounced as 'a person who never loved a woman but to betray her, and who never made an acquaintance among either young men or women but he injured and corrupted'.[3] As everyone knows, 'the social life of Robert Burns' (P. Hately Waddell's delicate phrase) was an obstacle for nineteenth-century commentators and editors,[4] from Wordsworth's squeamish and (in Hazlitt's view)

159

self-serving prevarication at Burns's 'infirmities', to the more resolute insistence of 'Gertrude', editor of 'The Family Edition' of Burns's works, that the 'excrescences of his genius' should be 'excluded altogether', to Stevenson's regret that Burns had 'lost his habits of industry, and formed the habit of pleasure'.[5] Leigh Hunt, inquiring into the 'universal regard' for Burns, traced his 'infirmities' to the 'ardent and enjoying temperament' which also rendered him 'a favourite with all the world'.[6] At the end of the nineteenth century, the poet laureate Alfred Austin, attending the unveiling of the Burns statue at Irvine, similarly opted to 'make what allowance [he] truthfully could for [Burns's] faults':

> as one could not deny, [Burns] was as weak as water in the presence of their native beverage and their native beauties. (Laughter.) He (the speaker) hoped the time would never come when it would be imputed as a fault to a poet to 'truly love the lasses, O', nor when it would be considered unbecoming in him to inspire his jaded music with something more than the Castilian fountain. Burns, he was prepared to admit, was convivial to a fault.[7]

Austin admitted that as an Englishman he had 'hesitated . . . whether he should come [to Scotland] and talk upon a subject about which they knew so much more and on which they felt so much more deeply than he could'. Like Hunt, he praised Burns as 'a universal favourite', attributing that popularity to his

> good fortune to be born in a lowly station of life, and therefore more near to Mother Earth, and better able to apprehend the enduring passions of the human heart . . . When he spoke in his mother tongue and as to the manner born he carried everything before him, and he bore them along delighted on the stream of his unsophisticated song. (Cheers.)[8]

Here the fortune of birth and lowly circumstances of Burns's life are brought forward as originary (maternal) sources of his passionate lyrical language; viewed in retrospect, he presents a natural aptitude for the 'enduring passions' which formed the core of Wordsworth's project in *Lyrical Ballads*. Yet, in Austin's hesitating estimation, Burns had also been 'weak as water' when confronted with other aspects of his native culture. The phrase 'weak as water' was clichéd, and the whole of Austin's speech was damned by the newspapers as 'tactless and factless' in that it fell 'far short . . . of the occasion and the poet'.[9] But Austin's remark was nevertheless telling in that it implicitly aligned Burns with another 'lowly' poet, John Keats, whose mortal name had by his own account been 'writ in water'.

John Gibson Lockhart diagnosed the lively 'cockney' idiom of Keats's poetry as the symptom of a 'diseased' imagination, a literary pathology which gave some credibility to the claims made by Shelley, Byron and others that Keats's consumption (a congenital susceptibility) had been brought on by hostile reviews.[10] In a similar manner, Burns's 'weakness' – his ardent mortality, 'convivial to a fault' – was perceived by some readers as intrinsic to both his literary genius and his early death. Thomas Duncan, for example, writing on 10 October 1796, aligned the 'indelicacy of our poet's humour' with his 'frequently faulty' versification and the 'radical misfortune' of his dialect.[11] With a firmer sense of the coherence of Burns's personality, Robert Heron traced his power as a writer to his 'native strength, Ardour, and delicacy of Feelings, passions, and affections' – qualities which also produced Burns's fatal lapses of 'drunkenness and licentious love'.[12] William Grierson's diary pursued the same analogy from a different angle, remarking that Burns's 'extraordinary genius may be said to have been the cause of bringing him so soon to his end'; his 'immortal works' had 'at last totally ruined his constitution', or, as Robert Louis Stevenson put it, 'He died of being Robert Burns'.[13]

This deep contradiction in the logic of Burns's reputation, superficially rendered as a tension between 'native strength' and moral 'blemishes',[14] informed the Romantic construction of Burns as a self-destructive genius. One of my concerns in this essay will be to suggest that Burns actually resisted this myth by pre-empting it, displaying a self-awareness which has proved resilient to the numerous attempts to define his unique identity as a writer. According to John Wilson, for example, Burns 'was born a poet, if ever man was'.[15] Explanations of his poetic and personal characteristics have typically invoked – and sought to illuminate – the 'obscure' identity which in the preface to *Poems, Chiefly in the Scottish Dialect* (1786) was one of Burns's strongest claims to public notice. This investment in 'obscurity' as a Burns family trait has proved curiously powerful and lasting; as recently as 1992, for example, one of the poet's biographers justified his researches by claiming that the 'origins' of the family (which are well known to have extended back into the seventeenth century) are still 'clouded'.[16] The obscure circumstance in which Burns 'was born a poet, if ever man was' has also been registered in the countering wish to dispel that original ambiguity, proving the authenticity of his 'nativity' (family background, birth, baptism, upbringing and education) implicitly by way of validating Burns's investment in *The Vision* as 'inspired Bard' of the 'native Muse'. Books such as *The Real Robert Burns* and *The Truth about Burns* (the latter reacting against 'ruthless' earlier biographies) explicitly announced their claims to revisionist authentication of the poet's life.[17] An identical suspicion of 'cloudiness' in the matter of Robert Burns is emphasised by a marginal note in the copy of James Currie's life of the poet in St Andrews University Library. In summarising

William Burnes's Kincardineshire background, Currie observes that '[h]is family having fallen into reduced circumstances, he was compelled to leave his home in his nineteenth year, and turned his steps towards the south, in quest of a livelihood'. A pencilled line beside this somewhat elliptical passage is accompanied by the charge, in a nineteenth-century hand: 'Ambiguity'.[18]

In these contexts of obscurity, indeterminacy and suspicion, the annual birthday toasts to the 'immortal memory' of Burns may be seen as a yearly ritual of affirmation and legitimation for a poet whose native circumstances seemingly threatened to compromise (rather than reinforce) the transparently 'unsophisticated' culture which he appeared to represent. And behind this troubling image of Burns was the strange affinity between the 'nameless Bard' and the powerfully 'obscure' focus of Romantic sublimity located by Edmund Burke in his *Philosophical Enquiry into the Origin of our Ideas of the Sublime and the Beautiful*: the shapeless figure of 'Death' in *Paradise Lost*.[19] This was an unhappy kinship, for it suggested that the mortal unravelling of Burns had been related to his sublime potential as the native poet of Scotland.[20]

NATIVE SOUNDNESS?

Our spirits rouze at an Original . . .[21]

It has been pointed out many times that Burns's popularity owed much to his success in responding to the revival of Scottish vernacular poetry, and his appeal to the late eighteenth-century cult of the 'primitive'.[22] The difficulties which stemmed from association with that second category have perhaps not been so fully appraised. Implicitly aligned against Johnsonian, metropolitan cultural values, the primitive was variously equated with pleasing simplicity, essential human feelings, the rural, the regional, the remote, the ancient. Its literary manifestations included James Macpherson's 'Ossian' poems *Fragments of Ancient Poems* (1760), *Fingal* (1762) and *Temora* (1763); Thomas Percy's *Reliques of Ancient English Poetry* (1765); James Beattie's *The Minstrel* (1771–4); Thomas Chatterton's 'Rowley Poems' (1777); Joseph Ritson's *Ancient Songs from the Time of King Henry the Third to the Revolution* (1790); Alexander Campbell's *History of Poetry in Scotland* (1798); Robert Bloomfield's *Farmer's Boy* (1800); and, later, James Hogg's *The Mountain Bard* (1807), and John Clare's collections of poetry such as *Poems Descriptive of Rural Life and Scenery* (1820).

One figure who was influential in this cultural movement was Hugh Blair, whose *Critical Dissertation on the Poems of Ossian* (1763) had welcomed Ossian's poems as 'genuine venerable monuments of very remote antiquity', adding in the second edition of 1765 that '[i]n Scotland, their authenticity was never called in question'.[23] The *Dissertation* was drawn from Blair's lectures on Rhetoric and Belles Lettres at Edinburgh University, and when published in 1783 the *Lectures* reiterated his praise for the 'plain and venerable manner of the antient times', celebrating Ossian's sublimity and wildness but also the more cultivated aspects of his 'beautiful and correct Metaphors'.[24] Meanwhile, the radical, *originary* preoccupation of contemporary literary fashion had been elaborated south of the border, in Edward Young's *Conjectures on Original Composition* (1759) and later in Thomas Warton's *History of English Poetry* (1774–81). In that book, Warton had sought 'to develope the dawnings of genius and to pursue the progress of our national poetry, from a rude origin and obscure beginnings', notably in poetry which 'transmitt[ed] to posterity genuine delineations of life in its simplest stages'.[25] David Fairer argues in the introduction to his edition of *The Correspondence of Thomas Warton* that the *History of English Poetry* encouraged a thoroughgoing transformation of British literary culture, such that the second half of the eighteenth century was 'more truly the Age of Warton than the age of Johnson'.[26] This gathering preoccupation with poetry's 'obscure beginnings' (personal and national) fostered the taste by which Burns's *Poems, Chiefly in the Scottish Dialect* would be enjoyed. It also formed the literary scene onto which William Lisle Bowles, Samuel Taylor Coleridge, Walter Scott, Charlotte Smith, Robert Southey, Helen Williams and William Wordsworth were subsequently to emerge.

As Ian McIntyre points out in his new biography of Burns, the poet had 'a pretty shrewd idea of the merit of his work' in *Poems, Chiefly in the Scottish Dialect*.[27] The preface to Burns's 1786 collection was very finely calculated to appeal to the prevailing fashion for 'originality': 'Unacquainted with the necessary requisites for commencing Poet by rule, he sings the sentiments and manners, he felt and saw in himself and his rustic compeers around him, in his and their native language'. Modestly deprecating any comparison with Allan Ramsay and Robert Fergusson (although 'he has often had [them] in his eye'), Burns announced himself as 'a Rhymer from his earliest years, at least from the earliest impulses of the softer passions', 'an obscure, nameless Bard'.[28] This preface was – and is – one of the canniest exercises in literary self-promotion ever penned. At a stroke, Burns had caught exactly the prevailing literary temper of the age, foregrounding the 'artless' qualities of simplicity, obscurity and vernacular originality which many contemporary readers relished. He was seeking quite deliberately to set out the terms on which his poetry would be read, and his early critical reception shows how fully he succeeded. According to his first readers, Burns's poems expressed 'native genius bursting through the obscurity of poverty' (*Edinburgh Magazine*, October 1786); 'artless and unadorned . . . flow[ing] . . . from the native feelings of the heart' (James Anderson, *Monthly Review*, December 1786); 'the force of native humour' (George Thomson, *London Chronicle*, July 1796); 'native brilliancy' (*Dumfries Journal*, August 1796); 'true effusions of genius ... promoted by its own native ardour as well as by friendly applause ... a power which nought can bestow, save native soundness' (Robert Heron, *Monthly Magazine*, June 1797).[29] Many other similar examples of 'native' approbation could be listed; but, for the moment, we might want to consider a simple question: was this echoing of Burns's own self-presentation quite as disinterested as it might at first appear? The forceful reaffirmation of Burns's preface by reviewers was entwined with a contrary strain in responses to Burns – a note of uncertainty, scepticism mingled with the 'friendly applause'. Was this 'nameless Bard' Robert Burns to be read with the indulgence which he sought? Was his 'obscurity' truly a guarantee of rustic authenticity, of '*native soundness*'? Were these poems indeed '*genuine* delineations of life in its simplest stages'?

The 'genuine' was a key concept in Warton's cultural lexicon. For him, 'genuine' denoted not only what was 'real' and 'true', it also defined what was 'native' in that it was of 'original stock', proceeding 'authentically' from its author or source.[30] The authenticity of Macpherson's ancient Scottish poems had been in question since their first publication in the 1760s, and debate about them continued well into the nineteenth century.[31] A similar controversy enveloped another 'obscure genius', the fifteenth-century cleric Thomas Rowley whose poems had been 'recovered' by Thomas Chatterton and published, after Chatterton's suicide, in 1777. Thomas Warton's *Enquiry into the Authenticity of the Poems Attributed to Thomas Rowley* (1782) proved that the Rowley poems were not in fact ancient verse, although Warton allowed that in other respects they were indeed 'genuine poetry': '[t]his youth, who died at eighteen, was a prodigy of genius: and would have proved the first of English poets, had he reached a maturer age'.[32] Chatterton the precocious youth might, in Warton's view, have achieved pre-eminence as an authentic, English national poet in his maturer years. Perhaps he would have done; certainly, John Keats regarded Chatterton as 'the purest writer in the English language'.[33] On the other hand, the 'unauthorised' register of Burns's 'dialect' poetry has dogged his reception right up to the present;[34] in its first manifestation, debate on this matter reflected the broader controversy between Johnsonian notions of linguistic decorum and the contrary fashion for 'unpolished' natural verse that was 'artless and unadorned'. The linguistic argument (focused neatly by Hugh Blair's 'corrections' of Burns's poems[35]) was, however, just one aspect of the larger question opened by *Poems, Chiefly in the Scottish Dialect*: how to authenticate Burns's claim to 'sing in his Country's service' as a genuine, native 'Scottish Bard', a successor to Ramsay, Fergusson and, perhaps, Ossian?[36] Burns's status as poet of his native place was rendered questionable (doubtful, and thus open to question) by the very obscurity from which his claim to aesthetic identity as a 'Scottish Bard' derived. Proving the legitimacy of Burns's 'nativity' would underline his cultural authority as a Scottish writer, and this imperative has produced the oddly paradoxical quest of those commentators who have sought to throw light on his 'obscurity' to prove that it was indeed genuine.

One of their strategies was to reiterate the various terms of Burns's self-presentation: his claim to native, rustic authenticity in the 1786 preface; his investment as 'inspired Bard' of the 'native Muse' in *The Vision*; his invocation of 'the rural scenes and rural pleasures of [his] natal Soil, in [his] native tongue' in the 1787 dedication.[37] Numerous commentators, as we've seen, applauded the 'native' qualities of the poems; a few, more perceptively, sought to trace the characteristics of his poetic voice to the circumstances of his origins – literally, to his birthplace and the authorising scene of Burns's nativity. It is in this obsession with verifying Burns's genealogy that we can detect most clearly the need to authenticate his claim to be poet of his native culture; to establish a bond between the poet's social milieu and its poetic articulation; to prove the legitimacy of Burns's conception and thus of the poetry which he created in later life. Ossian and Thomas Rowley shadow this quest back to the scene of the poet's nativity – ghostly witnesses to the contrary possibility that Burns's 'natural' poetry might arise from an obscurity which veiled the uncouth genius of the literary fake, the cultural betrayal of the 'Scottish Bard' revealed as a shapeless, nameless impostor.[38]

LEGITIMATING ROBERT BURNS

It was one of those births about which legends are told; but the present narrative is not concerned with legends. The facts are enough.[39]

The first chapter of Ian McIntyre's new *Life of Robert Burns* is a lively survey of Scottish contexts in the mid-eighteenth century embracing politics, literature, science, communications, industry, agriculture, religion, education and the church. This evocation of Scottish national life might well have served as an introduction to the biography, a narrative setting the cultural scene in which the poet would then have been introduced. In fact, McIntyre has opted to preface his cultural survey with a formal declaration of his subject's legitimacy. His book begins:

The entry in the Ayr parish register is of the briefest:
Robert Burns, lawful son to William Burns in Alloway, and Agnes Brown, his spouse, was born January 25, 1759; bapd. 26, by Mr William Dalrymple. Witnesses: John Tennant and Jas. Young.[40]

After this well-known certification of lawful parentage and baptism (duly witnessed), McIntyre reaffirms the nativity of his subject, then moves swiftly from the Ayr register to place Burns in a pantheon of international celebrities:

'Scotland's national poet was born', he writes, 'in the same year as William Pitt, Schiller and Mary Wollstonecraft, the near contemporary of Robespierre and Mozart, of Nelson and William Blake'.[41] The close of this first chapter circles back to the parish at Ayr, concluding: '[s]uch was the church into which Robert Burns was baptised in the penultimate year of the reign of George II[42] – although at this stage McIntyre has yet to finish his account of the birth. Burns's nativity is protracted further, in the next chapter, with the observation that a 'few days after the birth . . . in January 1759, there was a storm' and a quotation from Gilbert Burns's familiar anecdote about 'the young poet . . . carried through the storm to a neighbour's house'.[43]

McIntyre's account of Burns's birth, baptism and earliest days is the latest of many revisitings of those events, and it is striking to discover that this contemporary biographer repeats patterns and scenes of authentication which had been established in earlier accounts of his life. Obviously, Burns's biographers draw on a common fund of knowledge and sources, so that one would expect to find well-known and celebrated anecdotes repeated in even the freshest revaluation of the poet's life. What interests me, however, is the dynamic of McIntyre's narrative, setting out from the parish register recording the lawful birth and baptism of Scotland's national poet, only to return to the scene of baptism and, later, to another (secular) account of the circumstances of poet's birth. Thrice circled, the poet's origin, naming and the legitimacy of his inspiration are appropriately determined and consecrated.[44]

The beginnings of this Burns nativity rite, in biographical accounts and in the annual birthday celebrations in Burns clubs, can be traced back some 200 years. James Currie's introduction to the first collected edition of *The Works of Robert Burns* observed that 'this original genius . . . Robert Burns was in reality what he has been represented to be, a Scottish peasant' – an affirmation evidently intended to cancel doubts about the coincidence of 'reality' and 'representation' in the case of Robert Burns.[45] To enforce this authentication, Currie repeatedly invoked the poet's birth so that it became a kind of refrain in the biography: two brief references – 'Born in the condition of a peasant'; 'Robert Burns was, as is well known, the son of a farmer in Ayrshire' – were followed by Burns's autobiographical account in his letter to Dr Moore on 2 August 1787: 'I was born a very poor man's son'.[46] Twenty pages later, Currie warmed to the nativity theme once again:

Robert Burns was born on the 25th day of January 1759, in a small house about two miles from the town of Ayr, and within a few hundred yards of Alloway Church, which his poem *Tam o' Shanter* has rendered immortal. The name which the poet and his brother modernized into Burns, was originally Burnes or Burness.[47]

Two pages further on, Currie drew on Gilbert Burns's account of his parents as a further testimony:

> having built a house . . . with his own hands, [William Burnes] married in December 1757, Agnes Brown, the mother of our poet, who still survives. The first fruit of this marriage was Robert, the subject of these memoirs, born on the 25th of January 1759, as has already been mentioned.[48]

Gilbert Burns's narrative to Mrs Dunlop is followed, in turn, by the one written by the poet's tutor John Murdoch.[49] Currie said that the 'three relations' about the poet's forebears, birth and early life – by Burns himself, by his brother, and by Murdoch – served 'to authenticate each other', a statement which also betrayed a compelling need to establish the veracity of Burns's origin. Subsequent biographies proved that need both infectious and enduring – and readers caught it too: in the copy of Currie's edition in the University Library at St Andrews, readers have twice responded to Currie's narrative by calculating for themselves, in pencilled marginal notes, the year of Burns's birth and his age at death.[50]

BIGGININGS: PLACING BURNS'S NATIVITY

A peasant, born in a cottage that no sanitary inspector in these days would tolerate for a moment – (laughter) . . .[51]

A further important element in the authentication of Burns through reconstruction of his nativity was the place of the birth itself, the 'tabernacle of clay', as Murdoch described it, the edifice which would give physical substance to the 'reality' of his station in life as 'literally a ploughman'.[52] The 'auld, clay biggin' fashioned by the father's hands – mentioned over and over again in the Burns nativity narratives – is a kind of punning, substitutive figure for the conception of the child Burns inside the fleshly, amniotic 'biggin' of his mother's womb. The etymology of 'biggin' meaning a building, a cottage, or a cluster of houses, seems to have been separate from 'biggen', meaning to swell, grow larger, or to be pregnant, and also from 'biggin', meaning a child's cap (from the French *béguin*), but also – by analogy – the amnion or caul enveloping the foetus in the womb and regarded as a fortunate omen when retained on the child's head at birth. On the other hand, the *Scottish National Dictionary* also cites 'biggin', a building, as an extension of the verb 'big', the senses of which included 'To make a nest preparatory to hatching'. My point in tracing these verbal contexts is intended to suggest the range of associations that might be released by the invocation of 'biggin' at Burns's nativity: these include his paternal and maternal backgrounds, and also the superstitious auguries which informed narratives of the birth from *The Vision* onwards. Accounts of the physical 'biggining' of Burns, one might say, were crucial to the establishment of his subsequent social and cultural identity as a poet.

As we've seen, Currie noticed the 'small house about two miles from the town of Ayr, and within a few hundred yards of Alloway Church', but he added further details in a footnote:

> This house is on the right hand side of the road from Ayr to May-bole, which forms a part of the road from Glasgow to Port-Patrick. When the poet's father afterwards removed to Tarbolton parish, he sold his lease-hold right in this house and a few acres of land adjoining, to the corporation of shoe-makers in Ayr. It is now a country ale-house.[53]

Currie's account was repeated almost word for word in the 1814 Edinburgh edition of *The Poetical Works of Robert Burns*; the 1819 Ayr edition of *The Poems and Songs* added a few more details about the vernacular meaning of his place of birth:

> ROBERT BURNS, the eldest son of WILLIAM BURNES, originally from Kincardineshire, was born on the 25th of January, 1759, in that Cottage which, with its neighbours Allowa' kirk and the Auld Brig o' Doon, have acquired celebrity, as forming principal features of that charming portion of the classic ground of Caledonia. The Cottage is situated about two miles to the south of the town of Ayr, on the side of the road which runs through the district of Carrick to Portpatrick. The walls were originally of mud, and contained an apartment at each end, called a Butt and a Ben.[54]

The emphasis on ancestral and architectural *originality*, on the vernacular names for rooms in the cottage, and 'the classic ground of Caledonia' surrounding the birthplace, all reversed John Logan's early charge that Burns's 'novelty' stamped him as 'a *natural*, though not a *legitimate*, son of the muses'.[55] Furthermore, in the passage quoted above, we can see how Burns's birthplace, now precisely located in geographical terms, became identified as cultural *omphalos* through association with the 'biggining' of the poet's 'native genius'.

By 1819, 'that Cottage' was already well established as a shrine for literary pilgrims from Scotland and south of the border. In the summer of 1818, when the Ayr edition of *The Poems and Songs* was being readied for the press, John Keats and Charles Brown made their walking tour of Scotland visiting Burns's tomb at Dumfries on 1 July. Keats's sonnet 'On Visiting the Tomb of Burns', is a disquieting evocation of the brevity of Burns's life:

> The town, the churchyard, and the setting sun,
>   The clouds, the trees, the rounded hills all seem
>   Though beautiful, cold – strange – as in a dream
> I dreamed long ago. Now new begun,
> The short-lived, paly summer is but won
>   From winter's ague for one hour's gleam;
>   Through sapphire warm their stars do never beam;
> All is cold beauty; pain is never done
> For who has mind to relish, Minos-wise,
>   The real of beauty, free from that dead hue
>   Fickly imagination and sick pride
> Cast wan upon it! Burns! with honour due
>   I have oft honoured thee. Great shadow, hide
> Thy face, I sin against thy native skies.[56]

Keats associated Burns's northern landscape and 'native skies' with a cold, 'anti Grecian' spirit – recognising this at the same time as an outgrowth of English 'prejudice' against the Scots.[57] This visit to the grave, releasing a chilly apprehension of mortality, was an important stage on Keats's walking tour – not least because it established his encounter with Burns's native country as a passage from the place associated with Burns's death to the scene of his birth. 'I am approaching Burns's Cottage very fast', Keats wrote hurriedly to his friend John Hamilton Reynolds on 11 July 1818:

> We have made continual enquiries from the time we saw his Tomb at Dumfries – his name is of course known all about . . . One of the pleasantest means of annulling self is approaching such a shrine as the Cottage of Burns – we need not think of his misery – that is all gone – bad luck to it – . . . We were talking on different and indifferent things, when on a sudden we turned a corner upon the immediate Country of Air – the Sight was as rich as possible – I had no Conception that the native place of Burns was so beautiful – the Idea I had was more desolate, his rigs of Barley seemed always to me but a few strips of Green on a cold hill – O prejudice![58]

Keats's eagerness at the 'shrine' in prospect, coupled with the unexpected beauty of the landscape, wrought a surprising change in him: a banishment of 'prejudice' which (more significantly) amounted to a fresh 'conception' of Burns's native place and of the poet himself. Keats's approach to the birthplace effected, spontaneously, a personal identification with Burns's existence which also corresponded to the broadly nationalist purposes of the nativity narratives.

WITNESSING THE BIRTH

I think we can conceive him, in these early years, in that rough moorland country . . .[59]

The cottage itself was a disappointment for Keats (the curator irritated him, and he could only manage to write a flat, abortive sonnet on the occasion), but I want nevertheless to pursue the trajectory of Keats's walking tour as a voyage from the 'dead hue' of imagination at Dumfries, to the rich prospect of the cottage as a site of imagination's 'conception'. George Gilfillan's edition of *The National Burns* elaborated the birthplace motif in a direction that had already been signalled by Keats's letter. Gilfillan's is representative of the 'lurid' nineteenth-century accounts noticed by James Mackay, but there was also perhaps something more to his narrative than crude sensationalism.[60] The marriage of the parents, their early life together and the birth are presented by Gilfillan in a manner that clearly intimates a parallel with Christ's nativity:

> it was no golden land, only a humble house with a *but* and a *ben*, a hut, in which the boy Burns was to appear thirteen months afterwards; and beyond a piece of garden ground bordering on the sea, with the old road from Ayr to the south on its edge, a spot altogether consecrated to the genius of poverty and toil. But the 'golden land' lay in their mutual love, and that was soon to be sealed by the birth of the most extraordinary man in native power and genius Scotland ever produced.
>
> Thirteen months passed away in love and labour, the love sweetening the labour, the labour strengthening the love, till at last the consummation arrived. But Burns, who was not in the roll of common men, could not be like common men in the circumstances of his birth . . . It was fit that the handsel of Nature's great Scottish poet should be given by one of the genuine blasts of his own stormy sky.[61]

The reference to 'the handsel of Nature' was an echo of Burns's song 'There was a lad'. But, not content with hallowing the birthplace as the scene of a 'genuine' augury and 'consummation', Gilfillan went so far as to re-enact the natal scene itself, as if presiding over the poet's cradle:

> many years ago (in June 1846) we visited the 'auld clay biggin', at that time (and we believe still) a hostelrie for dispensing Burns' beloved beverage, and other good things of this life. We remember one rather

odd circumstance: when looking at the concealed bed in which the poet was born, our companion (the gifted Rev. Dr. W. B. Robertson of Irvine, the orator and poet of the West) exclaimed, 'Here's a laddie, here's wee Bobbie Burns!' A cry from the bed confirmed the words, and drawing near we tried to complete the *glamourie* of the scene by imagining that this boy who lifted up his arms and smiled was the inspired child to whose birthplace, in that humble cottage, the civilized world has flocked for well-nigh one hundred years.[62]

Gilfillan's wishful *glamour*, imagining Burns in his ('concealed') natal bed, arises from a deep and enduring need to give witness to the birth before 'the civilized world'. Here was originary vindication of Scott's contention that Burns was 'the child of passion and fancy', and of Coleridge's claim that Burns's genius had derived from childish inspiration, and was revealed in his ability to 'carry on the feelings of childhood into the powers of manhood; to combine the child's sense of wonder and novelty with the appearances, which every day for perhaps forty years had rendered familiar'.[63] The biblical tenor of Gilfillan's passage – 'that this boy who lifted up his arms and smiled was the inspired child'[64] – points further to the identification of Burns as prophet, a strategy calculated to efface his (equally childish) self-indulgence as a man.

The most remarkable account of Burns's prophetic election is probably the 'Spiritual Biography' which prefaces Hately Waddell's edition of *The Life and Works of Robert Burns* (1867). The life narrative is arranged in four parts which suggest the transcendental preoccupation of the narrative: 'Morning – On the Soil'; 'Mid-day – Above the Soil'; 'Gloaming – Return to the Soil'; 'Night, and After-Night – Underneath and Beyond the Soil'. As we might by now expect, the parenting and birth of the poet is explicitly paralleled with Christ's nativity:

It was of two such parents, thus briefly signalised – in many respects a lofty and remarkable pair; it was of such a mother above all, then in her twenty-seventh year, and doubtless to her glad relief, that Robert Burns was born, on the 25th of January, 1759: storms from the Atlantic that night prevailing, in which the gable of the new, half-seasoned, clay-built tenement gave way. Mother and child, for comfort and safety, were shortly afterwards removed to some neighbour's dwelling. Joy and merriment, we may believe, as well as bustle and anxiety, would abound on the occasion, and many sage auguries by wise women of the district would be made on the future of this boy; the pleasantest of which Agnes, with new-sprung maternal faith and hope, would thankfully treasure in her bosom. This son of hers, expelled by hurricanes from his cradle – why should not his destiny also be great, if not godlike?[65]

The stormy 'handsel' has been refigured as 'sage auguries by wise women' – again recalling 'There was a lad' and the gossiping palm-reader mentioned in that song. Those 'auguries' also invoke the 'good tidings of great joy' (Luke 2:10) which accompanied Christ's birth; similarly, the 'pleasantest' augury which Agnes Burns's 'maternal faith and hope . . . thankfully treasure[d] in her bosom' recalls Mary who 'kept all these things, and pondered them in her heart' (Luke 2:19).

'Let us look narrowly, reverentially for a moment, believing reader, into all this', Waddell continues:

> William Burnes the stern, taciturn, God-fearing man, and Agnes Brown the pure-hearted, truthful, loving woman, with the rich red hair and great dark eyes, have begotten a miracle; have become earthly co-editors for the world of a divinely-illuminated offspring. Is it not so? There can be no longer room for any reasonable doubt upon this subject. The finger of God is here. The simple-hearted Murdoch at last, with affectionate admiration, begins to be aware of this. William himself, according to tradition, already sees it, already knows it; and in whispers loud enough for the mother to hear (as if she knew it not!) reiterates in his decisive way, concerning this boy, that miraculous unfoldings shall yet come out of him. It was even so. Instincts like these in humble souls, from the mother and the night-watchers at Bethlehem downwards, are whispers from the invisible Shrine – infallible, eternal. The Prophet of the People, in short; the People's King, had been born at Alloway.[66]

John Murdoch, formerly one of James Currie's three authenticating voices, has become 'simple' witness to the miraculous nativity of Scotland's Messiah, Robert Burns. The desire for an empirical authentication of Burns, which dated from his first publication in 1786, has in Waddell's awe-struck sermon been overturned in favour of a renewed investment in mystery and an 'instinctive' awareness of divine providence at work in the 'obscurity' of the poet's origins. The rest of his life is treated in a similarly mystical fashion: '[i]t was one of the most remarkable circumstances of the social life of Robert Burns', Waddell says, 'that he was permitted from the first to worship, with a sort of adoration bordering on frenzy, the best, the most beautiful, and sometimes the most accomplished women, without offence or injury'.[67] All of this was of course 'pulpit trash', but intended to counter the charge (noticed at the start of this essay) that Burns's fleshly 'unfoldings' had a satanic power which 'injured and corrupted'. At his death, Waddell's Burns had 'overleaped and shaken off for ever' the 'entanglements' of the 'soil', entering 'the After-Life' of his posthumous reception:

He lives still for you and for the rest of us, because a portion of his earthly life remained still to live unexhausted, and due to posterity beyond himself, when he died. His life, in short, like his history, was an unfinished providence . . .[68]

The sublime possibility which had arisen from the obscure beginning of Burns's existence remains his most distinctive property after death, ambiguously 'living still . . . when he died'. Waddell deliberately framed himself as the minister of an 'unfinished providence', with Burns likened to Christ and (to follow Waddell's analogy) his editors and critics nominated as witnesses to the chaste authenticity of his life and word.

BURNS'S RESISTANCE TO ROMANTIC MYTH

Two hundred years dead, and yet his is one of the best known faces. But is it? Would you really recognise him if by some freak of time travel those two centuries ceased to stand between us?[69]

After his spiritual narrative of Burns's life, Waddell included as an appendix a grotesque testament to the poet's mortal existence: three engravings of his skull, based on the plaster cast taken in 1834 when his tomb was opened.[70] Waddell was interested in the skull as an 'anatomical comparison' for authentication of the recently-discovered 'Kerry Miniature' of Burns.[71] Even after his death, Burns's identity was traced from the obscurity of his native soil – in the exhumation of the skull (another 'auld, clay biggin') and in the pseudo-scientific phrenological examination to which the plaster cast was later subjected. George Combe's 'Observations on the Skull of Burns' traced the poet's predominant characteristics from the physical appearance of the bone. On examining the skull, Combe said that the poet had 'strong passions and great energy in action'; the organ of 'Philoprogenitiveness' (denoting love of offspring) was 'uncommonly [large] for a male head'; he had an 'ample endowment' in 'Acquisitiveness, Self-Esteem, and Love of Approbation', and his largest 'organs of moral sentiments' were 'Ideality, Wonder, Imitation, and Benevolence'.[72] The skull of a poet indeed: but Combe's final remarks return, surprisingly, to the notion that Burns's phrenological endowments had caused his downfall:

No Phrenologist can look upon this head, and consider the circumstances in which Burns was placed, without vivid feelings of regret. Burns must have walked the earth with a consciousness of great superiority over his associates in the station in which he was placed; of powers calculated for a far higher sphere than that which he was able to reach, and of passions which he could with difficulty restrain, and which it was fatal to indulge. If he had been placed from infancy in the higher ranks of life, liberally educated, and employed in pursuits corresponding to his powers, the inferior portion of his nature would have lost part of its energy, while his better qualities would have assumed a decided and permanent superiority.[73]

Here, the poet's 'superior' genius is seen as fatally at odds with the 'inferior portion of his nature' and 'the circumstances in which he was placed' from 'infancy': Burns's original situation in life – for so many critics the clouded source of his native strength, identity and achievement – had proved literally 'fatal' to him as a man. Combe has moved beyond the notion of Burns's antithetical nature noticed by Lord Byron, 'tenderness, roughness – delicacy, coarseness – sentiment, sensuality – soaring and grovelling, dirt and deity – all mixed up in that one compound of inspired clay!',[74] to disclose fatality as intrinsic to his existence as 'Scotland's Bard'.

'He died of being Robert Burns': Stevenson's claim invokes the self-consuming power of imaginative election, a predominantly masculine Romantic myth to which he would make a notable contribution himself. In the case of Robert Burns, congenial to a fault, dead on 21 July 1796 at the age of 37, Wordsworth's *Resolution and Independence* presented the enduring image:

> My whole life I have lived in pleasant thought,
> As if life's business were a summer mood;
> As if all needful things would come unsought
> To genial faith, still rich in genial good;
> But how can He expect that others should
> Build for him, sow for him, and at his call
> Love him, who for himself will take no heed at all?
>
> I thought of Chatterton, the marvellous Boy,
> The sleepless Soul that perished in its pride;
> Of Him who walked in glory and in joy
> Behind his plough, upon the mountain-side:
> By our own spirits are we deified;
> We Poets in our youth begin in gladness;
> But thereof comes in the end despondency and madness.[75]

Wordsworth's lines evoke the vulnerability of genius and imagination which he feared in his friend Coleridge, through a comparison with two other poets. The 'marvellous Boy' Chatterton, whose precocious gifts had been squandered, died in 1770 a suicide; Burns, here once again the 'nameless Bard' who came to public notice in 1786, is represented as a Christ-like figure of 'glory and joy' opening the furrow that would lead to despondency and an early grave. By pairing Burns with Chatterton, Wordsworth created a definitive Romantic image of 'deified' youth that was irrevocably doomed. Equally disconcerting was Wordsworth's twinning of two poets whose ambiguous originality mirrored his own insecurities. Yet Burns had already faced up to an interrogation on these matters himself:

> There, lanely, by the ingle-cheek,
> I sat and ey'd the spewing reek,
> That fill'd, wi' hoast-provoking smeek,
>   The auld, clay biggin;
> And heard the restless rattons squeak
>   About the riggin.
>
> All in this mottie, misty clime,
> I backward mus'd on wasted time,
> How I had spent my *youthfu' prime*,
>   An' done nae-thing,
> But stringing blethers up in rhyme
>   For fools to sing.

Having invoked Burns as a focus for his anxieties about writing poetry (and the capacities of his readers), Wordsworth moves in an opposite direction to recognise his own defence against despondency in the austere figure of the leech-gatherer, 'a man from some far region sent;/ To give . . . human strength, and apt admonishment'. In this encounter Wordsworth was, up to a point, following the example of *The Vision* where Burns's gloomy retrospect was succeeded by the arrival of his 'native Muse'. The similarity ends there, however, for Burns's poem effectively pre-empted the destructive teleology of 'gladness' and 'madness' by welcoming the muse as a figure calculated to play upon those mortal weaknesses regretted by Wordsworth and generations of commentators. She appears,

> bleezan bright,
> A tight, outlandish *Hizzie*, braw,
>   Come full in sight.

Not only does she appeal to the susceptibilities of Burns's 'social life':

> Down flow'd her robe, a *tartan* sheen,
> Till half a leg was scrimply seen;

> And such a *leg*! my BESS, I ween,
> Could only peer it;
> Sae straight, sae taper, tight and clean,
> Nane else came near it.

She also affirms his strategy of self-presentation in *Poems, Chiefly in the Scottish Dialect* by urging him: 'never murmur or repine;/ Strive in thy *humble sphere* to shine;/ . . . A *rustic Bard*'. Childlike, obscure, self-willed, careless, damaged, Burns (like Coleridge) cannot easily be reduced to the tragic category of 'mighty Poet in [his] misery dead', nor does Byron's list of antithetical qualities quite answer to the global presence of Burns's personality. Missing, perhaps, from all of these romantic attempts to bring Burns out of the mist as man and as poet is a facility remarked by Keats, and which Burns seems also to have understood more thoroughly than his biographers and critics: 'The Genius of Poetry must work out its own salvation in a man . . . That which is creative must create itself'.[76] If this was true of Scotland's '*own* inspired Bard', it also remains so for that '*well-known* Land'.

NOTES

1. *Lord Byron. The Complete Poetical Works*, ed. J. J. McGann, 7 vols (Oxford, 1980–93),V, p. 203.
2. *The Daily Scotsman* (26 January 1859).
3. 'Pulpit Trash', *The Daily Scotsman* (24 January 1859).
4. For the editorial 'censorship' of political, social and sexual aspects of Burns, see G. Ross Roy, 'Editing Burns in the Nineteenth Century', in Kenneth Simpson (ed.), *Burns Now* (Edinburgh, 1994), pp. 129–49.
5. *The Life and Works of Robert Burns. By P. Hately Waddell* (Glasgow, 1867), p. li; William Wordsworth, 'A Letter to a Friend of Robert Burns' (London, 1816), in *The Prose Works of William Wordsworth*, ed. W. J. B. Owen and J. W. Smyser, 3 vols (Oxford, 1974), III, p. 119; *The Family Edition. The Works of Robert Burns*, ed. 'Gertrude', 2 vols (Glasgow and London, 1874), I, p. 1; Robert Louis Stevenson, 'Some Aspects of Robert Burns' (1872), in *The Works of Robert Louis Stevenson*, 25 vols (London, 1911–12), III, p. 65. For Hazlitt's response to Wordsworth, see his 1818 lecture 'On Burns, and the Old English Ballads', in *The Complete Works of William Hazlitt*, ed. P. P. Howe, 21 vols (London, 1930–4), V, p. 129: 'poor Burns remains just where he was, and nobody gains any thing by the cause but Mr. Wordsworth, in an increasing opinion of his own wisdom and purity'.
6. 'Leigh Hunt on Robert Burns', *The Daily Scotsman* (24 January 1859).
7. See *The Autobiography of Alfred Austin. Poet Laureate 1835–1910*, 2 vols (London, 1911), II, p. 288, and 'The Poet Laureate on the Bard's Genius', *The Scotsman* (20 July 1896).
8. 'The Poet Laureate on the Bard's Genius', *The Scotsman* (20 July 1896).

9. *The Glasgow Herald* (22 July 1896), p. 6, and *The St Andrews Citizen* (25 July 1896), p. 4.

10. See, for example, Lockhart's diagnosis of Keats's poetical 'disease' in 'Cockney School of Poetry. No IV', *Blackwood's Edinburgh Magazine* (August 1818), 519. See also the Preface to *Adonais*, where Shelley writes: 'The savage criticism on his *Endymion*, which appeared in the *Quarterly Review*, produced the most violent effect on his susceptible mind; the agitation thus originated ended in the rupture of a blood-vessel in the lungs; a rapid consumption ensued'. *Shelley's Poetry and Prose*, ed. Donald Reiman and Sharon Powers (New York and London, 1977), p. 391.

11. Quoted from Donald A. Low (ed.), *Robert Burns. The Critical Heritage* (London and Boston, 1974), p. 115.

12. Memoir of Burns in the *Monthly Magazine* (June 1797), quoted from *Robert Burns. The Critical Heritage*, pp. 124–5.

13. *Apostle to Burns. The Diaries of William Grierson*, ed. John Davies (Edinburgh, 1981), p. 63; entry for Monday 25 July 1796; 'Some Aspects of Robert Burns', p. 70.

14. See, for example, the controversy in the *Glasgow Herald* (22 July 1896), following Alfred Austin's centenary speech.

15. John Wilson, 'On the Genius and Character of Burns', in *The Works of Robert Burns*, 2 vols (Glasgow, Edinburgh and London, 1855), I, p. xi.

16. James Mackay, *A Life of Robert Burns* (Edinburgh, 1992), pp. 17–26.

17. See J. L. Hughes, *The Real Robert Burns* (London and Edinburgh, 1922), and D. McNaught, *The Truth about Burns* (Glasgow, 1921), p. 13.

18. *The Works of Robert Burns; with an Account of his Life, and a Criticism on his Writings*, 2nd edn, 4 vols (London, 1801), I, p. 57, hereafter Currie, *Works of Robert Burns*.

19. See Edmund Burke, *A Philosophical Enquiry into the Origin of our Ideas of the Sublime and the Beautiful*, ed. Adam Phillips (Oxford, 1990), especially 'Section II. Obscurity', pp. 54–5.

20. For the Burkean association of indeterminacy, sublimity and 'Death', see in particular Lucy Newlyn, *'Paradise Lost' and the Romantic Reader* (Oxford, 1992), pp. 196–204.

21. Edward Young, *Conjectures on Original Composition* (1759), ed. Edith J. Morley (Manchester, 1918), p. 7.

22. See, for example, L. M. Angus-Butterworth, *Robert Burns and the 18th-Century Revival in Scottish Vernacular Poetry* (Aberdeen, 1969), and Marilyn Butler, *Romantics, Rebels and Reactionaries. English Literature and its Background 1760–1830* (Oxford, 1981), p. 35.

23. *A Critical Dissertation on the Poems of Ossian, the Son of Fingal*, 2nd edn (London, 1765), p. 133. For the 'sceptical' and 'mixed' responses to Ossian in Scotland and elsewhere, see Fiona Stafford, *The Sublime Savage. A Study of James Macpherson and the Poems of Ossian* (Edinburgh, 1988), pp. 163–80.

24. Hugh Blair, *Lectures on Rhetoric and Belles Lettres*, 2 vols (London, 1783), I, pp. 65, 307.

25. Thomas Warton, *The History of English Poetry, from the Close of the Eleventh to the Commencement of the Eighteenth Century*, 3 vols (London, 1774–81), I, pp. ii–iii.

26. *The Correspondence of Thomas Warton*, ed. David Fairer (Athens GA and London, 1995), pp. xviii–xix.
27. See *Dirt and Deity. A Life of Robert Burns* (London, 1995), p. 81.
28. *Poems, Chiefly in the Scottish Dialect, by Robert Burns* (Kilmarnock, 1786), pp. iii–v, hereafter *Poems* (1786), the text of the poems quoted here.
29. See *Burns. The Critical Heritage*, pp. 64, 71–2, 100, 104, 121, 124.
30. See in *OED* senses 2, 3 and 4a of 'genuine'. The word is related to 'ingenuous', the senses of which are also significant in relation to Burns's reception; they include 'freeborn', 'open, guileless, innocent, artless' and 'native' and 'natural'.
31. See Stafford, pp. 163, 170.
32. *History of English Poetry*, II, p. 157.
33. John Keats to J. H. Reynolds, Winchester, 21 September 1819, in *The Letters of John Keats*, ed. Hyder Rollins, 2 vols (Cambridge MA, 1972), II, p. 167. Keats's remark may well have been influenced by the Wartonian associations at Winchester; Thomas Warton's brother Joseph had been headmaster at Winchester School.
34. In the recent Penguin edition of *Robert Burns. Selected Poems*, ed. Carol McGuirk (London, 1993), p. xv, the 'non-standard, protean vocabulary' of the poems is recognised as 'confusing' yet 'central to his vision'.
35. See *Burns. The Critical Heritage*, pp. 81–2.
36. See the dedication to *Poems, Chiefly in the Scottish Dialect* (Edinburgh, 1787), p. v, hereafter *Poems* (1787).
37. See *Poems* (1786), pp. iii, 92, and *Poems* (1787), p. vi.
38. The need to establish national confidence in Burns's genealogy may well have been encouraged further by the sharply rising incidence of illegitimate births among the poor during the eighteenth century. For a pertinent discussion, see Alan Liu, 'The Tragedy of the Family: *The Borderers*', in *Wordsworth. The Sense of History* (Stanford, 1988), pp. 225–310 and especially p. 255.
39. Catherine Carswell, *The Life of Robert Burns* (London, 1930), p. 39.
40. Ian McIntyre, *Dirt and Deity. A Life of Robert Burns* (London, 1995), p. 1.
41. Ibid., p. 1.
42. Ibid., p. 11.
43. Ibid., p. 13.
44. For an identical pattern of consecration, see Franklyn Snyder, *The Life of Robert Burns* (New York, 1932), pp. 32–40, which opens with the parish register, then moves through William Burnes's and Agnes Brown's backgrounds and marriage, leading up to Robert's birth and baptism. See also Hugh Douglas, *Robert Burns – A Life* (London, 1976), pp. 21–2, where Burns's inheritance of 'the creative spark' from his mother is discussed before 'the arrival of her first child', thus 'taking us ahead of the story'.
45. Currie, *Works of Robert Burns*, I, p. 2.
46. Ibid., I, pp. 30, 33, 37.
47. Ibid., I, p. 57.
48. Ibid., I, p. 58.
49. Ibid., I, pp. 86–96.
50. See the copy of Currie, *Works of Robert Burns*, I, pp. 34, 219, in the Special Collections Department in the University Library, St Andrews.
51. Lord Rosebery's speech (and the audience response) at the centenary of Burns's death, reported in the *Glasgow Herald* (22 July 1896), p. 9.

52. Currie, *Works of Robert Burns*, I, p. 87; George Thomson, *London Chronicle* (July 1796), in *Burns. The Critical Heritage*, p. 99.
53. Currie, *Works of Robert Burns*, I, p. 57.
54. *The Poems and Songs of Robert Burns with a New Sketch of his Life* (Ayr, 1819), p. ii.
55. *English Review* (February, 1787), in *Burns. The Critical Heritage*, p. 76.
56. Quoted from *John Keats. Selected Poems*, ed. Nicholas Roe (London, 1995), p. 159.
57. *The Letters of John Keats*, ed. Hyder Rollins, 2 vols (Cambridge MA, 1972), I, p. 309.
58. *The Letters of John Keats*, I, pp. 322–3.
59. Robert Louis Stevenson, 'Some Aspects of Robert Burns', p. 50.
60. Mackay's own account is in fact sufficiently melodramatic: 'One can imagine poor William struggling through the stormy darkness to get his wife and baby safely lodged with a neighbour. By daylight, when the storm showed no sign of abating, he returned to the cottage to repair the ravages of the cruel west wind'. See James Mackay, pp. 27, 29.
61. *The National Burns*, ed. George Gilfillan, 4 vols (London, Glasgow and Edinburgh, 1879–80), I, p. iii. Compare *The Works of Robert Burns*, ed. William Scott Douglas, 6 vols (Edinburgh, 1877–9), I, p. 7, which has the cottage as 'a Mecca to northern patriots'.
62. *The National Burns*, I, p. iii.
63. See Scott's review in the *Quarterly Review* (February 1809), in *Burns. The Critical Heritage*, p. 199, and *Biographia Literaria*, ed. J. Engell and W. J. Bate, 2 vols (London and Princeton, 1983), I, pp. 80–1.
64. Compare Luke 2:40: 'the child grew, and waxed strong in spirit, filled with wisdom: and the grace of God was upon him'.
65. *The Life and Work of Robert Burns. By P. Hately Waddell* (Glasgow, 1867), p. xi.
66. Ibid., p. xi.
67. Ibid., p. li.
68. Ibid., p. lv.
69. Duncan Macmillan, 'An Altered Image of the Bard', *The Scotsman* (25 January 1996).
70. See the 'Appendix' in *The Life and Work of Robert Burns. By P. Hately Waddell*, pp. lxvii–lxxxi, and James Mackay, pp. 681–2.
71. Compare the recent (re)assertion, at the bicentenary of Burns's death, that Alexander Nasmyth's portrait of him is 'authentic beyond doubt'; 'An Altered Image of the Bard', *The Scotsman* (25 January 1996).
72. George Combe, 'Observations on the Skull of Robert Burns', in Robert Cox, *An Essay on the Character and Cerebral Development of Robert Burns* (Edinburgh, 1859), pp. 24–5.
73. Ibid., p. 26.
74. See *Byron's Letters and Journals*, ed. Leslie A. Marchand, 13 vols (London, 1973–84), III, p. 239.
75. Quoted from *William Wordsworth. Selected Poetry*, ed. Nicholas Roe (London, 1992), pp. 185–6.
76. Letter to J. A. Hessey, 8 October 1818, *The Letters of John Keats*, ed. Hyder E. Rollins, 2 vols (Cambridge MA, 1958), I, p. 374.

THE COTTER'S KAILYARD

Andrew Nash

A cotter lives in a cottage, a kailyard is a cabbage-patch. So far, so straightforward. But the fate of Burns's poetry in nineteenth-century Scotland, and particularly the fate of his then most admired poem 'The Cotter's Saturday Night', meant that it was the cultural authority of Robert Burns which was used by later writers and critics as a subtle and essential underpinning for the literary phenomenon in nineteenth-century Scottish culture which we know as Kailyard. It is an accepted thesis that the term Kailyard refers to a much wider spectrum of Scottish culture than the fiction which traditionally bears its name.[1] J. H. Millar, in an article in the *New Review* in 1895, labelled as the Kailyard School a trio of writers whose novel-writing careers began in the late 1880s: J. M. Barrie, Ian Maclaren and S. R. Crockett. The early novels of these three writers were internationally a popular success and were lauded by critics in Britain, North America and other parts of the English-speaking world. Kailyard is in truth a complex and widespread phenomenon, elusive in definition. Both admired and execrated by writers and critics in Scotland and beyond over the last 100 years, the Kailyard novels, with their discourse of the rural, the parochial, the domestic and the sentimental, have set the tone for many representations of Scotland from Barrie's Thrums and Maclaren's Drumtochty to the music-hall lyrics of Harry Lauder and such films as *Whisky Galore* (1949), *Brigadoon* (1954) and *Local Hero* (1983). In literature and other media, Kailyard is still with us, for good and ill, despite Hugh MacDiarmid's attempts to eradicate it with the intellectual equivalent of a flamethrower. Kailyard has been stretched to describe a general condition of Scottish culture. Frequently used in a rather generalised fashion as a synonym for Tartanry and referred to in present-day sociological studies,[2] Kailyard is now seen as part of the false stereotype which is marketed as Scotland's true national distinctiveness; a 'deformed' and '"pathological" discourse', readily ploughed in forms of popular culture, that is 'inadequate to the task of dealing with the reality of Scottish life'.[3]

The reason why Kailyard writing has acquired and retains such cultural significance is thus because of its perceived potential to market and validate an authoritative identity for Scotland. Modern-day attacks on modern-day Kailyard culture (which is usually seen as including television programmes like *Dr Finlay's Casebook* and (*Take the*) *High Road* and strip cartoons like 'Oor Wullie' and 'The Broons' in the *Sunday Post*) take place on the assumption that a simplistic, highly cheapening stereotype is in danger of being marketed as Scotland's cultural identity. In the 1890s, this is very much what happened. Contemporary readers of Barrie, Crockett and Maclaren understood this literature as imparting a mimetic description of life in Scotland and of what it meant to be Scottish. This essay will attempt to address one of the reasons why this might have happened – why readers had been encouraged to approach Scottish literature in a certain way, and why literature had come to hold such a powerful potential to market and validate an authoritative identity for Scotland. My argument is that the process of reception which was applied to Burns in the nineteenth century, which identified him as the national expression of Scotland, helped to prioritise certain subject matter as peculiarly distinctive to the Scottish literary capacity – subject matter that would be utilised by the Kailyard writers. More than that, Burns's influential, selective readers and critics also had a crucial effect in the establishing of a function for Scottish literature: literature was identified as the richest source available for understanding (or for constructing) Scottish identity. So, from being a figure who set about contesting the forms of cultural authority of his time, Burns was appropriated, and in a very strong way, by forces eager to impose their own patterns of cultural authority.

Nineteenth-century Burns critics did not make any radical departures from the already established conventions; far from it, the critical heritage was laid out firmly by critics of the Enlightenment period. The two seminal events in early Burns criticism were the review of *Poems, Chiefly in the Scottish Dialect* (1786) by Henry Mackenzie in *The Lounger*, and the first collected edition of the poems edited by James Currie in 1800. Mackenzie's name, which became in literary circles interchangeable with the title of his novel *The Man of Feeling*, was the paradigm of the Enlightenment ideal of common-sense philosophy and virtuous sensibility. His review typified the Enlightenment's general reception of Burns which seized on the rural and domestic characteristics of the poetry, enabling Burns to be accommodated to primitivist theories. It is significant that, in advertising the poems, Burns's publishers linked the work to advertisements for *The Lounger* and *The Mirror* (both periodicals edited by Mackenzie) and with Mackenzie's own novels. Marketed in this way, Burns became the 'Heaven-taught ploughman', and 'The Cotter's Saturday Night' was established as his most popular poem and declared to be his best. The poem is, above all, a celebration of a way of life, of 'the lowly train in life's sequester'd scene'. The 'toil-worn cotter' returns home from a cold November day to join his contented family in

a meal and a reading from the Bible. What Burns does that is most significant, however, is to designate the scene as being strongly characteristic of
Scotland:

> From scenes like these, old Scotia's grandeur springs,
> That makes her lov'd at home, rever'd abroad:
> Princes and Lords are but the breath of kings,
> 'An honest man's the noble work of God:'
> And certes, in fair virtue's heavenly road,
> The cottage leaves the palace far behind.
>
>   (163–8)[4]

Scotland's grandeur is thus declared to be best typified by scenes of simple
subsistence living and communal and familial bonding.

From the very beginning, Burns was being accommodated to philosophical
or political theories; and because of the nature of Enlightenment theories,
which, as in the case of Mackenzie, sought to fix strong ties between an
author and his text, biographical investigation was established as a primary
critical methodology. But, as Nicholas Roe's essay in this volume has suggested, instead of using biography to understand the poetry, the poetry was
used as a tool for the principal aim, which was the uncovering of Burns the
man. The kind of man that writers of the Enlightenment period were eager
to uncover was the man who not only wrote 'The Cotter's Saturday Night'
but who also experienced its sentiments; it established itself as Burns's most
popular poem because it offered the suggestion that the Enlightenment ideal
of 'virtuous sensibility' was evident in the *real* conditions of human life.
Burns *was* the cotter:

> [it] proves that the manners of our rustics can afford subjects for
> Pastoral Poetry more elevated and more amiable than those which are
> exhibited in Gay's 'Shepherd's Week'; that Pastoral Poetry needs not
> to employ itself upon the fictitious manners, and modes of life, but
> may, with higher poetical advantages paint the humble virtues, the
> simple pleasures, the inartificial manners of our peasantry, such as they
> *actually exist.*[5]

The stance adopted here easily allows for critical practice to be carried into
the realms of social history, and that is very much what happened.

James Currie's editorial judgements in the first collected edition of 1800
crystallised this idea that it wasn't just helpful to know Burns's life to understand his poetry; the two were entirely coexistent: 'If fiction be, as some
suppose, the soul of poetry, no one had ever less pretensions to the name of

poet than Burns', he argued.[6] Burns's poetry was not about art or imagination, it was about revealing reality, reality as felt by a ploughman in Scotland:

> the subjects on which he has written, are seldom, if ever, imaginary; his poems, as well as his letters, may be considered as the effusions of his sensibility, and the transcript of his own musings on the *real* incidents of his humble life.[7]

As we shall see, it is from this context that later critics would come to align the sensibility issue explicitly with topographical representation and national expression. Burns became identified as Scotland's Burns, and Scotland became identified as 'The Cotter's Saturday Night'. It is significant, in this context, that Duncan Macmillan has argued for Wilkie's painting *The Cotter's Saturday Night* (1837) as forming *'the* canonical image of Scottish art',[8] and the influence of Burns on the development of nineteenth-century Scottish genre painting is readily discernible. For example, Tom Faed depicts a 'Cotter's Saturday Night'-type setting in *The Scottish Emigrants' Sunday in the Backwoods* where a communal Bible-reading is taking place around a hearth in a humble cottage, the wall of which is neatly adorned by a portrait of Burns.[9] Nineteenth-century commentators were to make much of this canonical image which spread across disciplines, and the effect was not only to consolidate as a representation of Scotland the sentimental celebration of ruralism and domesticity, but also to make it the case that nineteenth-century Scottish identity was seen as predominantly literary. Literature was promoted as the best way of understanding Scotland, and it is partly because of this, I argue, that Kailyard writing was later to be received by its contemporary critics as a document of life in Scotland. The conventions of reading Burns that were established and built on throughout the century had made it the case that any Scottish literature, whether realism, romance or fantasy, was understood as revealing the constituents of Scottish identity.

Editions of the poems were crucial in imparting a specific view of Burns, and those of the early nineteenth century built on the work of Mackenzie and Currie. David Groves has analysed the editorial practice of William Motherwell in his coedition of 1834–6 where he expurgated much of James Hogg's notes in order to 'join the chorus of condescending, uncritical praise'.[10] Allan Cunningham's various editions beginning in 1834 furthered the importance of understanding the West of Scotland topography, and most of the editions were beginning to be accompanied by landscape illustrations. By encouraging readers to approach Burns's poetry with an accompanying set of visual references, editors were giving greater currency to the understanding of Burns as a poet who laid bare the realities of everyday life in Scotland in the manner of a tourist's guidebook. Indeed, when the tourist industry began to gather pace in mid-century, it was the land of Scott and the land of Burns that the guidebooks highlighted and to which the visitors flocked.

The most notable text that was to help tie Burns up with visual topography was *The Land of Burns* (1840), which featured a series of portraits by the pioneer of photography D. O. Hill, and descriptive prose directing the reader to topographical references. This text also presented to the reading public for the first time a highly influential essay by John Wilson, entitled 'The Genius and Character of Burns'. This long essay was also published separately before appearing again in what was to prove to be the most significant text (in terms of number of reprints) that the century was to produce: the 1843 edition, published by Blackie, entitled *The Works of Robert Burns; with Dr. Currie's Memoir of the Poet, and an essay on his Genius and Character by Professor Wilson*. This edition thus kept Currie's highly distorting biographical account and juxtaposed it with the long introductory essay by Wilson. These texts were seminal in influencing critical opinion of Burns. The 1843 edition was reprinted at least sixteen times between 1846 and 1878, Wilson's memoir was cited as being 'incomparably the best' at the 1859 centenary celebrations in Paisley,[11] and it was the 1847 reprint together with *The Land of Burns* and the Hogg/Motherwell text that the Boston Burns Club, for example, purchased in 1851.[12] Because of their success and widespread distribution, Wilson's articles, memoirs and editions gave an even stronger currency to established topics that would reverberate throughout the century: elevating the spiritual status of the poor, representing rural, peasant Scotland as the supposedly essential Scotland, understanding literature through topography, preserving the past through literature; and, significantly, understanding Scotland through literature. Such an emphasis on essentialism with regard to the definition of Scotland has left a sometimes troublesome, sometimes enabling legacy.

Writing in *Blackwood's Magazine* in 1819, Wilson described a 'depth of moral and religious feeling in the peasantry of Scotland' that could not be found in England; 'a great poet could not be born among the English peasantry', he argued, whereas Scotland was blessed by 'a spirit of poetry' because 'Religion', 'imagination' and 'a beautiful country' enables 'those higher and purer feelings which, in less happy lands, are possessed only by the higher ranks of society, [to be] brought into free play over all the bosom of society'.[13] Wilson is clearly groping for an identifiable national distinctiveness here, and he uses Burns's status as a peasant-poet to mark Scotland off from England:

> The fireside of an English cottage is often a scene of happiness and virtue; but unquestionably, in the 'Cotter's Saturday Night' of Burns, we feel, that we are reading the records of a purer, simpler, more pious

race; and there is in that immortal poem a depth of domestic joy – an intensity of the feeling of home – a presiding spirit of love – and a lofty enthusiasm of religion, which are all peculiarly Scottish, and beyond the pitch of mind of any other people.[14]

It is in the peasantry, Wilson is arguing, that you find the true Scotland; and in the same way as the Kailyard writers will be perceived as having translated their Scottishness into literature, Wilson consolidates the Enlightenment tradition by arguing that the peasantry of Scotland was 'not surveyed and speculated on by him [Burns] as the field of poetry, but as the field of his own existence'.[15] Such an approach erases the significance of point of view in the poetry. Because his criticism leads from the assumption that Burns is *'feeling'* 'The Cotter's Saturday Night', Wilson is unable to draw attention to the stance adopted by Burns vis-à-vis his immediate audience, which is established in the first stanza to be the lawyer Robert Aiken to whom the poem is dedicated. The significance of Burns's consciousness of describing the 'simple Scottish lays' to a refined, professional audience cannot be accommodated. To Wilson it's obvious: read Burns and you understand peasant Scotland, and, because peasant Scotland is unique, you understand what is unique to Scotland. This enables Burns's poetry 'to form a part of the *existence* of the Scottish peasantry',[16] and, in the same way as was to happen with Kailyard, to be *received* as social history, never mind its artistic technique: 'Burns's great calling here below was to illustrate the peasant life of Scotland. Ages may pass without another arising for that task; meanwhile the whole pageant of Scottish life has passed away without record.'[17]

Because Burns was seen as recording Scotland, then together with the international reception of Scott literature came to be identified as the way of understanding Scottish identity. With Burns, the Scotland that was being understood was Wilson's Scotland – rural, peasant, domestic Scotland – a Scotland which was to become the blueprint for the future course of Scottish literature. In this way, Wilson was able to use Burns to transmit his own political creed: in Burns's pictures of the poor, he argues, you do not see 'slaves sullenly labouring, or madly leaping in their chains, but in nature's bondage, content with their toil, sedate in their sufferings, in their recreations full of mirth – [they] are seen Free Men'.[18] That could hardly be a better description of the pictures of the poor to be found in such novels as J. M. Barrie's *A Window in Thrums* (1889), S. R. Crockett's *The Stickit Minister* (1893) and Ian Maclaren's *Beside the Bonnie Brier Bush* (1894). Wilson had established, through consolidating the presentation of Burns as Scotland personified, a blueprint for similar representations of Scotland in the future and had denied the validity of anything different, anything that in any way challenged the contentment of the poor. He had manipulated an identity for Scottish literature that was not only to restrict the scope available for future writers but also to manipulate the reader into approaching Scottish literature in a certain way. Literature dealing with the negative effects of Scotland's industrial development *did* exist, but it was subordinated in the canon because it could not be accommodated into the established idea of Scotland. It is only recently that such literature has begun to be recovered.[19] The archetype for the Kailyard and its hordes of international readers remained 'The Cotter's Saturday Night':

> he might have done far more good than he has done – had he delighted less in painting the corruptions of religion, than in delineating her native and indestructible beauty. 'The Cotter's Saturday Night' shews what he could have done – had he surveyed, with a calm and untroubled eye, all the influences of our religion, carried as they are into the inmost heart of society by our simple and beautiful forms of worship.[20]

The selective understanding of Burns that Wilson had consolidated from the Enlightenment period remained in force throughout the century. 'The Cotter's Saturday Night' was still identified as the key to his work and thus to Scottish national character: to a critic in 1849, the belief remained that 'everything else that he wrote may be considered as auxiliary to the purpose shadowed forth in that poem',[21] and that it was a poem where 'the rural scenes are real scenes'.[22]

In the second half of the century, the focus of criticism was still directed towards using the poem as a tool for understanding the man: Wilson had used 'The Cotter's Saturday Night' to defend the morality of Burns; and, apart from J. C. Shairp, who argued that the poem showed 'how Burns could reverence the old national piety, however little he may have been able to practise it',[23] this poem remained the evidence used by critics who were eager to rectify what they saw as wrongful prevailing opinion of Burns's moral character.[24] Biographies and editions remained the most significant output. In the opening speech of the internationally-reported 1896 exhibition marking the centenary of Burns's death, the chairman, Alexander Kirkpatrick, revealed just how strong the significance of Burns's life was: 'It was a life about which no biography or autobiography can tell us all we want to know. We want to get nearer to his life . . . Here you will see much of what you want to see. You will see the mirror on which he saw his own face.'[25] That biography was still at the forefront of Burns criticism is significant because of the way in which Burns had been identified as the personification of Scotland. What was said about Burns's character was understood as Scottish character. The poet laureate Alfred Austin, for example, speaking at the same 1896 centenary celebrations, argued that Scottish people found Burns 'extolling the very ideas of life and conduct which are at the root of Scottish character'. To an Englishman, Austin continued, these presented themselves as 'the strong foundation of adamantine will . . . self-reverence, self-control, self-denial, and, above all, the sanctifying grace of domestic piety'.[26] Such was the view of a prominent literary non-Scot. The extent of the equation of Burns with Scotland is driven home most succinctly by George Gilfillan's 1879 edition, which declared Burns to be 'the greatest National Poet that ever lived . . . a living image of his country . . . a microcosm of his nation'.[27] It was unanimous that by understanding Burns you were understanding Scotland. What is significant, in terms of the origins of the Kailyard, was that there was an acute awareness of the *need* to understand: 'The cause of a country is never utterly hopeless: the character of a people is never absolutely degraded; the sentence of national ruin is never finally and fatally sealed until popular song is silenced'.[28] The overwhelming tone of decadence is applied here to Burns and popular song; elsewhere it is Burns and the preservation of the perishing Doric.[29] Burns had become a lingering relic of what was seen as a fast-vanishing Scotland, and Burns-worship formed part of the nostalgic reminiscing for that Scotland which characterised the Scottish intellectual climate in the period after 1830. The taste for Kailyard owes a great deal to the tremendous amount of volumes of 'Reminiscences' published in the second half of the century which anecdotally recorded characteristics of Scottish life deemed to be fast vanishing away.[30] And one important manifestation of this condition of nostalgia can be seen existing as an intermediary between Burns and the Kailyard: the motivation behind the writing of Kailyard fiction can be linked to that behind the extensive production of song-collections made throughout the nineteenth century, a great number of which have since been derided for failing to deal with the real conditions of early industrial Scotland. Here again, Burns looms large.

It is significant that some of the most prominent Burns commentators of the early nineteenth century were the men who were at the centre of this song-collecting. Cunningham has already been mentioned. Robert Tannahill, R. A. Smith and William Motherwell were the early leaders of the Paisley Burns club formed in 1805. The most common aspect of all the early Burns clubs was the extensive number of imitations, odes and panegyrics to Burns that were delivered at the yearly celebrations. Robert Brown's exhaustive survey of the Paisley Burns clubs reveals the extent of this imitative practice, which often found a place in appendices to nineteenth-century editions, Blackie's 1843 text being particularly bountiful. Later in the century, the *Burns Chronicle* magazine would include a lengthy list of examples in the bibliographies of its early numbers. Many of these imitations delivered in the early meetings of the Burns clubs were subsequently published on their own standing in volumes such as Motherwell's *The Harp of Renfrewshire* (1819). The implication of this is that a 'living' literature was conceived and delivered under the banner of Burns. Instead of forwarding literature, the

Burns clubs could in this sense be argued to have frozen it, and in the process to have frozen a marketable Scottish identity at a time when it was perceived as moving into a stage of irreparable transition. It would be generalising to say that the early Burns clubs were wholly bad, as they undoubtedly provided a vital forum for the promotion and discussion of the arts in Scotland. But in their overriding emphasis on identifying Burns's poetry as a fixed archetype for the future development of Scottish literature, they helped to set up and fix a canon of taste that was to last throughout the century. The eagerness on the part of the clubs to establish a central place for Burns in the schools indicates just one facet of their attempts to identify in the minds of the Scottish people a national identity that came out of literature.

The conventions established for understanding Burns easily allowed him to become the ultimate example of the vanishing Scotland identified by the editors of the song-collections. Motherwell's motives are laid out in the introduction to his *Minstrelsy: Ancient and Modern* (1827). He identified a need to preserve a fast-dying culture, as 'the changes which, within this half century, the manners and habits of our peasantry and labouring classes, with whom this song has been cherished, have undergone, are inimical to its further preservation'.[31] Within this context, the declared reality of 'The Cotter's Saturday Night' took on an even greater significance; it became seen as a reality that had been captured and put in a frame to be immortalised forever: Alexander Webster called it 'a photograph from life',[32] and to another critic it was a 'picture . . . in print'.[33] The words 'picture' and 'photograph' are revealing. The poem is standing here as an act of social history: it has freeze-framed history so that it can always be a part of our own experience.

Linked to this predisposition for nostalgia was the reception of Burns by emigrant Scots now uprooted from their former rural lives – emigrants who would later afford Kailyard, and popular entertainers like Harry Lauder, an immense following. Wilson had drawn attention to the reception of Burns by exiled Scots and had used it to identify an essential Scotland that the exiles could draw out of Burns and live in again.[34] In an address at the unveiling of the statue of Burns in Central Park, New York, on 2 October 1880, George William Curtis addressed the crowds:

> Most of you, fellow citizens, were born in Scotland. There is no more beautiful country, and as you stand here, memory and imagination recall your native land . . . as if all the sadness of shaggy Scotland had found a voice![35]

'Essential Scotland', Curtis went on to declare, 'would live forever in the poet's verse'.[36] The extent of international interest in Burns can be observed by the exhaustive records of exhibitions, speeches and ceremonies assembled by James Ballantine in the *Chronicle of the Hundredth Birthday of*

Robert Burns.[37] Ballantine chronicles 872 celebrations across Britain, America and the colonies, and the one in Copenhagen. Incredibly, John McVie estimates that this figure represents only 5 per cent of the total number of celebrations that took place across the world.[38] The combination of Burns scholarship and Burns clubs meant that, everywhere, international Scottish identity was a 'Cotter's Saturday Night' identity.

American circles also appropriated Burns as a champion of liberty and egalitarianism;[39] and, although this was also a facet of British criticism,[40] the latter was more particularly characterised by a strong interest in the compatibility of Burns and religion, and it is in this context that I want now to identify how Burns criticism of the last third of the century is characteristic of a larger context on offer for understanding the Kailyard and late nineteenth-century literature generally – literature as a substitute religion. For this, we must return once more to the beginnings of the critical heritage to see how Burns became inextricably tied up with the issue of the moral function of literature.

As well as constructing Burns as Scotland personified, the bias towards biography in criticism had another effect. If it had been established that Burns's poetry *was* Burns, then this inevitably elevated the significance of Burns's private life, the ethics of which duly became a core component in any assessment of the poetry. Currie's introduction has been cited by Carol McGuirk as the origin of 'virtually every moralising picture and mythic obliquity in the critical heritage'.[41] Nineteenth-century critics would draw their judgements from this heritage, appropriating Burns for their own differing social and philosophical theories.

Currie's evaluation was that Burns's was a genius that had fallen short of its maximum realisation, and subsequent critics built on this emerging pattern of debate. Scott, with his Enlightenment entrenched belief in the importance of famous men leading by moral example, and Carlyle, with his search for a vitalistic prophet to replace God, concluded similarly that Burns had squandered his singular gift and had proved unable to assume his position as a leader of men. As the century wore on, the need, identified by Carlyle, Arnold and others, to find something to replace the worn-out garments of traditional Christianity became ever more acute, and the critical reception of Burns in the last third of the nineteenth century is indicative of the gradual development towards identifying literature as a substitute religion. It has been argued by Chris Baldick that it was at this time, and in response to the crisis over religion, that the academic discipline of English Literature was developed in the English universities.[42] With the growth in industrialisation and urbanisation, the widening spread of literacy and the explosion of the newspapers, orthodox religion was beginning to be seen as no longer equipped to serve a society so sharply transformed. The orthodox structures of the Church had fractured, in Scotland more so than in

England, into a tumult of ecclesiastical dissension. It has been argued that it
is in this context that the ideological motivation for Kailyard was born; that
it should be seen as a response to the need for a literature to perform an
ennobling and ethical function for the masses.[43] Burns criticism can be characterised as identifying the same need.

For Carlyle, Burns's 'memoirs' contained an 'important moral lesson',[44]
but whereas for him it was a negative lesson, for the vast majority of critics
in the last third of the century Burns came to be seen as a moral teacher and
his poetry as sermons. One critic identifies him as the incarnate of the
Second Coming: 'Mankind, astonished, heard God returning and calling to
them aloud in the songs of a ploughman'.[45] The Songs, which had been
purified from their coarse eighteenth-century origins, and 'The Cotter's
Saturday Night' were now equated with the Psalms[46] and cited as 'the best
and most frequently read sermon since apostolic times'.[47] Poetry and religion were seen as emanating from the same spirit,[48] and the poet was thus
able to be identified as a prophet. Carlyle would not have argued with the
following sentiments:

> It has been one of the worst errors of our modern religionists of all
> creeds for many generations, to ignore such manifestations of the
> Divine Mind; as if there was not a God in the Intellect as well as in the
> history of the Church and Tabernacle![49]

It was in this intellectual context that religious journalism, typified by the
Christian Leader and the *British Weekly*, rose up and allowed the likes of Ian
Maclaren and S. R. Crockett to move from being ministers in the church to
men of letters. The *Christian Leader* was where the bulk of Crockett's early
novels were first published, either in serialised form as in the case of *The
Lilac Sunbonnet* (1894), or as individual short stories that were later collected and published in novel form, as with *The Stickit Minister*. Crockett
eventually gave up his post as a Free Church minister in Penicuik to become
a full-time writer. Ian Maclaren, by contrast, remained first and foremost an
active minister, even when his earliest and most successful books, *Beside the
Bonnie Brier Bush* and *The Days of Auld Langsyne* (1895), proved both to
be well received by the establishment and to be outrageous best-sellers.
Both novels were collections of individual short stories that Maclaren had
published in the *British Weekly*. The editor of that newspaper was William
Robertson Nicoll, another former Free Church minister, who, as literary
advisor to the publishers Hodder and Stoughton, held a strong arm of
influence over the character of one particular branch of journalism and
book-publishing in the 1890s. Although J. M. Barrie's debt to this particular newspaper has been rather overstated, the *British Weekly* was a crucial

vehicle in the dissemination of the fiction of Ian Maclaren with its strong emphasis on the role of the church in town and village.

The *British Weekly* project which Nicoll fronted from 1886 was very much geared towards building bridges between journalism, literature and religion, and formed part of a body of opinion that, in reaction to the excessive ecclesiastical and denominational disputes that had developed, called for a rational religion that was expressly not based on any specific dogma or creed:

> I had always thought that religious papers did not give enough direct religious instruction, and that the leading articles should be mainly devoted to this, not to ecclesiastical matters or politics or literature chiefly, but to religion.[50]

Maclaren's fiction, which repeatedly elevates a simple, straightforward Christianity based on 'a gude word for Jesus Christ'[51] over the corrupting influence of ecclesiastical and doctrinal religion, must be seen in this context; indeed, it could be argued that he was hired by Nicoll for the exact purpose of transmitting a literary-religious message in the pages of the *British Weekly*. Thus the wider context for the Kailyard, so far as we restrict it largely to Maclaren, is to see this writing as following Carlyle in identifying the book (and the newspaper) as a potential pulpit.

Burns critics of the time were equally adept at identifying literature in this way. The *British Weekly*'s subtitle was 'A Journal of Social and Christian Progress', and it can thus be contextualised in the kind of contemporary thinking that stressed progress, advancement and the pursuit of knowledge as paramount in church and society. It was 'Rational Theology', 'the pursuit of knowledge' and 'a system of development' which emerged as the formula for society held by Alexander Webster, whose extensive writings on Burns and religion form the apotheosis of what was a flourishing practice. Webster outlined his own theology and then cited Burns as a great exemplum:

> To attain to rational conviction men must determine that the conditions of religious thought shall be such as enable the mind to act freely. There must be no bondage to any creed, no committal to any dogma, no fear of ecclesiastical power . . . But Burns saw that such was being done in effect by ecclesiastical power.[52]

Having established that Burns believed in universal salvation and in 'a good God, or the over-ruler of Nature and the Father of Man' and that he saw it as his life's work to rid his 'brethren' of the 'intellectual irreligion' that was their belief in the Devil,[53] Webster is able to present Burns as a critical voice on the church of his day – satirising the corruption in 'The Holy Fair', under-mining superstition in 'Tam o' Shanter', and generally challenging the power of the clergy and the lairds in the mould of a latter-day Hebrew prophet, because 'it has ever been the work of the prophet to oppose the Priest'.[54] The anonymous critic of the *Essay for the Working Classes* similarly saw 'The Cotter's Saturday Night' as fulfilling the 'noblest purpose . . . the diffusion of a system of pure religion',[55] and the Rev. James Forrest likewise declared that to Burns 'religion was not a matter of theological creeds and ecclesiastical observances, but rather a divine reality, native to the heart',[56] sentiments that were echoed by the Rev. George Gilfillan.[57] Burns's patrio-tism, argued Forrest, his humanitarianism and his celebration of the home, which were the keys to his poetry, formulated the '*sine qua non* of all religion'.[58]

The place that Burns took in this proclivity for prioritising the ethical function of literature which was, in part, characteristic of the 1880s and 1890s can be best summed up by J. Logie Robertson's note to 'The Cotter's Saturday Night' in his edition of 1889:

> It could be ill spared from any collection of Burns's poetry less on account of its poetical merit than because of its historical and ethical value. It contains many feeble lines, but in the descriptive it is a faithful transcript from peasant life, and in the reflective parts it bears testimony to the moral character of the author. It reveals at once his religion and his patriotism.[59]

What matters to this critic is Burns's morality and his fidelity to reality, not his Art. Robertson here brings together all the strands of the nineteenth century's reception of Burns.

It is also very relevant, in terms of the projection of literature and literary figures as replacements for Christianity, that the years 1870–1900 form an intense period of institutional manifestation of the Burns cult. Around 77 per cent of the Burns clubs formed before 1900 began in the period 1870–99, and this figure is not conspicuously inflated by the 1896 cente-nary year (the figure is nearly 65 per cent for the period 1870–95). Indeed, of those clubs which had been instituted much earlier in the century, many experienced a period of dormancy in the mid-century, only renewing activity in the 1870s and 1880s.[60] In addition, ten memorials were unveiled during the period 1872–92 compared with only four before those dates.[61] The Burns Federation was established in 1885, and in 1891 the *Burns Chronicle*. So, notwithstanding the fact that Burns bardolatry had clearly been born much earlier, the last third of the century was an especially significant time in the identifying and marketing of Burns as national poet and national Messiah.

It is this institutional manifestation of the Burns cult that was to so aggrieve Hugh MacDiarmid because, as we have seen, wherever Burns was marketed so was Scotland. With literature afforded such a crucial status in the construction of a national identity, it is not surprising that the kind of Scotland presented by the Kailyard novelists should similarly aggrieve MacDiarmid and that it should likewise prove that wherever Kailyard was marketed so was Scotland. This is why the selective realism of Kailyard novels – the charge of their having evaded the darker side of contemporary Scottish reality – has proved to be such an important and recurrent topic of discussion. 'The Cotter's Saturday Night' was a powerful, canonic national image, and the subject matter of the Kailyard novels and the way that readers responded to them is indicative of the pervasiveness of that image. For the most part, Barrie, Crockett and Maclaren write of villages that are resistant to and at times seemingly unaware of the outside world. Additionally, the range of social experience offered in Kailyard novels is almost entirely restricted to the poor, but very much to the comfortably-off poor. Like the cotter, the Kailyard families don't want anything more than porridge, but they also don't have to worry where the next bowl is coming from.

Kailyard novels celebrate the values of family and community. Ian Maclaren's fiction can perhaps best be described as the creation of a Godly Commonwealth village. A story in *The Days of Auld Langsyne* presents a tyrannous Episcopalian factor who refuses to renew the lease of his tenant farmer unless farmer Burnbrae agrees to leave the Free Church. Burnbrae duly refuses and leaves his farm. The iconic image of the 'Cotter's Saturday Night' is threatened, and this allows Maclaren to indulge in some anti-city, pro-country sentiment:

> a townsman may be born in one city and educated in a second, and married in a third, and work in a fourth. His houses are but inns which he uses and forgets, he has no roots and is a vagrant on the face of the earth. But the countryman is born and bred, and marries and toils and dies on one farm . . . His roots are struck deep in the soil, and if you tear them up his heart withers and dies . . . For it is not a house this farmer leaves: it is his life.[62]

Burnbrae's farm holdings are put up for auction, and the parish rallies round. Another farmer, Drumsheugh, calls for the people to bid high prices for Burnbrae's stock: 'there's ae thing in oor poo'er. We can see that Burnbrae hes a gude roup, an', gin he maun leave us, that he cairries eneuch tae keep him an' the gudewife for the rest o' their days' (DALS, 69). And this they do. But that is not all. Burnbrae makes a stirring plea to the landowner himself, Lord Kilspindie. His argument is that throughout history the farmer and the Earl have lived happily side by side: 'For twa hundred years an' mair there's been a Baxter at Burnbrae and a Hay at Kilspindie, ane wes juist a workin' farmer, an' ither a belated earl, but gude freends an' faithfu' (DALS, 88–9). Moved by the simplicity of the rhetoric, Lord Kilspindie makes sure that the lease is returned to Burnbrae. The cotter is contented with his lot, and, in so being, could teach the Earl a thing or two. As we have seen, this was very much the nineteenth-century interpretation of Burns's poem. To cap it all, the parish honourably returns all of Burnbrae's stock free of charge, and the strength of the Godly Commonwealth is reasserted. The cotter can go back to his farm and cottage.

The family, which is at the heart of Burns's image, is identified in Kailyard novels as the key to understanding Scottish character: 'So much of what is great in Scotland has sprung from the closeness of the family ties', writes J. M. Barrie in *Margaret Ogilvy*; 'You only know the shell of a Scot until you have entered his home circle'.[63] Kailyard takes us into the home circle, it allows us to glimpse the family content by the fireside and frequently explores the pains of family break-up. In another Maclaren story, in *Beside the Bonnie Brier Bush*, Flora Campbell runs away from her home rather than face the Session over 'a case of discipline' (BBBB, 129). It is typical of Maclaren that he does not stoop to tell us the nature of Flora's crime; she had simply 'gone astray'. Without his daughter, Lachlan Campbell is a lost man, and once more the 'Cotter's Saturday Night' image is the one evoked by Maclaren in order to dramatise the nature of his loss:

> The minister walked with Lachlan to the foot of the hill on which his cottage stood, and after they had shaken hands in silence, he watched the old man's figure in the cold moonlight till he disappeared into the forsaken home, *where the fire had gone out of the hearth*, and neither love nor hope were waiting for a broken heart. (BBBB, 133; my emphasis)

Campbell reaches for the Bible, just as the cotter had done. But in it he has scored out the name of his daughter where her mother's name and his are written. With Maclaren, however, there is always a happy ending. Flora is persuaded to return by the kindly intervention of another villager, and in the Bible the returning prodigal writes her name, reasserting the 'Cotter's Saturday Night' picture.

Maclaren's novels milked established conventions, and the reading public loved it. Reacting against these conventions, against the cultural authority that had been applied to Burns and 'The Cotter's Saturday Night', was to become part of the rationale of the twentieth-century Scottish Renaissance movement. In the first editorial of the first edition of *The Scottish Chapbook* (August 1922), Hugh MacDiarmid, or C. M. Grieve as he then was, anticipates 'A New Movement in Scottish Literature'. The Kailyard is identified as being part of the old movement: 'Scottish writers have been terrified even to appear inconstant to established conventions.

(Good wine would have needed no 'Bonnie Brier Bush'.)'⁶⁴ The challenge of being inconstant to established conventions, of breaking out of the nineteenth century's construction of Burns and Scotland, was what lay before MacDiarmid and the 'New Movement in Scottish Literature'.

NOTES

1. This was the critical approach taken, for example, by Ian Campbell in *Kailyard* (Edinburgh: Ramsay Head Press, 1981).
2. See, for example, David McCrone, *Understanding Scotland: The Sociology of a Stateless Nation* (London and New York: Routledge, 1992).
3. Colin McArthur, introduction to *Scotch Reels: Scotland in Cinema and Televison* (London: BFI Publishing, 1982), pp. 2–3.
4. *The Poems and Songs of Robert Burns*, ed. James Kinsley, 3 vols (Oxford: Clarendon Press, 1968), I, p. 151.
5. Robert Heron, *Observations made in a Journey through the Western Counties of Scotland* (1793), quoted in Donald Low (ed.), *Robert Burns: The Critical Heritage* (London: Routledge, 1974), p. 97 (my emphasis).
6. James Currie, 'Criticism on the writings of Burns', *The Works of Robert Burns, with an Account of his Life* (1800), quoted in *Robert Burns: The Critical Heritage*, p. 132.
7. Ibid. (my emphasis).
8. Duncan Macmillan, 'The Canon in Scottish art: Scottish art in the canon', *Scotlands*, 1 (1994), 87–103 (p. 91; his emphasis).
9. For a reproduction of this picture, see Mary McKerrow, *The Faeds: A Biography* (Edinburgh: Canongate, 1982), p. 100.
10. David Groves, 'James Hogg on Robert Burns', *Burns Chronicle*, 100 (1991), 51–9 (p. 53).
11. Robert Brown, *Paisley Burns Clubs 1805–1893* (Paisley: Alexander Gardner, 1893), p. 229.
12. 'Boston Burns Club, America', in J. W. Egerer, *A Bibliography of Robert Burns* (Edinburgh and London: Oliver & Boyd, 1964), pp. 317–18 (p. 317).
13. John Wilson, 'Some Observations on the Poetry of the Agricultural and that of the Pastoral District of Scotland, illustrated by a Comparative View of the Genius of Burns and the Ettrick Shepherd', in *Blackwood's Magazine*, 4 (February 1819), quoted in *Robert Burns: The Critical Heritage*, p. 309.
14. Ibid., p. 310.
15. John Wilson, 'The Genius and Character of Burns' (1840), reprinted in *Essays: Critical and Imaginative*, vol. III (Edinburgh and London: William Blackwood, 1857), 1–211 (p. 1).
16. 'Some Observations . . .', op. cit., p. 315 (my emphasis).
17. 'The Genius and Character of Burns', op. cit., p. 177.
18. Ibid., p. 224.
19. See William Donaldson, *Popular Literature in Victorian Scotland* (Aberdeen: Aberdeen University Press, 1986); William Findlay, 'Reclaiming Local Literature: William Thom and Janet Hamilton', in *The History of Scottish*

Literature: Volume 3, Nineteenth Century, ed. Douglas Gifford, gen. ed. Cairns Craig (Aberdeen: Aberdeen University Press, 1988), pp. 353–75.

20. 'Some Observations . . .', op. cit., p. 316 (my emphasis).

21. Samuel Tyler, *Robert Burns as a Poet and a Man* (Dublin: James M'Glashan, 1849), p. 60.

22. Ibid., p. 55.

23. Principal Shairp, *Robert Burns* (London: Macmillan, 1879), p. 196.

24. See, for example, Peter Livingston, *Poems and Songs; with Lectures on the Genius and Works of Burns*, 8th edn (Dundee: John Durham, 1871), p. 19; [A Scotchwoman,] *Robert Burns: An Inquiry into Certain Aspects of his Life and Character and the Moral Influence of his Poetry* (London: Elliot Stock, 1886).

25. Quoted in *Burns Chronicle*, 6 (1897), 13.

26. Ibid., pp. 28–9.

27. George Gilfillan, 'Life of Burns', in *The National Burns* (London, Glasgow, Edinburgh: William Mackenzie, [1879?]), IV, p. cv.

28. Alex M. Walker, *A Lecture on the Poems and Songs of Burns* (Tunbridge Wells: John Colbran, 1860), pp. 42–3.

29. For this, see, for example, P. Hately Waddell, *Genius and Morality of Robert Burns* (Ayr: Ayrshire Express Office, 1859), pp. 4–17; R. W. Hunter, *A Hundred Years After: Burns under the Light of the Higher Criticism* (Edinburgh, 1896), p. 5; Lord Rosebery's speech at the Dumfries centenary celebrations, *Burns Chronicle*, 6 (1897), 46.

30. The pioneering work was E. B. Ramsay's *Reminiscences of Scottish Life and Character* (1857), which went through twenty-two editions within fifteen years.

31. *Minstrelsy: Ancient and Modern*, with an Historical Introduction and Notes by William Motherwell (Glasgow: John Wylie, 1827), p. cii.

32. Alexander Webster, *Burns and the Kirk: A Review of what the Poet did for the Religious and Social Regeneration of the Scottish People* (Aberdeen: A. Martin, 1889), p. 66.

33. *Burns: An Essay for the Working-Classes of Scotland. Part I: His Influence as a Moral Teacher and Social Reformer* (Edinburgh: MacLachlan and Stewart, 1872), pp. 20–1.

34. 'The Genius and Character of Burns', op. cit., p. 227.

35. George William Curtis, *Robert Burns: An Address* (New York, printed for private circulation, 1880), pp. 5, 8.

36. Ibid., p. 21.

37. *Chronicle of the Hundredth Birthday of Robert Burns*, collected and edited by James Ballantine (Edinburgh and London: A. Fullarton, 1859). For further records of Burns's reception by emigrant Scots, see 'Burns in America: a late nineteenth-century view', in *Robert Burns: The Critical Heritage*, pp. 439–40 (p. 439); William Brown, 'Burns and New Zealand', *Burns Chronicle*, [7] (1958), 69–73.

38. John McVie, *The Burns Federation: A Bi-Centenary Review* (Kilmarnock: Burns Federation, 1959), p. 33.

39. For this, see 'Burns in America: a late nineteenth-century view', op. cit., p. 440; Wallace Brue, 'The Influence of Robert Burns on American Literature', *Burns Chronicle*, 1 (1892), 43–6.

40. See, for example, Livingston, p. 23; Tyler, p. 56; and Webster, passim, who integrates a religious and political argument.

41. Carol McGuirk, 'The Politics of *The Collected Burns*', in W. N. Herbert and Richard Price (eds), *Gairfish Discovery* (Bridge of Weir: Gairfish, 1991), p. 37.
42. Chris Baldick, *The Social Mission of English Criticism 1848–1932* (Oxford: Clarendon Press, 1983).
43. See Peter Keating, *The Haunted Study: A Social History of the English Novel 1875–1914* (London: Secker & Warburg, 1989), p. 338; Thomas Knowles, *Ideology, Art and Commerce: Aspects of Literary Sociology in the Late Victorian Scottish Kailyard* (Gothenburg: Acta Universitatis Gothoburgensis, 1983); A. Whigham-Price, 'W. Robertson Nicoll and the Genesis of the Kailyard School', *Durham University Journal*, 86:1 (1994), 73–82.
44. Donald A. Low, introduction to *Robert Burns: The Critical Heritage*, op. cit., p. 42.
45. Hately Waddell, p. 46.
46. Ibid., pp. 26–7; and George Gilfillan, 'Life of Burns', op. cit., I, p. xxii.
47. Hunter, p. 12.
48. See, for example, the introduction to 'The Cottar's Saturday Night' in *The Complete Works of Robert Burns*, ed. William Scott Douglas (London: Swan Sonnenschin, 1890), p. 65.
49. Hately Waddell, p. 26.
50. Quoted in T. H. Darlow, *William Robertson Nicoll: Life and Letters* (London: Hodder and Stoughton, 1925), p. 69.
51. Ian Maclaren, *Beside the Bonnie Brier Bush* (London: Hodder and Stoughton, 1894), p. 87.
52. Webster, pp. 25–6.
53. Ibid., pp. 46, 90.
54. Ibid., p. 24.
55. *Burns: An Essay for the Working-Classes of Scotland*, op. cit., p. 22.
56. Rev. James Forrest, 'The Religion of Burns', *Burns Chronicle*, 2 (1893), 95–104 (p. 97).
57. George Gilfillan, 'Life of Burns', op. cit., IV, pp. ciii–civ.
58. Forrest, op. cit., p. 102.
59. Note to 'A Cottar's Saturday Night', in Robert Burns, *Selected Poems*, ed. with an Introduction, Notes and Glossary by J. Logie Robertson (Oxford: Clarendon Press, 1889), p. 206.
60. This is true of Kilmarnock, Greenock and Paisley: see James A. Mackay, *The Burns Federation 1885–1985* (Kilmarnock: The Burns Federation, 1885), pp. 9–21; D. M'Naught, 'Kilmarnock Burns Club', *Burns Chronicle*, 4 (1895), 90–9; Charles L. Brodie, 'Greenock Burns Club: A Sketch of its History', *Burns Chronicle*, [5] (1927), 124–30, James Thomson, 'Paisley Burns Club: A Sketch of its History', *Burns Chronicle*, [5] (1927), 131–4.
61. For these figures, see 'The Posthumous History of Robert Burns', *Burns Chronicle*, 1 (1891), 14–38.
62. Ian Maclaren, *The Days of Auld Langsyne* (London: Hodder and Stoughton, 1895), pp. 55–6.
63. J. M. Barrie, *Margaret Ogilvy* (1896) (Uniform Edition, London: Hodder and Stoughton, 1932), pp. 18, 122.
64. C. M. Grieve, 'A New Movement in Scottish Literature', repr. in *Hugh MacDiarmid: Selected Prose*, ed. Alan Riach (Manchester: Carcanet, 1992), pp. 3–8 (p. 5).

MACDIARMID'S BURNS

Alan Riach

The American poet Charles Olson, prompted by an invitation to a conference, responded with 'Letter for Melville 1951'.[1] Appended to the title was
the following note:

> *written to be read AWAY FROM the Melville Society's 'One Hundredth
> Birthday Party' for MOBY DICK at Williams College, Labor Day Weekend,
> Sept. 2–4, 1951.*

An angry assault upon the academic conference (a 'false and dirty thing')
and the organisers ('a bunch of commercial travellers'), the letter was directed
at Melville scholars who, in Olson's view, had betrayed and cheapened the
great writer by reducing him to what Olson's biographer calls 'a clichéd
banquet commodity': 'carry my damnations to each of them', wrote Olson,

> as they sit upon their arse-bones variously
> however differently padded.

Eight years later, the 1959 Edinburgh Festival commissioned the composer
Iain Hamilton to produce a work to celebrate the bicentenary of the birth of
Robert Burns. Burns was already a clichéd banquet commodity and a
national monument. Hamilton, immersed in Schoenbergian theories of
dodecaphonic music bristlingly antagonistic to melody and lyricism, presented his *Sinfonia for Two Orchestras*, and the performance was received
with outrage. John Purser explains:

> Hamilton, knowing well enough that most of Scotland would be
> hoping for something more akin to the splendid and cheerfully tonal
> work of a Cedric Thorpe-Davie . . . produced a powerful and uncom-
> promising essay in which he honoured Burns, not in the remembrance,
> but by producing the most adventurous Scottish score of his day.

198

It was, Purser judges, 'a courageous act'.[2]

Two creative responses to two conventional forms of celebration, one academic, the other public: together, they illustrate the overlaps between the fields of creative artistry, academic commodification and public dominion. It's essential to keep these discrete but overlapping fields in mind when we come to MacDiarmid, because his understanding of the tensions and the conflicts of interest between them was acute, and that acuity energises all his writings and speeches about Burns.

It would be a straightforward job to discuss MacDiarmid's Burns in Harold Bloom's terms. The anxiety of influence is clear enough. I remember telling MacDiarmid that I thought that no-one could really go forward in Scotland until they'd done to him what he'd done to Burns. He smiled cheekily and said: 'Yes, but I'm much more difficult to deal with'.

But Burns wasn't easy to deal with, and MacDiarmid spent a lot of time and energy, reams of paper and oceans of ink, trying to write him into his proper space. A discussion of MacDiarmid's Burns takes us to the heart of the conflict between popularity and élitism which runs through all Mac-Diarmid's work (and was of deeper concern to Burns than many suspect).

C. M. Grieve did not grow up under the influence. His father, James Grieve, was such a devout Presbyterian that he refused to have Burns's poems in the house. 'Burns', MacDiarmid wrote, 'was taboo in my father's house and quite unknown to me as a boy.'[3] Yet in 'Kinsfolk' MacDiarmid seems fond enough of his memory of his father to present him without irony in a light reminiscent of 'The Cotter's Saturday Night': 'a kindly, gin conscientious, man':

> Fearless but peacefu', and to man's and God's
> Service gi'en owre accordin' to his lichts
> But fondest o' his ain fireside o' nichts.
> (*Complete Poems*, p. 1,148)[4]

But MacDiarmid said he wished his home life as a child had acquainted him with Burns as it had his teacher, friend and mentor, F. G. Scott, in whose home Burns was more popular among the family than the Bible. And at school, MacDiarmid claimed, he learned only one or two of the more hackneyed love songs.[5] Burns would have been 'in the air' though, and Burns club celebrations around 25 January would have been familiar enough. But it was as a young journalist in Wales in 1911 that Grieve met Keir Hardie, whose love for Burns must have offered a spontaneous example of poetry taken up into a political context by an imposing personality, mediated less by academic interest or conventional morality than by immediate apprehension of the appropriate words and sentiments.[6]

After the First World War, Grieve's burgeoning interest in Scottish literature brought together his intellectual concerns, patriotism and personality. It was one thing to recognise the popular bourgeois Burns cult and its clubs and to see Burns as the source of innumerable polite platitudes; it was another thing to hear Burns effortlessly quoted by a man such as Keir Hardie; and it was another thing again to read G. Gregory Smith's *Scottish Literature: Character and Influence* (1919) and to find a scholarly, academic description of Burns as a poet to be classed with Ramsay and Fergusson as authors of the final efflorescence of poetry in vernacular Scots before the long decline.

In 1922, as a delegate of the Montrose Burns club, Grieve attended the annual conference of the Burns Federation in Birmingham. The re-election of Duncan McNaught to the presidency of the Federation prompted a sonnet praising the man 'Whose service followed where the great song sped!' but also hinting at what was to come:

> Burns International! The mighty cry
> Prophetic of eventual brotherhood
> Rings still, imperative to be fulfilled.
> M'Naught, who follows you must surely try
> To take his stand where, living, Burns had stood
> Nor save on this foundation can he build.
>
> (p. 1,224)

Grieve's declaration at the conference drew attention not only to his faith but also to his own unique qualifications to speak it: 'I believe in the future of Scottish literature just as I believe in the continuance of Scottish Nationality which our presence here on this occasion exemplifies; and of which such an accent as mine is surely an incorruptible witness'.[7] There is slippage here between the chauvinism inherent in the occasion, the love of country and of literature courageously affirmed as dynamic (rather than as nostalgic or retrospective), and the personal disposition made evident in that last part of the sentence (both arrogant and curiously minifying, a soldier's pledge to a higher cause). This complexity of responses developed. In 1924, Grieve was writing for the London-based journal *The New Age*, and, in an article ostensibly reviewing John Buchan's anthology of Scottish poetry, *The Northern Muse*, he focused on the possibility of reviving vernacular Scots as a medium for poetry in an international context, rather than one merely local, regional or couthily national.

Grieve quotes Buchan's introduction referring to 'the high flights of Burns and Dunbar', and comments: 'The highest flights of the former – from any high European standard – may seem like the lamentable efforts of a hen at soaring; no great name in literature holds its place so completely from extra-literary causes as does that of Robert Burns'. The article ends with a prophecy that a new movement for the revival of the Scots vernacular is allying itself with a realistic Scottish nationalism 'with a pronounced Sinn Fein element' and that

> subversive tendencies are at work which may undermine the odious apathy and the false senses of humour and pathos which have hag-ridden Scottish letters; and, given a little group of determined, ruthless and competent artists, the latent potentialities of the Scottish vernacular may be realised in ways of consequence to European literature however abhorrent and unnatural to contemporary Scottish conventionalists.[8]

It was a point that Hugh MacDiarmid was to demonstrate with acute reference to Burns in his second collection of Scots lyrics, *Penny Wheep*. Just as the first, *Sangschaw* (1925), had collected twenty-seven poems in Scots, then ended with one poem in English and one in French, so *Penny Wheep* (1926) follows forty-four Scots poems with three English ones. The Scots poems frequently evoke a rural world, a farmer's Scotland, the world of agricultural workers, and an emotional world immediately recognisable from, but instantly unfamiliar to, the world of Burns's works. They evoke this world again and again, only to move away from it, deliberately and often shockingly, refocusing or translating the idiom into a modernist or symbolist mode. The diminutive affection of 'Wheesht, Wheesht' achieves an un-sentimental, atheist chill with the realisation that this love song is also an elegy. In 'Exephemeride mare' ('From the ephemeral sea'), 'Egypt herrings' are glimpsed as they disappear in 'an emeraud sea' like dreams 'in deeps/ Thocht canna faddom'. 'Tam' was 'a man for the weemun', but in death he is truly at last 'Himsel' – alane'. Duncan Gibb o' Focherty, like Tam, seems to have blundered out of Burns's world and into the modern cosmos, and cannot expect benevolence from a patriarchal God, but rather the victorious laughter of the poet's persona taking God's place in Duncan's startled, upturned view.

It is in the poems dealing explicitly with sex that MacDiarmid's achievement is most evident. In 'Sabine', a young woman looking for help to procure an abortion is given a moralistic scolding by a farmer's wife. The poet's sympathy is with the girl's wry, fearful, admonishing laughter: 'Ye'd better gi'e me what I seek/Than learn what I've to gi'e'. What she has 'to gi'e' is the shocking realisation of the poem's sympathies in the context of the pious sentimentalism of Burns's Christian devotees. And the implication that the farmer is himself the father of the young woman's unborn, soon-to-be-aborted child is a shock made more effective by the way in which he is relegated to the poem's background (though he is its 'narrator'), while the confrontation takes place between the voices of the young woman and the farmer's wife. The rueful, courageous, humorous tone of the poem has precedents in Burns himself, in Burns's use of voice and stance in poems such as 'Robert Burns' Answer' (perhaps better known as 'The Reply to a Tailor'),[9] but the freshness with which MacDiarmid gets the sense of human creaturality and the shift of central sympathy and concern to the young woman remain. Even when Burns is celebrating the independent choice of women, the male imperatives are dominant (as in the beautiful song 'The rantin dog the Daddie o't'). MacDiarmid's curiosity about the woman's experience is different, and runs through 'The Love-Sick Lass', 'Wild Roses', 'In Mysie's Bed', 'Scunner', 'Servant Girl's Bed', 'Empty Vessel' (which is perhaps a kind of sequel to 'Sabine') and 'The Fairmer's Lass' (which links back to both 'Sabine' and 'Empty Vessel'). These poems, plus the rural context of poems such as 'Jimsy: An Idiot' ('He tak's the licht o' Heaven/As a gargle for his mooth'), all seem to reflect decisively both on the sentimental ruralism of Burns's idolators and on the sentimentalism of Burns at his worst.

They are placed alongside other poems in Scots where the subjects, tones and emotions are clear contrasts. 'The Deid Liebknecht' for example, while it is a 'translation' from Rudolf Leonhardt, is a poem equally Scots in language, tone and timbre, but it is urban, not rural, full of workers and factories, not farmyards and countryfolk, and the revolutionary moment which it evokes is fraught with ambiguity: is the smile on the face of the corpse a blessing that the prophecy of liberation has been fulfilled? Liebknecht's blood floods the skies as Marlowe's Christ's blood streams in the firmament; both are saviours, but both are seen fearfully by the damned below. The vision of liberated workers ('like emmits skailin everywhere') is far from being a call to arms such as 'Robert Bruce's March to Bannockburn' ('Scots Wha Hae') or 'The Dumfries Volunteers' ('Does haughty Gaul invasion threat?'). By carefully charting a course *away from* Burns, MacDiarmid, post-Freud, post-Marx, post-Nietzsche, brings these Scots vernacular poems into the twentieth century, and the twentieth century into Scotland.

Penny Wheep ends with the rich Scots of 'Gairmscoile', then the delicate English of 'A Herd of Does' and the elegy for Anna Akhmatova, and finally the seventeen-stanza diatribe, 'Your Immortal Memory, Burns!' – a conclusive gesture of contempt, placed at the close of the book. Every year, 'to thee, O Burns', MacDiarmid perorates, 'The punctual stomach of thy people turns'.

> From wame to wame
> Wags on your fame,
> Once more through all the world
> On fronts of proud abdomena unfurled.
>
> These be thy train,
> No-Soul and No-Brain,

And Humour Far-From-It,
Bunkum and Bung, Swallow-All and Vomit.

(p. 77)

The verse-form is brilliantly chosen. The tight, cramped rhythms and monosyllabic vocabulary emerge like small belches from a dyspeptic Vice-Chancellor, the pinched lines glitter like mean eyes in a polished face, the unmitigated regularity of the rhymes reflecting a mind that feels safe only with procedure, the lurching outward movement of each stanza's last line like a moment's uncontrollable flatulence. The structure itself is an exposure of the flow and empty rhetoric of innumerable Burns orations or popular eulogies such as the song 'universally adopted as a Burns anniversary hymn',[10] 'The Star o' Rabbie Burns'. To counter all this, MacDiarmid invokes a trinity more than merely Romantic: along with 'Soul' and 'Brain' there is also required a quality of 'Humour' that demands insight, spontaneity and wit.

Yet while this is the final poem of *Penny Wheep*, the last five lines of Part I of 'Gairmscoile' (the poem which ended the earlier section of poems in Scots), haunt one's memory of the book and seem a more fitting conclusion to it:

> *It's soon', no' sense, that faddoms the herts o' men,*
> *And by my sangs the rouch auld Scots I ken*
> *E'en herts that ha'e nae Scots'll dirl richt thro'*
> *As nocht else could – for here's a language rings*
> *Wi' datchie sesames, and names for nameless things.*

(p. 74)

The point here, of course, is that MacDiarmid was not only attacking the Burns clubs and the sentimental vernacular versifiers, but he was also offering the Scots language itself as something far more radical, freshly attuned to international contemporary ideas in psychology and politics. The Burns poem in cramped English is a downbeat ending to the book, coming after the strength of MacDiarmid's declaration of faith, uttered in a rich, magniloquent Scots. Once again, the relations and interconnections between the worlds of pedagogy, popular culture and creative literary endeavour are in dynamic tension in his thinking.

From the turn of the century, at least since the 'Whistle-Binkie' anthologies of the 1890s, there had been a number of genuinely popular poets writing in vernacular Scots. Many of their poems entered the memories of generations of Scots all over the world as recitation pieces, learned at school or Sunday school, forming an attachment to the rural and agricultural Scotland which, while not entirely erased, was quite foreign to the world of cities and heavy industries. There is no need to gainsay the work of Charles Murray, David

Rorie, Violet Jacob, Marion Angus and others, to make the point that these poets were not concerned to engage with the ideas of Nietzsche, Marx or Freud. The reactionary aspect of even their best poems was anathema to the MacDiarmid whose declared faith and hope lay in 'the future of Scottish literature' and 'the continuance of Scottish nationality'. The significant words in those phrases are 'future' and 'continuance'. Even the scholarly work of a vernacular revivalist like Lewis Spence was to be categorised as no more than antiquarianism: pottering about in the prison-house of language. MacDiarmid wanted a breakout.

At the same time as he was writing the poetry, he was producing hundreds of articles syndicated to Scottish newspapers the length and breadth of the country. His attacks on the Burns cult became notorious; his attacks on Burns's legacy to Scottish literature became infamous; and his attacks on Burns himself became scandalous. The quantity of MacDiarmid's (or C. M. Grieve's) writings on Burns and the Burns cult was peculiarly appropriate to the extent to which the opposition had perpetrated their atrocities:

> A judiciously-selected anthology of extracts from the innumerable orations on 'The Immortal Memory' is another long-overdue task which would tax the resources of the most competent wit. A volume could undoubtedly be compiled which would be an immortal scream. Mr Mencken's selected *Americana* pale in comparison . . . [A]ll manner of essentially non-literary persons – ministers, schoolmasters, law lords, and what not – have, year in and year out, conspired to bury Burns under an ever-increasing cairn of the most ludicrous and inapposite eulogy. The enormities of praise that have been heaped upon him beggar description. They are peerless products of people with no sense of proportion – no intuitive appreciation of literature – no sense of literary latitude and longitude to guide them – floundering from one fatuous misconception to another, almost as if they were trying to excel each other in saying the last word upon something which their first word, their very angle of approach, showed that they were constitutionally incapable of saying anything that was not the very essence of irrelevance and fatuity.[11]

That comes from the first part of an essay on the Burns cult published as part of a series of 'Contemporary Scottish Studies' in the *Scottish Educational Journal* in 1926. In the second article, the claim that Burns was a 'typical Scot' is quickly dismissed: he was a typical Scot 'of his age, inspissated with English influences':

> He did not inaugurate a new era in Scottish literature. He merely crowned the tendencies which had been long at work. Patriotically we

owe little to him. His use of the vernacular was exiguous – eked out with English. His attitude to women was wholly unreal; his songs to any of them might as easily have been addressed to any other – or to some abstraction – for all of precise psychology that transpires from them . . . The truer Burns, in his relation to women, is to be seen in *The Merry Muses* . . . Most of his work rings psychologically false.[12]

Yet MacDiarmid (or C. M. Grieve in this instance) claims: 'Burns is proba-bly the most powerful lyrical poet the world has ever seen'. He blames the cultural history of Scotland for shackling this Pegasus to a shambling carthorse, for insisting that Burns's 'wonderful power of song' and 'unique passion' had to be manifested behind 'an irrelevant array of trite platitudin-isation', so that 'even yet' he is revered for 'the orthodox externalities' and 'all that is . . . most disfiguring of his genius rather than for the essence of that genius in itself'. 'Historically, Burns is to be discerned as a safety-valve – a means of 'working off' Scottish sentiment amenably to the tendency to progressive Anglicisation which had set in so strongly by his day.'[13] These are complex, interwoven criticisms, and proceed from a concern with more than one priority. That the Burns clubs had produced no valuable literary study of Burns or scholarly annotated editions of his letters, let alone shown any support for contemporary Scottish poets or Scottish literature of any kind outwith Burns himself and his literary kin, was a criticism levelled at the academic and educational establishment as much as (if not more than) at the club members themselves. And in the famous slogans which Mac-Diarmid broadcast in the early 1920s, 'Not Burns – Dunbar!' and 'Back to Dunbar!', he was addressing other poets, writers and artists in the first instance, hoping to generate a more radical creative dynamic than that prevailing.

It is in his poetry of the period that Burns features most memorably, and the marvellous, rippling eloquence of the opening pages of *A Drunk Man Looks at the Thistle* (1926) crystallises MacDiarmid's argument with lucid immediacy. MacDiarmid begins his great poem in a country world, a rural Scotland familiar from the lyrics of *Sangschaw* and *Penny Wheep* and from Burns himself. The literal and figurative imagery easily suggests the village pub and the drunk man's drinking companions, Cruivie and Gilsanquhar ('called as was the custom not by their surnames but by the names of their farms', as MacDiarmid himself noted).[14] These fall behind as the drunk man has stumbled off the road and lies sprawling in a ditch looking up at the thistle, rearing between him and the moon in the night sky, an uncultivated weed on the bank between the road and the surrounding farmland. The dis-cursive nature of the poem takes its bearings from a setting deliberately reminiscent of – and clearly different from – Burns's 'Tam o' Shanter'.

Where Burns's poem is characterised by appetite, pace, exhilaration, satisfaction and healthily derisive laughter (the moral is doomed from the start), MacDiarmid's poem begins in enervation, surfeit, satiety, exhaustion and disgust, a ballad metre sustaining parentheses, digressions, crazy shifts of attention, passionate and abortive grapplings; and no moral, doomed or otherwise, is vouchsafed by this voice. MacDiarmid's 'narrative' frame is quickly made secondary to the voiced concerns of the drunk man. Yet voice is the key to both poems, and in both poems voice is a subtle, slippery, quick and clever thing. The similarity between them lies in the speed with which judgements are perceptible in vocal tone. And MacDiarmid draws attention to this from the very first line, an echo of Burns's 'Willie brew'd a peck o' maut': 'We are na fou, we're nae that fou'[15] – a warning that the drunk man isn't as drunk as he might seem to be: things are not as they appear.

The inevitable consequence of polite, platitudinous Burnsians upon pop-ular and academic commentary has been an emphasis upon the moral admonition in Burns's poem: 'pleasures are like poppies spread' (line 59), and 'ye may buy the joys o'er dear' (line 223) (where 'ye' is Biblical rather than Scots, as the 'wages of sin' metaphor makes clear). But these are vacuous illustrations of what Marshall Walker has called the 'smugly pompous English couplets and pulpit gravity', which are clearly comic and intended to be so. 'After such a night Tam can have nothing to fear either from such paltry homiletics or from his killjoy Kate . . . Burns's mock-heroic, like his work as a whole, is as affirming as the final "Yes" of Joyce's *Ulysses*.'[16]

MacDiarmid understood this aspect of the poem immediately and intu-itively. In the introduction to *The Golden Treasury of Scottish Poetry* (1940), MacDiarmid refers to Edwin Muir's contention 'that Scots may serve our emotions but that we cannot think in it' and regards the example which Muir gave in *Scott and Scotland* (1936), 'where, in "Tam o' Shanter", Burns breaks into pure English for a few lines of reflective poetry', as being a 'poor' example, and one 'susceptible of a very different explanation'. Muir's expla-nation was that Burns used English as the language of a reflective mood. MacDiarmid, whose provenance of voice was much closer to Burns than Muir's, recognised the false dichotomy inherent in Muir's argument and knew that Burns was being ironic at the expense of the genteel and the pious.[17]

Moreover, there is a subtextual humour that links both poems in a general way, inexplicable from textual analysis but approachable from a knowledge of context and voice. The rural 'setting' of *A Drunk Man* and the 'drunken-ness' of the first person singular are clearly fabrications: they allow for a structure to be held in the mind as we read the poem, with the promised return to sobriety and to Jean. But they do not make the poem *literally* the product of a drunk man any more than they insist upon a realist narrative pressure as a component of the lyrics, interpolations, philosophical discursions and translations which multiply in intricate elaborations over the length of its 2,685 lines.

In an inverted sense, 'Tam o' Shanter' has most frequently been taken to be a literal rendition of a traditional ghost story, with the full *son et lumière* effects being sought after in countless recitations. Yet there is an explanation for the poem which locks fancy and reality together more accurately in the context of a rural, agricultural farming community. The poem is a sober man's response to the demands of his wife for an explanation: he has come home drunk or hung over, riding in on his best 'gray mare' Meg, and the horse is missing its tail. What happened? Tam's explanation is the poem. The literal answer is that one of his drunken cronies cut it off for a lark in high spirits before he set off from the inn in Ayr. Such a jape would have been instantly recognisable by MacDiarmid and perfectly fitting in the worlds of Lewis Grassic Gibbon or George Douglas Brown, or in the Dumfriesshire where C. M. Grieve spent his boyhood. Yet such an obvious subtext has escaped a good many academic commentaries and skewed numerous readings of the poem. It does nothing to diminish the raciness, vigour and flight of the poem, as the tale (and the performance of it) has to be convincing. Every recitation of the poem is a rehearsal for the final performance promised, to Kate, who will be the most sceptical audience of all. Such an understanding of the dynamics of Burns's poem adds qualities of humour and irony melding sophistication and earthiness with unsuspected dexterity. Such understanding MacDiarmid would have recognised intuitively in Burns, and enjoyed, beyond the critical assaults upon his poetic achievement and his literary legacy.

Implicitly in the lyrics, explicitly in *A Drunk Man*, MacDiarmid begins with 'what's still deemed Scots and the folk expect' but intends, as he says, 'to spire up syne in visible degrees/To heichts whereo' the fules ha'e never recked'. Once he's transported us there, he'll 'whummie' us: 'souse the craturs in the nether deeps'. In these sixth and seventh stanzas, MacDiarmid's plan to set out from and move beyond Burns is clear enough; there is no reason to be fooled by the infectious humour of the following pages of spectacular invective, evoking Burns and Burns Suppers at which 'some wizened scrunt o' a knock-knee/Chinee turns roon to say, "Him Haggis – velly goot!"/An' ten to wan the piper is a Cockney'.

As with 'Tam o' Shanter', the immediacy of the voice conceals another meaning. These rambling verses about Burns and Burns clubs (lines 37–120) are the luring entrance to the poem. They foreshadow the Burns of line 723 ('wha's bouquet like a shot kail blaws'), where the bouquet of blanched cabbage is shorthand for the legacy of Burns in the domestic moral tales of village Scotland in the works of Ian Maclaren, S. R. Crockett and others. Yet they do not prepare us for the deeper tides of thought running through the later parts of the poem, the psychosexual self-questioning ('A' thing wi' which a man/Can intromit's a wumman', lines 965–6), or the 'Letter to Dostoevsky' (lines 1,745–2,023), or 'Metaphysical Pictures of the Thistle' (lines 2,056–183).

It is unnecessary to itemise a concordance of references to Burns in the poem or in MacDiarmid's later work to make the essential points about their relationship. But MacDiarmid's running battle with Burns continued in prose, in newspaper and journal articles and in public speeches. A number of points should be noted here, as they are less well known and some quite unsuspected.

Two key texts changed the understanding of Burns in the twentieth century: Catherine Carswell's biography of 1930 and David Daiches's critical study of 1952.[18] The letters, edited by J. De Lancey Ferguson and *The Merry Muses*, edited by James Barke and Sydney Goodsir Smith, expanded the *plenum*; but as revolutionary reassessments, Carswell and Daiches broke new ground historically. MacDiarmid was certainly keen to draw attention to them, welcoming Carswell's biography and saying that the introductory chapter to Daiches's book and William Power's essay on Burns were essential reading. But more broadly, their work should be considered in the context of the dynamic of MacDiarmid's effort.

On 21 January 1928, MacDiarmid launched an attack in a speech for the Glasgow Branch of the Scottish Nationalist Movement. It was widely reported and massively denounced by leading lights in Burns club circles. Burnsians, keen on temperance, abstinence and reverent pieties, turned on MacDiarmid all the venom of their repressions. MacDiarmid responded in print in an article in the Glasgow *Evening Times* (26 January) entitled 'Is Burns Immortal? The Lopsidedness of Scots Literature: An "Almost Worthless" Cult':

> Is Burns immortal? I hope not – for humanity's sake. In reply to Dr Rosslyn Mitchell, who claims that Burns has permeated European thought, I would point out that there is an increasing disposition today to ask whether democracy has not failed, to realise that lip-service to brotherhood does not always promote it, and that, in any case, we have to face the fact that civilization is being threatened by its hordes of submen.[19]

In the light of all this, MacDiarmid concluded that he had no objection to Burns dinners on Temperance grounds: 'The drinking at Burns dinners is one of the few elements in the programme which have had my invariable and hearty approval. I prefer my Burnsians "speechless".'

He continued the attack in syndicated articles in local Scottish newspapers. In *The Stewartry Observer* (9 February), 'The Burns Cult Bombshell' by 'a

Special Correspondent' (MacDiarmid himself) reported 'Mr Grieve's declaration that the best thing Scotland could do with regard to Burns was to set itself deliberately to forget for the next quarter of a century that he ever existed'. Printed beside articles on the 'Dalbeattie Burgh Band Social' and local crime reports, adverts for 'Sanita's Fluid to Prevent Pyorrhea (The ideal mouthwash)' and the Haugh-of-Urr v. Palnachie Carpet Bowling District League results, MacDiarmid's column was an affront to the complacency of his environment. 'Mr Grieve . . . has acted as foreign literature critic for the *New Age* (London), and written extensively on Russian, French, German, Spanish and other literatures . . . He is therefore in an unusually good position to view Burns from the standpoint of world letters, and contends that Burns has no living literary influence whatever.'

In the March issue of the pro-Gaelic *Pictish Review*, MacDiarmid had a more reflective article on 'Scottish Nationalism and the Burns Cult' in which he set out the focus of his concerns under the following headings:

(1) The Burns Cult; (2) the question of Braid Scots revival, (a) generally, and (b) for literary purposes (two very different and by no means interdependent things); (3) the relation of these to Scottish cultural and political nationalism; and (4) to Scotland's international status; (5) Burns' precise quality and value, (a) as a poet, (b) as a Scotsman, and (c) in relation to world literature and thought.

He quotes A. N. Whitehead: 'The soul cries aloud for release into change. It suffers too much from claustrophobia. The transitions of humour, wit, irreverence, play, sleep, and, above all, art are necessary to it.' And he identifies Burns with these 'agencies of claustrophobia'.

Following the publication in 1930 of Catherine Carswell's *The Life of Robert Burns*, MacDiarmid was prompted to write a series of three articles for the *Scottish Educational Journal* under the byline of James Maclaren entitled 'Burns: The Next Step'. In the first article (12 February), MacDiarmid commented that Carswell's book elicited a storm of condemnation which was 'all to the good' and that Carswell brought Burns the man ('as distinct from the poet') 'into a better perspective'. Along with J. De Lancey Ferguson's edition of the letters, Carswell's book 'has put us in general possession of a great mass of new material; and has done the further service of exposing to some degree the extraordinary machinations of the Burns Federation in denying access to this'. According to MacDiarmid, Carswell had written in *The Spectator*: 'On the eve of publication steps were taken by the Burns Federation to have my book suppressed or mutilated'. And apparently, Carswell herself was sent a bullet in the post, a pointed threat from an anonymous critic.

On 19 February, MacDiarmid declared that he had 'the profoundest respect for Mrs Carswell's biography' and called it 'a very valuable and timely piece of work . . . biographical studies of many other kinds, will come; and they will not displace Mrs Carswell's book'. But on 26 February he added that the next step now was to produce an adequate critical discussion of the value of Burns's poetry, and suggested a number of questions that might prompt such discussion. Though MacDiarmid's personal correspondence with Carswell reveals that their relationship began at cross-purposes, they developed a strong and lasting friendship and a warm respect for each other.[20]

It was David Daiches who took up MacDiarmid's challenge to produce a critical exposition of Burns's poems twenty years later, and in 1962 Daiches confirmed MacDiarmid's recognition of Dunbar when he defined the three poets thus: 'Dunbar, Burns and MacDiarmid are the great Scottish trio'.[21] But in 1933, MacDiarmid was less concerned with singing in their company than with emphasising the differences between them. Writing in the Douglasite weekly *The Free Man* on 28 January, he was clear about his privileging of Dunbar over Burns: '[E]nthusiasm for Burns is generally most prominent in people who have little or no use for most of what is accepted as the greatest poetry of the world . . . Dunbar, on the contrary, is singularly modern. He was a superb craftsman.' Lacking both the 'large-hearted humanitarianism' of Burns and the 'broad-minded humanity' of Scott, he appealed to MacDiarmid: 'One man genuinely concerned about poetic form is worth thousands with the woolly sentiments about poetry which are generally prevalent . . .'.

And yet this is not to deny MacDiarmid's later affection for some of the qualities which he repudiates here. In 1957, for example, in *The Southern Annual* (issued by the *Southern Reporter*, a Scottish Border newspaper emanating from Selkirk), he writes a warm tribute to W. H. Ogilvie, 'the Grand Old Man of Border Song', placing him in the tradition of Hogg and the Border Ballads. In his poetry, MacDiarmid tells us, 'there is nothing . . . of modern experimentalism. It is none the worse for that. It appeals to a far greater public than any "highbrow stuff" can hope for.' This is not a complete *volte-face*, however: 'While it is seldom that a golden coin appears amongst the silver in a man's pocket nowadays, the latter has its uses. And so it is with poetry.'

A similar tone is conveyed by his introduction to what Robert Creeley has called 'a curiously genteel collection' of Burns's *Love Songs* in 1962.[22] 'Burns was a great song-writer rather than a great poet. This accounts largely for a much greater world-wide vogue than any of the great poets has had. That vogue is not lessening.' MacDiarmid complained that new and better settings of Burns's songs failed to make any headway, that Scotland had changed utterly since Burns's time, and that 'Post-Burnsian Scottish poetry (and little of it is Song!) gives off a great sense of warmth and offering, like a dog when it loves you. It is soggily and indiscriminately affectionate.' But he also was pleased to be included in Lady Antonia Fraser's anthology of *Scottish Love Poems*,[23] and took such inclusion to signify a more recognisably warm humanity in his own work than critics of his austere political imperatives would allow.

> [I]t is the way of life that some child's nursery rhyme has an immortality denied to most of the great epics, and whatever criticism one may bring to bear, or however difficult it may be to account for the phenomenon, the simple fact remains that these songs are immortal, and that through them Burns has an international acceptance no other poet equals.[24]

Only three years prior to this acceptance of Burns's 'immortality', MacDiarmid had pointed out that the works of Sir David Lindsay had enjoyed a vogue for two centuries, as Burns's works had done, and were to be found cheek-by-jowl with the family Bible in 'cottages and castles all over the country'. But, he added, 'how many Scottish houses today hold a volume of his work, how many Scots have read any of it? Is it possible that Burns's great vogue may similarly disappear?'[25]

The contradictions here are perhaps best exemplified in two uses of a quotation from Burns's 'Jolly Beggars'. In the last pages of *Lucky Poet*, MacDiarmid quotes this verse:

> A fig for those by law protected!
>   Liberty's a glorious feast!
> Courts for cowards were erected
>   Churches built to please the priest.

He follows this with a long commentary beginning 'in these lines began the Revolution of Revolutions, compared with which the French Revolution is but a ripple on the sea of change. The Revolution of Burns is an insurrection of the naked spirit of man.' After the commentary, he adds, in italics, '*Vive l'anarchie!*'[26] In *Burns Today and Tomorrow*, published six years later, MacDiarmid quotes the same verse, gives the same commentary (attributing it to James Douglas), and then adds: 'Nonsense!' – dismissing as 'useless' what he earlier affirmed and celebrated.[27]

The tangles spring from passionate concern. In *Lucky Poet*, he also quotes D. H. Lawrence's letter to Catherine Carswell: 'I read just now Lockhart's bit life of Burns. Made me spit! Those damned middle-class Lockharts grew lilies of the valley up their – ,to hear them talk. My word, you can't know Burns unless you can hate the Lockharts and all the estimable bourgeois and upper classes as he really did – the narrow-gutted pigeons.'[28] Yet in 1959, MacDiarmid was writing in the establishment *Burns Chronicle* an article on foreign translations of Burns: 'there is a vast new audience opening up for Scotland's National Poet in the Soviet Union, in China, in Czechoslovakia, Bulgaria, Hungary and elsewhere'. And discussing Burns's influence in the upmarket glossy *Scottish Field*, he writes in the same year: 'Burns owes his vast reputation to the fact that, albeit imprecise and contradictory, he was on . . . the side of the poor and oppressed, the side of justice and mercy and peace'.

Part of the explanation for this is that in the late 1950s there were numerous opportunities for MacDiarmid to talk on Burns not only in Scotland but also in Eastern Bloc countries. Having rejoined the Communist Party in 1956, he was well treated by the Party and travelled widely under the Party's wing. His best friend Norman MacCaig commented that it must have been like joining a free international travel agency.[29] Again in the *Burns Chronicle* in 1968, MacDiarmid comments: 'I have always had to look beyond Scotland for intelligent readers – and found them particularly (as Burns himself has done to an astonishing extent) in the "Iron Curtain" countries'.

How are we to bring MacDiarmid's Burns to a final account? In the mass of writing, the contradictions, the early prose polemics, the later consolations and praise, the verve and velocity of the poetry, the tensions between academic analysis, creative transformation and popular understanding, what was MacDiarmid doing with Burns? Did he succeed?

MacDiarmid's most succinct and splendid judgement is 'The Last Great Burns Discovery' (1934), a short story in which a Burns idolator ('in the direct line of Duncan McNaught') leads the narrator through an overgrown garden to a ruined outdoor toilet near a cottage where Burns himself had lived: 'It was an august moment . . . Burns himself had used that very place, that very seat . . .'. The story ends with regret that the pail was no longer there: '"If only . . ."/We left it at that'.[30]

MacDiarmid's most direct summary of the cult is still in the 1990s desperately appropriate:

> It has denied his spirit to honour his name.
> It has denied his poetry to laud his amours.
> It has preserved his furniture and repelled his message.
> It has built itself up on the progressive refusal of his lead in regard to Scottish politics, Scottish literature, and the Scottish tongue.[31]

And MacDiarmid's most extensive commentary is to be found in *Lucky Poet* and *Burns Today and Tomorrow*. In the latter, MacDiarmid notes, 'All that Burns wanted was "ae spark o' Nature's fire/That's a' the learning I desire." Well,' he remarked, 'it is not enough and less so today than ever.' But he also pointed out 'the supreme power of Burns's finest line – "Ye are na Mary Morrison".'[32]

Why should that line have struck MacDiarmid so forcefully? Perhaps the answer is to be found in Robert Creeley's comment on MacDiarmid's reflection that 'T. S. Eliot was right when he said that Burns was a decadent representative of a great alien tradition, a tradition, that is to say, alien to the tradition of English letters'. Creeley writes:

> MacDiarmid's repetition of the key word three times in one brief sentence is . . . revealing. He especially is caught in a curious classicism of intellectually proposed program, just that he *wills* the Scots language to reassert its coherence and its people also to become politically an independent and articulate collective.[33]

For MacDiarmid, all that potential resides in the value of the difference between 'Ye are na' and 'You are not' when the words are charged with a human meaning that any articulate adult might comprehend. So Creeley continues:

> Paradoxically, it is Burns who most knows and is whatever 'the tradition' may be said to be, because it is more than a place and time, however actual both are as obvious terms. Quite literally, it is the intense factor of human experience, of *feelings*, hot and cold, rough and smooth, pleasure and pain, *all* the particulars of language as an economy of *physical* existence, which become increasingly displaced as a demanding and abstracting 'system,' of whatever kind, translates their directness into a referential of generalising orders.[34]

Perhaps MacDiarmid understood that aspect of Burns intuitively too.

Success, then, or failure?

MacDiarmid failed. Careerist academics still turn Burns into a commodity, fetishised in conferences, books like this, essays like this: an object of study. And the public still make less of poetry than they might; they retreat from its quicknesses and depths. And the Burns cult is still the fiasco that it was when MacDiarmid decried it in 1928. Of all the women and men who attended Burns Suppers throughout Scotland and throughout the world, in Canada, in America, in Australia, in New Zealand, in January 1996, how many knew the meaning of the death, on the 23rd of that month, of Norman MacCaig?

MacDiarmid failed, because he expected too much of people.

Yet he succeeded too. Burns is read today in a different way. The Burns cult may be known for what it is. The teaching of Scots – literature and language – is possible today. The best academics are able to perceive and to convey the quicknesses and depths. There are still people who can quote Burns accurately and according to his spirit, as Keir Hardie must have quoted him to Grieve. And there still are those citizens who will have none of his best qualities diminished, and who, as I know, might lean across a table in an Edinburgh bar, politely to point out your mistake in quoting a half-remembered verse, with unsentimental pleasure in the sharing of the poem, a common property, an authority resident in the culture which Burns's poems, and MacDiarmid's, still inhabit.

NOTES

1. Charles Olson, 'Letter for Melville 1951', in George F. Butterick (ed.), *The Collected Poems of Charles Olson Excluding the 'Maximus' Poems* (Berkeley, Los Angeles and London: University of California Press, 1987), pp. 233–41. See also Tom Clark, *Charles Olson: The Allegory of a Poet's Life* (New York and London: W. W. Norton & Co., 1991), p. 207.

2. John Purser, *Scotland's Music: A History of the Traditional and Classical Music of Scotland from Early Times to the Present Day* (Edinburgh: Mainstream, 1992), p. 253.

3. Hugh MacDiarmid, in Alan Riach (ed.), *Lucky Poet: A Self-Study in Literature and Political Ideas, Being the Autobiography of Hugh MacDiarmid (Christopher Murray Grieve)* (1943; Manchester: Carcanet Press, 1994), p. 191. Henceforth, *LP*.

4. Page references to MacDiarmid's poems are to W. R. Aitken and Michael Grieve (eds), *The Complete Poems of Hugh MacDiarmid* (1978; Manchester: Carcanet Press, 1993–4). Henceforth, *CP*. References to *A Drunk Man Looks at the Thistle* are by line number. Line numbers to this poem are noted in Kenneth Buthlay's annotated edition (see note 10 below) and in Alan Riach and Michael Grieve (eds), *Hugh MacDiarmid: Selected Poems* (Harmondsworth: Penguin Books, 1994).

5. Hugh MacDiarmid, '*Satori* in Scotland', in Karl Miller (ed.), *Memoirs of a Modern Scotland* (London: Faber and Faber, 1970), pp. 55–60 (p. 57).

6. MacDiarmid's comments on Keir Hardie's knowledge of Burns are to be found in Hugh MacDiarmid, *Burns Today and Tomorrow* (Edinburgh: Castle Wynd Printers, 1949), pp. 5, 10, 34. Henceforth, *BTT*. This will be republished in 1996 in Alan Riach (ed.), *Albyn: Shorter Books and Monographs by Hugh MacDiarmid* (Manchester: Carcanet Press, 1996).

7. Hugh MacDiarmid, in Alan Bold, *MacDiarmid: Christopher Murray Grieve. A Critical Biography* (1988; London: Paladin Grafton Books, 1990), p. 161.

8. Ibid., p. 182. The original provenance of each quotation from MacDiarmid's journalism and fugitive prose is given in the text of the essay; all articles cited will be collected in Angus Calder, Glen Murray and Alan Riach (eds), *The Raucle Tongue: Hitherto Uncollected Prose by Hugh MacDiarmid*, 3 vols (Manchester: Carcanet Press, 1996–7).

9. Robert Burns, 'Robert Burns' Answer', in James Kinsley (ed.), *Burns Poems and Songs* (London: Oxford University Press, 1969), pp. 224–6. Compare, for example, the shifts in vocal tone in lines 31–66, especially.

10. Kenneth Buthlay (ed.), *Hugh MacDiarmid: A Drunk Man Looks at the Thistle* (Edinburgh: Scottish Academic Press, 1987), p. 11.

11. Hugh MacDiarmid, in Alan Riach (ed.), *Contemporary Scottish Studies* (1926; Manchester: Carcanet Press, 1995), p. 355.
12. Ibid., pp. 359–60.
13. Ibid., p. 360.
14. Kenneth Buthlay, op. cit., p. 5.
15. James Kinsley, op. cit., pp. 378–9.
16. Marshall Walker, *His Power Survives: Robert Burns 1759–1796. A Bicentenary Essay* (Hamilton, New Zealand: Avizandum Editions, Department of English, University of Waikato, 1995), p. 26.
17. Hugh MacDiarmid, 'Introduction', in idem (ed.), *The Golden Treasury of Scottish Poetry* (1940; Edinburgh: Canongate, 1993), pp. xiii–xliii (pp. xxvi–xxvii).
18. Catherine Carswell, *The Life of Robert Burns* (London: Chatto & Windus, 1930); David Daiches, *Robert Burns* (London: Bell and Sons Ltd, 1952).
19. See note 8 above.
20. Alan Bold (ed.), *The Letters of Hugh MacDiarmid* (London: Hamish Hamilton, 1984), pp. 419–32.
21. David Daiches, 'Hugh MacDiarmid: The Early Poems', in K. D. Duval and Sydney Goodsir Smith (eds), *Hugh MacDiarmid: A Festschrift* (Edinburgh: K. D. Duval, 1962), pp. 21–47 (p. 47).
22. Robert Creeley, 'Introduction', in idem (ed.), *The Essential Burns* (New York: The Ecco Press, 1989), pp. 3–16 (p. 5).
23. Lady Antonia Fraser (ed.), *Scottish Love Poems* (Edinburgh: Canongate, 1975). See also Hugh MacDiarmid, 'Introduction 1976', in Alan Riach (ed.), *Contemporary Scottish Studies by Hugh MacDiarmid* (Manchester: Carcanet Press, 1995), pp. 443–9.
24. Hugh MacDiarmid, 'Introduction', in idem (ed.), *Burns: Love Songs* (London: Vista Books, 1962), pp. 5–8 (p. 8).
25. Hugh MacDiarmid, 'Robert Burns: His Influence', in Duncan Glen (ed.), *Selected Essays of Hugh MacDiarmid* (London: Jonathan Cape, 1969), pp. 177–82 (p. 177).
26. *LP*, pp. 417–18.
27. *BTT*, pp. 58–9. See note 6 above.
28. *LP*, p. 5 (the passage is repeated on p. 193).
29. Alan Bold, *MacDiarmid: Christopher Murray Grieve. A Critical Biography* (1988; London: Paladin Grafton Books, 1990), p. 471.
30. Hugh MacDiarmid, 'The Last Great Burns Discovery' (1934), in Alan Riach (ed.), *Selected Prose by Hugh MacDiarmid* (Manchester: Carcanet Press, 1992), pp. 99–102.
31. Hugh MacDiarmid, 'The Burns Cult' (1934), in ibid., pp. 103–5 (p. 104).
32. *BTT*, p. 33. See note 6 above.
33. Robert Creeley, op. cit., p. 4.
34. Ibid., pp. 4–5.

BURNS'S ART SPEECH

Seamus Heaney

There is something about the poetry of Robert Burns and about the figure of Burns himself that makes me uneasy about lecturing on him at all. The convention of the lecture as such and the kind of discourse that it entails belong to the world which Burns's contemporaries would have called Rhetoric and Belles Lettres and Robert Crawford has shown in his book *Devolving English Literature* that this was a world towards which Burns had genuinely ambivalent attitudes.[1] He could manage to function in it – very capably – yet he also maintained a certain detachment from it. It held, after all, the keys to the kingdom of high culture, and, in spite of Burns's natural confidence in his own vernacular possessions, he still shared the general presumption that high poetic achievement could only occur and could certainly only be recognised within that kingdom. But Burns also realised that his hearth culture was essential to the carrying power of his poetry; something in him knew that the speech which belle-lettristes would have called unlettered and the company which high society would have called low were the very things that guaranteed the force of his utterance. His instinct must have told him that his 'nugget of harmony'[2] had better be mined out of the deep strata of the Scots that he had spoken as a child and youth. To put it another way, Burns knew that his 'sound of sense'[3] originated in the undersong of the spoken tongue, in a speech-world where people cracked rather than conversed and where they wrought at rhymes rather than composed poetry. So that part of Burns speaks to a part of me that would prefer to crack than to lecture, a part which has survived out of that older rhyme world which was still vestigially present when I was growing up in rural Ulster half a century ago.

Rhyme, of course, persists as a central concern in poetic culture, high and low, and has been making something of a comeback in the last couple of decades. Just because it was suppressed by some of the great practitioners earlier in the century does not mean that it did not survive as a more or less

216

determining factor in the modernist consciousness. And in several literatures outside English, it has never been dislodged to anything like the same extent. In Russian, for example, the deployment of rhyme continues to be a vital element in the art, and in fact it was in conversation with a Russian poet a few years ago that I found myself positioned again where Burns had once been positioned, at that old crossroads where the local and the learned traditions meet. I was talking – indeed I was cracking – to the late Joseph Brodsky, and in his merry way he raised the question of what was the best rhyme in English for 'love'. Dove? Move? Shove? 'No, no,' said Joseph, 'the best rhyme is Auden's: Diaghelev!' So, Round One to the Russians. But then I had a question for Joseph. What, I asked him, was the best rhyme for 'mahogany'; and I had the satisfaction (for once) of not being answered back. So I quoted two lines to him from a poem made by a local bard in County Tyrone in praise of the character and possessions of his parish priest – two lines in which the end-rhyme was perfect when judged by this man's own particular 'sound of sense':

> His furniture's made of the finest mahogany
> And he perfumes his hair with *eau de cologne*.

Round Two to Tyrone.

But I am running ahead of myself, even if it happens to be in the right direction. I want to talk about Burns autobiographically, because I have known his name and some of his poems for as long as I can remember, and this is an opportunity to celebrate that old familiarity. But I also want to explore how my original at-homeness with the poet has become part of a more developed understanding of the importance and the operation of poetry in general. To begin with, however, I want to cite another piece of Brodsky wisdom, this time from his essay on Derek Walcott. 'Poets' real biographies', he writes there,

> are like those of birds . . . their real data are in the way they sound. A poet's biography is in his vowels and sibilants, in his meters, rhymes and metaphors . . . With poets, the choice of words is invariably more telling than the story they tell . . .[4]

The way Burns sounded, his choice of words, his rhymes and metaphors, all that collapsed the distance which I expected to feel between myself and the schoolbook poetry I encountered first at Anahorish Elementary School and subsequently at St Columb's College, Derry. I'm almost certain that I knew his lines 'To a Mouse, On turning her up in her Nest, with the Plough, November, 1785' before I went to secondary school, but it wasn't any previous acquaintance with the poem that gave me a special relationship to it when I met it again in *The Ambleside Book of Verse*. In those days, when it came to poetry, we all braced ourselves linguistically. And rightly so: everybody should be in good verbal shape when faced with a page of verse. In our case, however, we expected that the language on the written page would take us out of our unofficial speaking selves and transport us to a land of formal words where we would have to be constantly on our best verbal behaviour. 'Hail to thee, blithe spirit' fulfilled these expectations perfectly, as did the elevation of 'Tyger, tyger, burning bright'. But next comes this:

Wee, sleeket, cowran, tim'rous *beastie*.[5]

and this was different. In a single monosyllable, even before a metre or a melody could get suggested, a totally reliable aural foundation had been laid in place. The word 'wee' put its stressed foot down and in one pre-emptive vocative strike took over the emotional and cultural ground, dispossessing the rights of written standard English and offering asylum to all vernacular comers. To all, at least, who hailed from somewhere north of a line drawn between Berwick and Bundoran. 'Wee' came on strong. It was entirely untwee. It neither beckoned nor beguiled. It was just suddenly and solidly there in front of you, like a parent or a pillar, and there it remains to this day, *omphalos* of the pre-literary and even the pre-literate life, irreducible, undislodgeable and undeniably true. A bit like what Burns himself was like at his best, the Burns whom Walter Scott remembered, for example, as a person 'strong and robust' with 'a sort of dignified plainness and simplicity', expressive of 'perfect self-confidence, without the slightest presumption', and exhibiting thereby a 'perfect firmness, but without the least intrusive forwardness'.[6]

Big claims, you may feel, for a wee word; but not, I would argue, exaggerated claims. Both as a matter of poetic fact and a matter of personal reminiscence, the opening of Burns's poem to the mouse is a decisive occurrence. It gets into the boundless language of poetry by reason of its totally unchallengeable rightness as utterance, its simultaneous at-oneness with the genius of English and Scottish speech; and it got under my official classroom guard and into the kitchen life, as it were, of my affections by reason of its truth to the life of the language that I spoke while growing up in mid-Ulster, a language where trace elements of Elizabethan English and Lowland Scots are still to be heard and to be reckoned with as a matter of pronunciation and even, indeed, of politics.

'Wee, sleeket, cowran, tim'rous *beastie*' – 'sleeket' was something else that slipped under the guard, as a sleeket thing might be expected to, since the word had connotations of plausibility as well as silkiness and slinkiness. And the line built quickly and securely on that 'wee' foundation. The mouse, for example, was not cowering but 'cowran', a participle as careless about its final *g* as we ourselves were in our schoolyard speech. It was a beastie, not a beast, the way a John among us became a Johnnie or a Hugh a Hughie or, indeed, a Robert a Rabbie. And the whole thing, I knew, had to be spoken in a more or less County Antrim accent, an accent I happened to be familiar with from my trips to the fair hill in Ballymena where the farmers said 'yin' and 'twa' for 'one' and 'two' and in general spoke a tongue that was as close to Ayrshire as to County Derry.

There is no need, I suppose, to keep going on in this fashion, because what I am describing is a common enough phenomenon. It is always a pleasure to find your subcultural life being represented with accuracy and without condescension in a high cultural context – and in its own way, in its own time, *The Ambleside Book of Verse* did provide just such a context. Nowadays, however, as well as recognising the documentary accuracy of the language, I can also rejoice in what we might call its poetic verity. By which I mean its earworthiness, the way it is as firm within itself and as buoyant inside our hearing as a boat beneath an oarsman. 'Wee, sleeket, cowran, tim'rous *beastie*': the line comes on like a reassuring 'There, there, there, there'; the four stresses of the four adjectives establish the largeness and largesse of the human agent on the scene. The poetic feet have a benevolent tread and step into the poem as surely and unthreateningly as the plough-man coming to inspect the ruined nest. Indeed, what is being sounded forth beat by metrical beat is that independence which was so often remarked upon as an attractive and indispensable part of the poet's own make-up – what Scott called his 'perfect firmness'.

Moreover, it is because the melody of confidence gets established in the first line that the rhetorical exclamation of the second one – 'O, what a panic's in thy breastie!' – carries real emotional weight. I can, of course, imagine Spike Milligan using a burlesque Scoto-Goonish accent and putting these words through it as through a synthesiser in order to send them up; but the point is that it would indeed require such genuinely comic gifts as Spike's to rock the line on its emotional keel. 'O, what a panic's in thy breastie' has a scramblier movement than the first line, but it is a move-ment which springs from sympathy rather than mimicry. There is nothing remotely Disney-like going on here: this is not mere skilful verbal simulation of the behaviour of a frightened mouse but an involuntary outrush of fellow feeling. And as the address to the unhoused mouse continues, the identifi-cation becomes more intense, the plough of the living voice gets set deeper and deeper in the psychic ground, dives more and more purposefully into the subsoil of the intuitions until finally it breaks open a nest inside the poet's own head and leaves him exposed to his own profoundest forebod-ings about his fate. The last stanza feels weird, in the strictly Anglo-Saxon sense:

> Still thou art blest compar'd wi' me!
> The present only toucheth thee:
> But, Och! I backward cast my e'e
>   On prospects drear!
> An' forward tho' I canna see,
>   I guess an' fear.

What has happened here is truly, almost literally, a discovery. From a hiding place in the foggage of the poet's own consciousness, his wee, cowran, tim'rous soul has been panicked out into a bleak recognition of its destiny. The sturdy, caring figure who overshadowed and oversaw the panic of the mouse at the beginning has been revealed to himself as someone less perfectly firm, less strong and robust than he or the reader would have ever suspected. In other words, Burns's mouse gradually becomes a sibylline rather than a sentimental element in the poem – so much so that, by the end, the reader feels that the bleakness of Lear's heath must have overtaken the field at Mossgiel on that wintry November day in 1785 when 'crash! the cruel coulter passed/ Out thro' thy cell'.

And it is a matter of the profoundest phonetic satisfaction that the exclamation 'Och' should be at the centre of this semi-visionary final stanza. For if 'wee' is the monosyllable that takes possession of the cultural and linguistic ground at the start, 'och' is a kind of *nunc dimittis* positioned near the end. 'Och' springs us from the domestic into the disconsolate. It is a common, almost pre-linguistic particle, one of those sounds that 'haven't been brought to book . . . living in the cave of the mouth';[7] and while it is certainly a cry of distress, it is by no means a venting of self-pity. If 'ouch' is the complaint of the ego, 'och' is the zen of ultimate resignation and illumination. Here, and in the countless instances in which it has been uttered by men and women *in extremis* since time immemorial, it functions as a kind of self-relinquishment, a casting of the spirit upon the mercy of fate, at once a protest and a cry for help.

Of course, I am aware that I am overdoing it a bit here, but I believe that I am still not misrepresenting the poetic truth of the matter, which has precisely to do with the raising of common speech to the power of art. 'Och' strikes a note of grief and wisdom which the poem as a whole elaborates and orchestrates. It is what Nadezhda Mandelstam called 'the nugget of harmony' and the guarantee of Burns's genius as a poet of the Scots and English tongues, for 'och', like 'wee', also belongs north of that Berwick/Bundoran line where the language of Shakespeare and the Bible meets the language of Dunbar and the ballads and where new poetic combinations and new departures are still going on.

The language missing in these same areas is, of course, Gaelic, whether of the Scots or Irish variety, yet I have always taken it to be a promising fact that the expression 'och' lies every bit as deep in the Irish larynx as in the English or Scots. Twenty-five years ago, for example, when I was trying to coax a few lyric shoots out of the sullied political compost of Northern Ireland, I wrote a poem called 'Broagh' which could just as well have been entitled 'Och'.[8] Its immediate subject was my recollection of an outlying part of our farm in the townland of Broagh on the banks of the River Moyola in Co. Derry, but its poetic quest was to bring the three languages I've just mentioned – Irish, Elizabethan English and Ulster Scots – into some kind of creative intercourse and alignment and thereby to intimate the possibility of some new intercourse and alignment among the cultural and political heritages which these three languages represent in Northern Ireland. I very much wanted to affirm the rights of the Irish language to be recognized as part of that Ulster mix, to correct the official, east-of-Bann emphasis on the province's ur-languages as Ulster Scots and Elizabethan English. None of this appeared, however, in the story the poem told: instead, it was meant to be implicit in the way it sounded, in the vocabulary and voicing of the lines, in the connotations and allusiveness of word and image, in the way the poem tapped into the shorthand and coding that are constantly operating beneath the first level of Ulster speech. Ultimately, it all came down to the ability to say Broagh, to pronounce that last *gh* as it is pronounced in the place itself; the poem, in other words, was just one tiny move in that big campaign of our times which aims to take cultural authority back to the local ground and to reverse the colonising process by making the underprivileged language of the native the normative standard. Whitehall ministers would have called the place Broa, but they would have been wrong. Their pronunciation in this instance was no sign of entitlement; on the contrary, it revealed a certain incapacity. But everyone native to Northern Ireland, Protestant or Catholic, Planter or Gael, whatever their separate myths of linguistic exile from Irish or Ulster Scots – each one of them could say Broagh, each one of them was fitted to dwell at least in phonetic amity with the other, and it was at just this level of primal utterance that I wanted to locate the irreducible vocal unit upon which a desirable language might be constructed.

I think, in other words, that we can prefigure a future by reimagining our pasts. In poetry, however, this prefiguring is venturesome and suggestive, more like a melodic promise than a social programme. It is not the blueprint for a better world which might spring from the forward-planning intelligence of a social engineer. Rather, it arises from the cravings of the spirit as expressed in language, in all of those patiences and impatiences which language embodies. I wish, therefore, that in those days when I was studying *The Ambleside Book of Verse* in my English class, somebody had told me to look at another poem which we would eventually meet in our Irish class and to compare it with Burns's poem to the evicted mouse. This was 'An Bunnán Buí' by the Irish language poet, Cathal Buí MacGiolla Ghunna, a native of Ulster who followed, according to his most recent editors, 'the career of rake poet', who died three years before Burns was born and whose work is 'marked by a rare humanity' and a 'finely-judged blend of pathos and humour'.[9]

MacGiolla Ghunna was a significant presence to me in my mid-teens when I was beginning to be able to read and feel my way into poetry in the Irish language. Significant because he was a northern voice and part of a group of Ulster poets whose work, like Burns's, was sustained out of the past by a long and learned literary tradition; but this once privileged tradition subsisted in the poets' time as part of a culture that was oral, rural and more and more dislodged from its previous high cultural authority. MacGiolla Ghunna and his older brothers in the art like Seamus Dall MacCuarta and Art MacCumhaigh, for example – still retained something of the *techne* and the status of the bardic poet, but the Gaelic order which once supported the bardic schools had been shattered over the seventeenth century, beginning with Elizabeth's decisive campaign against Hugh O'Neill, continuing with the Cromwellian depredations and culminating in the Williamite defeat of the Stuart cause at Derry, Aughrim and the Boyne. The poets' biographies showed the consequence of these defeats in the Gaelic world, but Brodsky's law applied to them as well, in that their biographies were also present in the way they sounded. Their words and intonations belonged to an Ulster Irish in which I felt completely at home, since it was that particular strain of the language which had been taught to me in Derry; so when I read MacCuarta's 'Fáilte do'n Éan' or MacCumhaigh's 'Úr Chill Ui Chreagain' or MacGiolla Ghunna's 'An Bunnán Buí', I experienced something of that domestic familiarity I had known when I first read 'To a Mouse'. And I could also have said what John Hewitt said of his experience of reading the poets of the Ulster Scots tradition in Ulster; the verse written by 'The Rhyming Weavers' had produced in Hewitt the same kind of recognition as the work of these Gaelic northerners produced in me, 'some feeling that, for better or worse, they were my own people . . .', a feeling issuing from a susceptibility 'in stanza, couplet or turn of phrase, [to] some sense of the humanity that was in them'.[10]

But still, leaving aside the ethnic solidarities and divisions of Ulster, it would have been interesting as a purely literary exercise to have read 'An Bunnán Buí' alongside 'To a Mouse'. In the Irish poem, the rake poet is in mourning because he has just discovered the carcass of a bird frozen into the ice of a winter lake and this awakens a mood of foreboding, a fear that his addiction to drink will be the end of him. The bird is a mighty one, a yellow bittern, and the tragedy and omen of its death come home to the poet all the more forcefully because its very name – bunnán buí, yellow bittern – echoes his own name, Cathal Buí – Yellow or Fair-haired Cahal or Charles. As in the Burns poem, there is an increasing convergence, as the stanzas proceed, between the tender and the tragic aspects of the situation, a sense of fatal link between the poet exposed to poverty and danger and the creature foraging for dear life until the day of its death; just as there is also the same huge sense of proportion, a cosmic perspective within which the man and the mouse or the man and the bird end up as big or as small as each other by the conclusion of the poem. The third and fourth stanzas go like this:

> I am saddened, bittern, and broken-hearted
>   To find you in scrags in the rushy tufts
> And the big rats scampering down the ratpaths
>   To wake your carcass and have their fun.
> If you had got word to me in time, bird,
>   That you were in trouble and craved a sup,
> I'd have struck the fetters off those loch waters
>   And have wet your thrapple with the blow I struck.
>
> Your common birds do not concern me,
>   The blackbird, say, or the thrush or heron,
> But the yellow bittern, my heartsome namesake
>   With my looks and locks, he's the one I mourn.
> Constantly he was drinking, drinking,
>   And by all accounts I am just the same,
> But every drop I get I'll down it
>   For fear I might get my death from drouth.
>   (Translation: Seamus Heaney)

And here are those stanzas in the original:

> A bhonnáin óig, is é mo mhíle brón
>   thú bheith romham i measc na dtom,
> is na lucha móra ag triall chun do thorraimh
>   ag déanamh spóirt is pléisiúr ann;
> dá gcuirfeá scéala in am fá mo déinse
>   go raibh tú i ngheibheann nó i mbroid fá dheoch,
> do bhrisfinn béim ar an loch sin Vesey
>   a fhliuchfadh do bhéal is do chorp isteach.
>
> Ni hé bhur n-éanlaith ata mise ag éagnach,
>   an ion, an smaolach, ná an chorr ghlas –
> ach mo bhonnán buí lán den chroí,
>   is gur cosúil liom féin é ina ghné is a dhath;

bhíodh sé choíche ag síoról na dí,
    agus deir na daoine go mbím mar sin seal,
is níl deor dá bhfaighead nach ligfead síos
    ar eagla go bhfaighinnse bás den tart.[11]

Needless to say, it's another source of satisfaction to me that *och* reappears at the phonetic centre of this poem in the word *loch* and the word *deoch* – which happens to mean 'drink' in Irish. It functions there like a signal broadcast forward into Broaghville, an optative *och*, as it were, a pointer towards a future that is implicit in the mutually pronounceable elements of the vernacular speech of Planter and Gael. Even if we grant the deeply binary nature of Ulster thinking about language and culture, we can still try to establish a plane of regard from which to re-envisage the recalcitrant elements in the situation and reposition ourselves in relation to them. And that plane, I believe, can be projected from fundamentally reliable starting points in poems and poetry. I wish, as I said earlier, that somebody had asked me years ago, 'Have you ever noticed how the "prophetic soul", as Hamlet called it, deepens the note in those two poems by Burns and MacGiolla Ghunna? How poems that might have stayed touching get closer to something tragic? How their given note arrives out of the literary tradition but ends up in the place that Ted Hughes calls the place of "ultimate suffering and decision in us"?'[12] Moreover, I wish all this not because I believe the reading of the two poems would have helped me into some better civic posture, some higher commitment to the notion of diversity, for example; instead, I wish it because, to quote Joseph Brodsky one last time, good poetry is a tonic and defence against that which is the final enemy, namely 'the vulgarity of the human heart'.[13]

None of us wants fake consolation in the face of real problems. None of us wants Disney when what we need is Dante. But in discovering a similar sense of vulnerability and sympathy in Burns and MacGiolla Ghunna, and in recognising that their art speech not only inhabits a similar literary and linguistic middle state but is also capable of prospecting the deeper levels of their poetic being, I believe one is doing more than merely introducing a feel-good factor, some corollary of the old Ulster saw that there are faults on both sides. Poetry operates more opulently than that. The terms of its understanding are not dictated by the circumstances that pertain but are commensurate with the poet's intellectual and imaginative wavelength. Those rats in the Irish poem, for example, for all of their anthropomorphic jollity, are every bit as far from Disneyland as Burns's mouse. I feel, indeed, that they could have escaped from Villon or that they might return from the bittern's wake to join up with the rattons Burns hears squeaking under the rigging of the thatch in his poem 'The Vision'. They're a bit macabre and a bit macaronic, archetypal and vernacular all at once, and as such they (and the poem which they inhabit) belong equally to the parish and the universe.

This suggestive phrase, 'the parish and the universe', is the title of an essay by Patrick Kavanagh.[14] In it, Kavanagh is concerned with the way in which the local can be winnowed by the boundless and set free within it, the way in which poetry can create conditions where 'the word for family/ is also the word for departure'.[15] And it is this very transformation which has concerned me in this essay. I wanted to do more than state the obvious truth that Burns's poetry was particularly congenial to natives of Ulster, whatever their allegiance, not only because of a common language, but also because of a shared sense of confidence and embattledness. Obviously, poetry is a domestic art and finds its most telling reach within the acoustic of its first language and language-group. But I wanted to affirm a supplementary truth, namely that poems and poets do not become available to their audience on the simple basis of ethnic or linguistic kinship. Burns is a world poet because of his genius, not because of his Scottishness. There is nothing determined about the reach of poetry, either for the writer or the reader of it: it is, as Keats said, a matter of surprise by fine excess, what Robert Frost calls in 'Birches' a going above the brim, a getting away from earth awhile in order to come back and begin over.

I am well aware, of course, that one of the ways in which this liberation and amplification of the parish truth occurs in Burns's poetry is through the merging and modulation of Ayrshire Scots and literary Scots with an English that is variously Scots or Standard in its colouring. Even though I did concentrate on the language of 'To a Mouse', I may have given less attention to this aspect of his writing than was warranted. In fact, I would have greatly enjoyed talking about it in far more detail, not in order to proclaim Burns's vernacular authority by decrying the southron elements in his art speech (for I believe that Professor Jack has put paid to that prejudice in his genially contrary reading[16] of Burns as a Sassenach poet): rather, I would have enjoyed taking soundings of the swift, deep flow which his poetry achieves because it is a confluence of so many different linguistic tributaries. But Thomas Crawford's wonderfully close and convincing readings[17] of individual poems have rendered such an exercise superfluous. I suppose that what I chiefly want to do is to emphasise the 'art' bit in my title over the 'speech' bit, and this is why I have felt free to cross the linguistic border into Irish – even though, in fact, there was no real border to cross. In the land of poetry the frontiers are open, citizenship comes from inner freedom in the creator and the creation, and this in turn promotes a salubrious inner freedom in the reader. If you think, for example, about Li Po by the Yellow River and Tam o' Shanter by the banks of Doon and Cathal Buí on the shores of Vesey's Lake, the fact that all three are drinking men in crisis in a watery scene is secondary to the fact that each of them arrives in profile in

the mind's eye and walks over the threshold of memory as a singular, buoyant creature born out of a language's impulse to rejoice in itself.

So, while one cannot help but feel confirmed and gratified by the democratic solidarity implied by Burns's use of the speech of his local district, one
has to be clear that the mere use of dialect is not enough to ensure artistic
success. 'I'll tell you about dialect, so I will', my old friend and headmaster,
the short-story writer Michael McLavery used to say; 'dialect's nothing
but a typesetter's headache'. And while there may be a certain extremity in
his position, we all know what he means. What produces the art is not the
medium, but what is made of it. For example, I am predisposed to like
Burns's 'The Twa Dogs' because of its unfoolable, realistic sense on the
world, its uncorny, wily humour and its unmitigated sense of justice, but I
could say that about Burns's letters as well; what distinguishes it as a poem
is the way it combines tonal verity and technical virtuosity – the pitch of the
voice and the musical trueness of it. It is because of a special mixture of
intimacy and documentary accuracy in the art speech of the poem that none
of the humour is at the expense of the dogs and none of the virtuosity is
knowing. And the same is true of the two poems about Poor Mailie, the
author's 'pet yowe' that strangled herself at the end of the rope. There is a
beautifully limpid quality about the dying words which she wishes to be
carried to her master and relayed by him to her family. To call them gentle is
to miss the adequacy that underwrites them, something hard to name, less
dewy-eyed than pathos, more sympathetic than irony:

> My poor toop-lamb, my son an' heir,
> O, bid him breed him up wi' care!
> An' if he live to be a beast,
> To pit some havins in his breast!
> An' warn him, what I winna name,
> To stay content wi' *yowes* at hame;
> An' no to rin an' wear his cloots,
> Like ither menseless, graceless brutes.
>
> An' niest my *yowie*, silly thing,
> Gude keep thee frae a *tether string*!
> O, may thou ne'er forgather up,
> Wi' onie blastet, moorlan *toop*;
> But ay keep mind to moop an' mell,
> Wi sheep o' credit like thysel!

Even Burns's humorous rhyming is distinguished by a compensatory emotional fidelity to the subjects which are being made fun of. If you compare

what he does with what Byron or Auden do in a similar vein, you find that the pair of them tend to be show-offs, and the more deadpan and one-up their performance is, the better. Burns, on the other hand, retains a certain protectiveness towards those very things which bring out the verbal scamp in him. In 'Tam o' Shanter', for example, the poise of the rhymes in the following famous lines is altogether characteristic:

> Nae man can tether time or tide;
> The hour approaches Tam maun ride;
> That hour, o' night's black arch the key-stane,
> That dreary hour he mounts his beast in;
> And sic a night he takes the road in,
> As ne'er poor sinner was abroad in.

Let me put it like this: if I were asked to find a way of writing that was equidistant from the naivety that rhymes 'mahogany' with 'cologne' and the deadpan-ness which makes such a rhyme an exercise in clued-in gamesmanship, I would point to these lines. There is something as bountiful about the feeling here as there is about the sense of supply. The one is an effect of the other, of course; it is as if my title were exercising its right to pun, since here, by dropping the 'h' from heart, we might speak with some justification of Burns's ''eart speech'. The words are as kind to Tam as they are kinned to one another. That run of feminine rhymes is carried away with itself, as they would say in Ulster, and cannot quite suppress its relish of its own sportiveness; but neither can it forget the suppressed panic in Tam o' Shanter's breast, and it is this double susceptibility in the writing that makes it so beguiling.

Being able to get carried away is, of course, a crucial gift when it comes to poetry. 'What reasonable man', Czeslaw Milosz asks in his poem 'Ars Poetica?',[18] 'would like to be a city of demons,/ who behave as if they were at home, speak in many tongues,/ and who, not satisfied with stealing his lips or hand,/ work at changing his destiny for their convenience?' And the answer expected here, but not necessarily desired, is Plato's answer: no reasonable man or woman would want to be susceptible to that kind of visitation. Control freak a poet cannot afford to be, but must, on the contrary, be prepared to go with the flow. And it is out of the submerged quarrel between the reasonable man in Burns and the city of demons which he contained that his best poems arrive. A great number of Burns's contemporaries thought of those demons as sexual, emissaries from caverns 'grim an' sootie', sent by 'Auld Hornie . . . Nick, or Clootie', but nowadays we have added to their horde the geniuses of the different languages that were available to him. Burns, we gratefully realise, opened his door to a great variety of linguistic callers. He gladly let his lips and hands be stolen at one moment by the language of Beattie and Thomson and at the next by the voices of his neighbours. In fact, his subjectivity only became totally available in situations which were performative or, if you prefer Milosz's way of thinking, when he was possessed by a spirit. 'Holy Willie's Prayer' is the masterpiece of such possession and performance, but his gift for it is everywhere. The first line or two of each epistle, for example, open the door to different visitors, each one corresponding under the name of Burns but each displaying different potentialities in the pitch and rhythm of his utterance. Who, after all, could shut the door on the agility and genuine accommodation in the voice that addresses Doctor Blacklock?

> Wow, but your letter made me vauntie!
> And are ye hale, and weel, and cantie?
> I kend it still your wee bit jauntie
>   Wad bring ye to:
> Lord send you ay as weel's I want ye,
>   And then ye'll do –

And who could have guessed that such a jongleur of the vernacular could reappear and be equally convincing in the role of minstrel boy addressing the master minstrel, James Lapraik?

> While briers an' woodbines budding green,
> An' Paitricks scraichan loud at e'en,
> An' morning Poosie whiddan seen,
>   Inspire my Muse,
> This freedom, in an *unknown* frien',
>   I pray excuse.

Even the songs, perhaps most of all the songs, required a surrender of the Burns who sat down to breakfast (as Yeats would have called him) to the Burns who had been reborn as the melody of inwardness:

> Had we never lov'd sae kindly,
> Had we never lov'd sae blindly!
> Never met – or never parted,
> We had ne'er been broken hearted. –

> Fare-thee-weel, thou first and fairest!
> Fare-thee-weel, thou best and dearest!
> Thine be ilka joy and treasure,
> Peace, Enjoyment, Love and Pleasure! –

> Ae fond kiss, and then we sever!
> Ae fareweel, Alas, for ever:
> Deep in heart-wrung tears I'll pledge thee,
> Warring sighs and groans I'll wage thee. –

The drama is one that is played out in every poet between the social self and a deeper self which is the locus of 'the ultimate suffering and decision in us', and I have to confess that when I began rereading Burns for this essay, I did so with a prejudice, a pre-judgement made before I had sufficiently immersed myself in the work. From my memories of the poems that I knew, and particularly those in the Standard Habbie metre, I had got it into my head that the social self had been given too much of an upper hand. I remembered the Burns stanza as one which set its cap rather too winsomely at the reader; but in fact Burns's deep poetic self inheres in something much bigger and older and more ballad-fastened, so to speak, as well as in something as intimately laid down in himself as the insinuation and stealth of both his humour and his sexuality. The potency of his songs is in itself enough to prove how surely he could find his way into a previousness, but that feeling of broaching the race's oldest survival-truths is present everywhere. One of my own favourite instances comes in the meeting of the poet with Death in 'Death and Doctor Hornbook', in particular the recognition in the last couple of lines of the following quotation that Death too has to survive by the sweat of his brow, that he's one of the toilers, that it is an achievement for him too simply to keep going:

> 'Weel, weel!'" says I, 'a bargain be't;
> 'Come, gies your hand, an' sae we're gree't;
> 'We'll ease our shanks an' tak a seat,
>   'Come, gies your news!
> 'This while ye hae been mony a gate,
>   'At mony a house.'

> 'Ay, ay!' quo' he, an' shook his head,
> 'It's e'en a lang, lang time indeed
> 'Sin' I began to nick the thread,
>   'An' choke the breath:
> 'Folk maun do something for their bread,
>   'An' sae maun *Death*.'

The access to world-sorrow comes in the intonation, the sound of sense in that concluding cadence. The utterance matches the contours of immemorial utterances made to the same effect. To call it folk wisdom or proverbial truth is to rob it of its specific emotional gravity within the dramatised setting. Death is a neighbour recognised on the road. He doesn't, for example, cut the thread of life but nicks it, and in that acutely refreshing and totally unshowy vernacular touch, Burns gives a glimpse of the other, more intimate power that he so often broaches. So I want to end by quoting and commenting briefly upon a poem whose subject is, in fact, the poet's middle state not just between Belles Lettres and Braid Scots, or between Ayr and Edinburgh, or between *Ça ira* and 'God Save the King', but between the vocation of poet and the behaviour of a reasonable man, between the call to open the doors of one's life to the daimonic and prophetic soul and have one's destiny changed by it, between that choice and the temptation to keep the doors closed and the self securely under social and domestic lock and key. Whether to be the cotter or Saint Paul, as it were. Here, therefore, beginning with the second stanza, is the opening of 'The Vision':

> The Thresher's weary *flingin tree*
> The lee-lang day had tir'd me;
> And when the Day had clos'd his e'e,
>   Far i' the West,
> Ben i' the *Spence*, right pensivelie,
>   I gaed to rest.
>
> There, lanely, by the ingle-cheek,
> I sat and ey'd the spewing reek,
> That fill'd, wi' hoast-provoking smeek,
>   The auld, clay biggin;
> And heard the restless rattons squeak
>   About the riggin.
>
> All in this mottie, misty clime,
> I backward mus'd on wasted time,
> How I had spent my *youthfu' prime*,
>   An' done nae-thing,
> But stringing blethers up in rhyme
>   For fools to sing.
>
> Had I to guid advice but harket,
> I might, by this, hae led a market,
> Or strutted in a Bank and clarket
>   My *Cash-Account*;
> While here, half-mad, half-fed, half-sarket,
>   Is a' th' amount.

I started, mutt'ring blockhead! coof!
And heav'd on high my wauket loof,
To swear by a' yon starry roof,
    Or some rash aith,
That I, henceforth, would be *rhyme-proof*
    Till my last breath –

When click! the *string* the *snick* did draw;
And jee! the door gaed to the wa';
And by my ingle-lowe I saw,
    Now bleezan bright,
A tight, outlandish *Hizzie*, braw,
    Come full in sight.

Ye need na doubt, I held my whisht;
The infant aith, half-form'd, was crusht;
I glower'd as eerie 's I'd been dusht,
    In some wild glen;
When sweet, like *modest Worth*, she blusht,
    And stepped ben.

Green, slender, leaf-clad Holly-boughs
Were twisted, gracefu', round her brows,
I took her for some SCOTTISH MUSE
    By that same token;
And come to stop those restless vows,
    Would soon been broken.

This is Burns's *aisling*, and its transcultural allegiance to the Gaelic heritage in Scotland is made clear by his calling each section of it a *duan*, a term he found in Macpherson and which is simply the word for a poem in Irish and Scots Gaelic. The *aisling* genre had immense popularity in Ireland during the late seventeenth and eighteenth centuries, although in her Irish setting the Muse was politicised into an image of the maiden Hibernia, a Hibernia Tacta, as it were, violated by and in thrall to the heretic English invader. So the genre's primal function as a vehicle for the myth of access to poetic power got submerged as it became more and more a manifestation of the Jacobite strain in Irish politics during those decades when the Irish Gaels were left without leadership or a plan for resurgence. But the Art MacCumhaigh who wrote an *aisling* about a maiden coming to kiss him awake at dawn in the churchyard at Killycreggan[19] would surely have recognised the commingling of the erotic with the local and the national in

Burns's lines. And the sexually-entranced Sir Thomas Wyatt, whose dawn visitor once took him 'in her armes long and smale' and 'Therewithal swetely did [him] kiss/ And softely said, *dere hert, howe like you this?*'[20] Wyatt too would have smiled with a delicious remembrance 'When click! the *string* the *snick* did draw;/ And jee! the door gaed to the wa''.

By citing these parallels, I mean to commend the poem's ability to do what T. S. Eliot said that the most potent poetry could do, namely 'unite the most ancient and the most civilized mentality'.[21] And yet it is not the ancient thematic respectability of the 'The Vision' which makes it such a credible poetic event. There are, of course, echoes of the Muses singing to the farmer Hesiod, of Dante about to give up in the middle of his journey and being saved by Beatrice, and of the White Goddess whose presence Robert Graves would have recognised immediately in the lines that I've just quoted. But this poem is not simply a case of an archetype being selected from the myth kitty: the personal expense of Burns's poetic vocation is embodied deeply in its speech and drama. The initiate's fear of the divine call, the poet's temptation to go easy on himself: these are indeed part of the story which the poem tells, but they are also present in the way that it sounds. The reluctance (call it the rel*och*tance) to face the next move, the desire to let the harp pass, to do a Caedmon and substitute the business of the daytime self for the dreamwork – all this comes through and comes true in the words themselves. And so too does the miraculous lightening and alleviation of that mood as a brightness falls from the air and everything that is viscous and sluggish yields miraculously to something far more lightsome and visionary. When I read 'The Thresher's weary *flingin tree*/ The lee-lang day had tir'd me', the limberness of the flail travels fleetly up my arm only to meet the actual drudgery of farmwork coming leadenly down; but when 'click! the *string* the *snick* did draw', I know that 'the next bright bolt'[22] has fallen and I come through the reasonable man's demurrals every time. So, even though a part of me will always agree with Milosz's admonition at the end of his 'Ars Poetica?' that 'poems should be written rarely and reluctantly,/ under unbearable duress and only with the hope/ that good spirits, not evil ones, choose us for their instrument',[23] I am still nevertheless persuaded that Burns did right to let his door go to the wall and that he did not fail the Muse or us or himself as one of poetry's chosen instruments.

NOTES

1. Robert Crawford, *Devolving English Literature* (Oxford: Clarendon Press, 1992), pp. 88–110.
2. Nadezhda Mandelstam, *Hope against Hope* (Harmondsworth: Penguin Books, 1975), p. 225.

3. Lawrance Thompson (ed.), *Selected Letters of Robert Frost* (London: Jonathan Cape, 1965), p. 79.
4. Joseph Brodsky, *Less Than One* (New York: Farrar Straus & Giroux, 1986), pp. 164–5.
5. All quotations from Burns's poems are taken from Angus Calder and William Donnelly (eds), *Robert Burns: Selected Poetry* (London: Penguin Books, 1991).
6. Donald A. Low (ed.), *Robert Burns: The Critical Heritage* (London: Routledge and Kegan Paul, 1972), p. 262.
7. Lawrance Thompson, op. cit., p. 191.
8. Seamus Heaney, *Wintering Out* (London: Faber & Faber, 1972), p. 27.
9. Sean O Tuama and Thomas Kinsella, *An Duanaire 1600–1900: Poems of the Dispossessed* (Dublin: Dolmen Press, 1991), p. 133.
10. John Hewitt, *Rhyming Weavers* (Belfast: The Blackstaff Press, 1974), p. vii.
11. Sean O Tuama and Thomas Kinsella, op. cit., p. 134.
12. Ted Hughes, 'Notes on the Chronological Order of Sylvia Plath's Poems', in Charles Norman (ed.), *The Art of Sylvia Plath* (London: Faber & Faber, 1970), p. 194.
13. Joseph Brodsky, *On Grief and Reason* (New York: Farrar Straus & Giroux, 1995), p. 210.
14. Patrick Kavanagh, *Collected Pruse* (London: MacGibbon & Kee, 1967), pp. 281–3.
15. Peter Sirr, *The Ledger of Fruitful Exchange* (Loughcrew: The Gallery Press, 1996), p. 33.
16. R. D. S. Jack, 'Burns as Sassenach Poet', in Kenneth Simpson (ed.), *Burns Now* (Edinburgh: Canongate Academic, 1994), pp. 150–66.
17. Thomas Crawford, *Burns: A Study of the Poems and Songs* (Edinburgh: Oliver & Boyd, 1960).
18. Czeslaw Milosz, *Bells in Winter* (New York: Ecco Press, 1978), pp. 30–1.
19. Sean O Tuama and Thomas Kinsella, op. cit., pp. 176–81.
20. Kenneth Muir (ed.), *The Collected Poems of Sir Thomas Wyatt* (London: Routledge and Kegan Paul, 1963), p. 28.
21. T. S. Eliot, *The Use of Poetry and the Use of Criticism*, rev. edn (London: Faber and Faber, 1964), p. 119.
22. Robert Graves, *Selected Poems* (Harmondsworth: Penguin, 1974), p. 116.
23. Czeslaw Milosz, op. cit., p. 31.

NOTES ON CONTRIBUTORS

MARILYN BUTLER's books include *Romantics, Rebels and Reactionaries: English Literature and its Background 1760–1830* (Oxford University Press, 1981). She is Rector of Exeter College, Oxford.

ROBERT CRAWFORD's most recent collection of poetry is *Masculinity* (Cape, 1996). He is Professor of Modern Scottish Literature in the School of English, University of St Andrews.

DOUGLAS DUNN's *Selected Poems* was published by Faber and Faber in 1986. He is Head of the School of English, University of St Andrews, and Director of the University of St Andrews Scottish Studies Institute.

SEAMUS HEANEY's most recent collection of poetry is *The Spirit Level* (Faber and Faber, 1996). He was awarded the 1995 Nobel Prize for Literature.

A. L. KENNEDY's books include *Looking for the Possible Dance* (Secker and Warburg, 1993), *So I Am Glad* (Cape, 1995) and *Original Bliss* (Cape, 1997).

KIRSTEEN McCUE is Director of the Scottish Music Information Centre, based in Glasgow. She holds a doctorate on the work of Burns as a song-collector.

CAROL McGUIRK's books include *Robert Burns and the Sentimental Era* (1985; reprinted by Tuckwell in 1996). She teaches in the Department of English and Comparative Literature at Florida Atlantic University.

SUSAN MANNING's publications include *The Puritan-Provincial Vision: Scottish and American Literature in the Nineteenth Century* (Cambridge University Press, 1990). She is a Fellow of Newnham College, Cambridge.

ANDREW NASH holds degrees from the universities of Dundee and Edinburgh, and is now a graduate student in the School of English, University of St Andrews, where he is writing a doctoral thesis on Kailyard and the imaging of Scotland.

ALAN RIACH's books include *Hugh MacDiarmid's Epic Poetry* (Edinburgh University Press, 1991). General editor of Carcanet's MacDiarmid 2000 edition, he is Senior Lecturer in the Department of English, University of Waikato, New Zealand.

NICHOLAS ROE's books include *Wordsworth and Coleridge: The Radical Years* (Clarendon Press, 1988). He is a Professor in the School of English, University of St Andrews.

INDEX

Literary works referred to are by Burns unless otherwise indicated.

Grant, Anne, 41
Graves, Robert, 232
Grierson, William, 161
Grieve, C. M., *see* MacDiarmid, Hugh
Grose, Captain Francis, 15–16, 94, 110–11
Groves, David, 183

'Hallowe'en', 15–16, 106
'Hallow-Fair' (Fergusson), 64
Hamilton, Elizabeth, 41
Hamilton, Ian, 198
Hardie, Keir, 199, 200, 213–14
Hawthorne, Nathaniel, 138–40
Heaney, Seamus, 83
'Heaven-taught', 2, 23–4
Henderson, George, 49
Henderson, T. F., 62
Herbert, George, 127
Herd, David, 53
'Here's a health to them that's awa', 98
Heron, Patrick, 88
Heron, Robert, 161
Hesiod, 232
Hewitt, John, 222
'Highland Mary', 146–7
Hill, D. O., 184
Hill, Reverend Rowland, 115
history, power of, 102
Hogg, James, 183
Holmes, Oliver Wendell, 136, 138, 144
'Holy Fair, The', 64–5, 106, 126
'Holy Willie's Prayer', 60, 119–22, 129, 228
homoerotica, 10–12
Hopkins, Gerard Manley, 127
Hough, Graham, 121
Howff, The, 23
Hughes, Ted, 113, 123, 129, 224
humanitarianism, 89
humility, 59
Hunt, Leigh, 160
Hyslop, Mrs, 27

iambic tetrameter couplets, 68
identity, from skull, 173–4
ideology, 58–84
imaginative language, lacking for religion, 126–7
imitations, of Burns, 187
infatuation, 31–3

irony, 60–1, 75
    in form and statement, 67
Irving, Washington, 151

Jack, R. D. S., 225
Jacob, Violet, 204
Jacobite songs, 52, 109–11
Jacobitism, 103–4
Jacob's dream, 116
James, Henry, 154
Jamieson, Burns, 121
Jesus Christ, in Calvinism, 117
'John Anderson my Jo', 14, 48, 49
'John Barleycorn', 148
'Johnnie Cope', 109
Johnson, James, 40, 42, 45, 48, 49, 86
Johnson, Dr Samuel, 2, 5–7
Johnston, Captain William, 95
'Jolly Beggars, The' ('Love and Liberty — A Cantata'), 65, 79–82, 211
Jonson, Ben, 133

Kailyard, 180–95
Kavanagh, Patrick, 225
Keats, John, 60, 160, 164, 168–70
Kelman, James, 80
Kilpatrick, Nelly, 43, 44
Kinsley, James, 13, 40, 73
Kirk
    and cultural authority, 117, 129
    politics, 105–6
Kirkpatrick, Nelly, 27
Knox, John, 115, 124

'Laird o' Cockpen, The' (Nairne), 49–52
'Lament, The', 67
language, in letters, 118
Lapraik, John, 93
Lauder, Harry, 180, 188
Lawrence, D. H., 211
legitimacy, of birth, 165–6
Leonard, Tom, 80
Leonhardt, Rudolf, 202
Lewars, Jessie, 48
Libertarian beliefs, 35–6
Lincoln, Abraham, 136
Lindsay, Miss, 27
Lindsay, Sir David, 60, 62, 211
literature, seen as pulpit, 191